# CBT at Work
### FOR
# DUMMIES®
A Wiley Brand

## by Gill Garratt

**CBT at Work For Dummies®**

Published by: **John Wiley & Sons, Ltd.,** The Atrium, Southern Gate, Chichester, www.wiley.com

This edition first published 2016

© 2016 John Wiley & Sons, Ltd., Chichester, West Sussex.

*Registered office*

John Wiley & Sons Ltd., The Atrium, Southern Gate, Chichester, West Sussex, PO19 8SQ, United Kingdom

**For details of our global editorial offices, for customer services and for information about** how to apply for permission to reuse the copyright material in this book, please see our website at www.wiley.com.

The right of the author to be identified as the author of this work has been asserted in accordance with the Copyright, Designs and Patents Act 1988.

Wiley publishes in a variety of print and electronic formats and by print-on-demand. Some material included with standard print versions of this book may not be included in e-books or in print-on-demand. If this book refers to media such as a CD or DVD that is not included in the version you purchased, you may download this material at http://booksupport.wiley.com. For more information about Wiley products, visit www.wiley.com.

Designations used by companies to distinguish their products are often claimed as trademarks. All brand names and product names used in this book are trade names, service marks, trademarks or registered trademarks of their respective owners. The publisher is not associated with any product or vendor mentioned in this book.

For general information on our other products and services, please contact our Customer Care Department within the U.S. at 877-762-2974, outside the U.S. at (001) 317-572-3993, or fax 317-572-4002. For technical support, please visit www.wiley.com/techsupport.

For technical support, please visit www.wiley.com/techsupport.

A catalogue record for this book is available from the British Library.

ISBN 978-1-119-06738-2 (hardback/paperback); ISBN ePDF: 978-1-119-06736-8 (ePDF)

ISBN 978-1-119-06737-5 (ebk)

Printed and bound in Great Britain by TJ International Ltd, Padstow, Cornwall, UK

10 9 8 7 6 5 4 3 2 1

# Contents at a Glance

Introduction ........................................................ 1

## Part I: Getting Started with CBT at Work ................ 7
Chapter 1: Reducing Your Anxieties at Work with CBT ........................ 9
Chapter 2: Discovering How CBT Works ........................................ 19
Chapter 3: Using CBT to Change Unhelpful Thinking .......................... 33
Chapter 4: Working in Healthy Ways ......................................... 47

## Part II: Benefits, Bonuses and Added Value for All ....... 61
Chapter 5: Looking after Yourself at Work .................................. 63
Chapter 6: Impressing Employers with Your Professional Integrity ........... 79
Chapter 7: Putting CBT to Work . . . at Work! .............................. 97

## Part III: Working with CBT (Work and You) .............. 115
Chapter 8: Feeling Positive about Your Work ................................ 117
Chapter 9: Matching Your Personality to Your Job ........................... 131
Chapter 10: Creating Your Own Philosophy for Work .......................... 147
Chapter 11: Exploring Your Relationships at Work ........................... 161

## Part IV: Using CBT in Your Organisation ................... 175
Chapter 12: Taking Action! Implementing CBT at Work ........................ 177
Chapter 13: Seeing CBT as a Positive Force in the Workplace ................ 197
Chapter 14: Communicating the Benefits of CBT to Other People .............. 213
Chapter 15: Introducing CBT Methods to Your Organisation ................... 231

## Part V: Next Steps and the Future ......................... 255
Chapter 16: Transferring Your CBT Practice to New Situations ............... 257
Chapter 17: Adapting to the Inevitable Changes at Work ..................... 271
Chapter 18: Revising and Maximising Your Work Opportunities ................ 281
Chapter 19: Exploring Additional Practices for Health and Wellbeing ........ 291

## Part VI: The Part of Tens ................................. 301
Chapter 20: Ten Top Tips to Train You in CBT ............................... 303
Chapter 21: Ten Pointers to Maintain Your CBT Practice ..................... 311
Chapter 22: Ten Tips for Maximising Success in the Workplace ............... 319
Chapter 23: Ten Invaluable Ideas for CBT Resources ......................... 327

Index ............................................................... 333

# Table of Contents

*Introduction* ............................................................................. *1*

About This Book .............................................................. 2
How to Use This Book ....................................................... 3
Foolish Assumptions ......................................................... 4
Icons Used in This Book ..................................................... 5
Beyond the Book .............................................................. 5
Where to Go from Here ...................................................... 6

*Part I: Getting Started with CBT at Work* ....................... *7*

**Chapter 1: Reducing Your Anxieties at Work with CBT** ............. .9

Coping with Changing Roles at Work ................................... 10
  Stressing out at work .................................................. 10
  Taking charge of your emotions ..................................... 10
Thinking Rationally to Troubleshoot Your Emotions ................ 11
  Meeting the CBT basics ............................................... 11
  Tackling tough times with CBT ...................................... 13
Recognising Problems in the Workplace ............................... 14
  Experiencing conflict between your beliefs and actions ........ 14
  Admitting your struggles ............................................. 15
  Looking after yourself at work ...................................... 15
Discovering the Benefits of the CBT Problem-Solving Method .... 16
  Increasing a company's productivity and positivity ............. 16
  Being an ambassador for CBT ........................................ 17
  Selecting the work life you want ................................... 17
  Becoming balanced professionally and personally .............. 18

**Chapter 2: Discovering How CBT Works** ........................... .19

Understanding Cognitive Behavioural Therapy ...................... 19
  Introducing the components of CBT ................................ 20
  Deciding whether you want to use CBT ............................ 21
  Realising that you can change if you want ........................ 23
Meeting the ABCs of CBT ................................................. 23
  Thinking scientifically ................................................ 24
  Simplifying CBT methods ............................................. 24
  Becoming a detective of your emotions ........................... 26
  Your feelings ........................................................... 27

Tackling Your Unsettling Feelings ....................................................29
    Connecting thinking and feelings.......................................29
    Concentrating on what you're thinking ............................30
    Discovering what pushes your buttons .............................31
    Creating a CBT toolkit ........................................................32

## Chapter 3: Using CBT to Change Unhelpful Thinking . . . . . . . . . . . . . .33

Observing Your Behaviour at Work........................................34
    Viewing yourself in terms of your helpful beliefs ...........34
    Viewing others in terms of your beliefs ............................35
    Identifying helpful and unhelpful beliefs ........................35
    Seeing damaging beliefs at work........................................36
    Noticing negative thinking at work....................................37
    Watching for catastrophising thinking..............................38
    Deciding if some of your beliefs need changing ..............39
Building Yourself a CBT Toolkit ............................................39
    Tooling up to take control ..................................................39
    Keeping your CBT toolkit prepared ..................................41
Choosing to Use Your CBT Toolkit ........................................42
    Getting smarter at using your CBT toolkit........................42
    Exercising your brain muscles............................................43
    Checking your alerting strategies......................................43
    Deciding when to implement your CBT toolkit................44
    Practising the routines........................................................44
    Demanding more of yourself in a helpful way.................45
    Using your toolkit to gain a little peace ...........................45

## Chapter 4: Working in Healthy Ways . . . . . . . . . . . . . . . . . . . . . . . . .47

Discovering Your Environment at Work.................................48
    Looking at your physical surroundings ............................48
    Describing the psychological environment......................50
    Recognising conflicting influences ...................................53
Changing Your Attitudes in the Workplace...........................55
    Recognising the importance of attitudes.........................56
    Challenging your expectations of comfortable conditions ...........57
    Identifying your preferred way of working.......................58
    Exploring new attitudes ......................................................58
    Creating the best outcomes ...............................................59
Using CBT to Adjust Your Workplace Emotions ...................59
    Implementing healthy work routines ...............................60
    Dealing with obstacles ........................................................60

## Part II: Benefits, Bonuses and Added Value for All ........ 61

### Chapter 5: Looking after Yourself at Work ...................... 63

Allowing Yourself to Be Number One ........................................ 63
    Replacing selfishness with enlightened self-interest ..................... 64
    Viewing yourself honestly ................................................ 64
    Reflecting on your behaviours ........................................... 65
    Valuing yourself ......................................................... 66
    Treating yourself with respect ........................................... 67
Taking Responsibility for Yourself ........................................... 67
    Recognising the need to take care of yourself ........................... 68
    Rationalising why you're important ...................................... 68
    Needing to earn a living ................................................. 69
    Considering how much work means to you ................................ 70
    Being responsible for your own happiness ............................... 70
Being Your Own Best Friend .................................................. 71
    Assessing whether your work habits are healthy ......................... 71
    Realising others don't always care ...................................... 72
Investing in Your Overall Health .............................................. 73
    Placing yourself in context .............................................. 73
    Replacing your bad work habits and routines ............................. 74
    Making efforts to assist your health ..................................... 75

### Chapter 6: Impressing Employers with Your Professional Integrity ....................................... 79

Ensuring Your Firm Hires a Responsible Person – You! ........................ 80
    Preparing for work ...................................................... 81
    Analysing a job description .............................................. 81
    Recognising your skills and abilities ..................................... 82
    Facing the fear of being found out ...................................... 83
    Succeeding at interviews with CBT ...................................... 84
    Negotiating your pay ................................................... 84
Taking Responsibility for Yourself as a Dynamic Employee .................... 85
    Assessing the situation ................................................. 85
    Prioritising the work .................................................... 86
    Meeting expectations ................................................... 86
    Becoming aware of your weaknesses .................................... 87
    Going beyond the boundaries ........................................... 87
    Being bold and audacious in your job .................................... 89
Benefitting the Organisation .................................................. 91
    Working out where you stand ............................................ 92
    Valuing your place at work .............................................. 92
    Influencing the work culture ............................................. 93

**Chapter 7: Putting CBT to Work . . . at Work!** . . . . . . . . . . . . . . . . . . .**97**

Identifying Problem Areas at Work ........................................................... 97

　Dealing with anger at work .............................................................. 98

　Handling anxiety about work ......................................................... 100

　Feeling depressed about work ....................................................... 100

　Lacking self-confidence at work .................................................... 100

　Being neglected at work ................................................................. 101

　Facing bullying at work .................................................................. 102

　Replacing low self-worth with self-acceptance ........................... 103

　Suffering from scared feelings at work......................................... 104

　Having guilty feelings ..................................................................... 104

　Thinking twice before going to work ill ....................................... 104

　Dying to hide away! Embarrassment and shame at work............ 105

　Making mistakes in work................................................................ 106

　Defusing frustration at work.......................................................... 106

　Crying at work ................................................................................. 107

Targeting Unsettling Emotions ............................................................... 107

　Allowing yourself to accept the difficult emotions..................... 108

　Telling another person of your struggle ....................................... 108

Implementing CBT Techniques for Work-Related Problems ................ 110

　Addressing your discomfort one step at a time ........................... 111

　Finding an example where CBT could've helped.......................... 112

　Applying the technique to your problem ...................................... 112

　Maintaining vigilance for your emotional outlook ...................... 113

**Part III: Working with CBT (Work and You)** .............. **115**

**Chapter 8: Feeling Positive about Your Work** . . . . . . . . . . . . . . . . . .**117**

'Keeping It on the Sunny Side!' Working at Optimistic Thinking........... 117

　Expecting the best outcome........................................................... 118

　Squashing NATs – like the bugs they are!..................................... 118

　Implementing positive body language .......................................... 119

　Playing the 'glad' game.................................................................... 120

　Counting your blessings ................................................................. 121

　Reflecting at the end of the day .................................................... 121

Increasing Favourable Interactions at Work......................................... 121

　Engaging with other people............................................................ 122

　Nodding and smiling to give you a breather ................................ 122

Putting Your Job into Perspective ......................................................... 123

　Dividing your time ........................................................................... 123

　Prioritising your day........................................................................ 123

　Letting time heal your wounds ...................................................... 124

　Gaining perspective on the grand scheme .................................... 124

Taking in the Wider View to Catch Important Opportunities ............... 125
    Being open to experience ................................. 126
    Increasing your luck and fortune ............................ 126
Optimising Your Chances of a Positive Work Climate ........................... 128
    Studying optimism ....................................... 129
    Hedging your bets at work ................................. 129
    Brightening your work future with CBT ....................... 130

**Chapter 9: Matching Your Personality to Your Job** .............. **131**
Considering the Personality Types ............................. 131
    Looking inwards or outwards ............................... 132
    Analysing your personality's origins ......................... 133
    Testing for personality types .............................. 134
    Avoiding typecasting people ............................... 136
Taking a Look at Your Own Personality ......................... 136
    Reacting to personality feedback and tests ................... 137
    Finding out how you prefer to work ......................... 137
    Identifying your positive attributes .......................... 138
    Admitting your unhelpful characteristics ..................... 138
    Tweaking the self-defeating parts of your
        character with CBT ................................. 138
Linking Personality Types to Different Jobs ..................... 139
    Choosing a job you can enjoy .............................. 140
    Imagining the worst at work ............................... 142
    Tying mental health to different professions ................. 142
Adopting the Role of a Successful, Happy Worker ................ 143
    Auditioning for the part of your job ......................... 143
    Acting in your own best interests ........................... 144
    Getting into character .................................... 145

**Chapter 10: Creating Your Own Philosophy for Work** ............ **147**
Delving into Your Attitudes toward Work ........................ 147
    Identifying how you view work ............................. 148
    Appraising what you want from work ........................ 149
    Aiming to get what you want from your job .................. 150
    Discerning your values about work .......................... 150
Identifying Dissonances between Your Beliefs and Your Actions ........ 152
    Handling differing views and attitudes toward work ............ 153
    Unearthing conflicts in your professional and personal views ... 154
Pinpointing Unhelpful Beliefs with CBT .......................... 155
    Picking up on tensions ................................... 156
    Devising a holding bay ................................... 156
    Agreeing to differ and not losing face ....................... 157
Staying Put or Leaving Your Job ............................... 157
    Making tough decisions .................................. 159

**Chapter 11: Exploring Your Relationships at Work** . . . . . . . . . . . . . . **161**

Taking a Hard Look at Your Colleagues . . . . . . . . . . . . . . . . . . . . . . 162
Categorising your workmates . . . . . . . . . . . . . . . . . . . . . . . . . 162
Appraising the horrors and the lovelies . . . . . . . . . . . . . . . . . 163
Seeing the character types in work . . . . . . . . . . . . . . . . . . . . 164
Dealing with people you can't stand . . . . . . . . . . . . . . . . . . . 166
Considering the Way You Come across at Work . . . . . . . . . . . . . . . 167
Thinking about self-presentation . . . . . . . . . . . . . . . . . . . . . . 167
Picturing yourself at work . . . . . . . . . . . . . . . . . . . . . . . . . . . 168
Remembering how you were before work . . . . . . . . . . . . . . . 170
Seeing yourself in different roles . . . . . . . . . . . . . . . . . . . . . . 171
Making Friends at Work . . . . . . . . . . . . . . . . . . . . . . . . . . . . . . . . . 172
I'll be there for you . . . . . . . . . . . . . . . . . . . . . . . . . . . . . . . . . 172
Not everyone can be your best buddy . . . . . . . . . . . . . . . . . . 173
If you want a friend, get a dog! . . . . . . . . . . . . . . . . . . . . . . . . 174

**Part IV: Using CBT in Your Organisation** . . . . . . . . . . . . . . . . . . . **175**

**Chapter 12: Taking Action! Implementing CBT at Work** . . . . . . . . . . **177**

Gaining Insight into Yourself with CBT . . . . . . . . . . . . . . . . . . . . . 177
Doing your homework . . . . . . . . . . . . . . . . . . . . . . . . . . . . . . . 178
Understanding your motivation . . . . . . . . . . . . . . . . . . . . . . . 178
Becoming conscious of your actions . . . . . . . . . . . . . . . . . . . 179
Seeing the CBT Methods in Action . . . . . . . . . . . . . . . . . . . . . . . . 180
Practising before acting . . . . . . . . . . . . . . . . . . . . . . . . . . . . . 180
Realising that the time has come to act . . . . . . . . . . . . . . . . . 182
Speaking louder than words – with actions! . . . . . . . . . . . . . 183
Spiralling out of control: Negative thoughts running wild . . . 186
Spiralling negative thoughts . . . . . . . . . . . . . . . . . . . . . . . . . . 187
Halting the unhelpful thoughts . . . . . . . . . . . . . . . . . . . . . . . . 188
Applying the ABC model . . . . . . . . . . . . . . . . . . . . . . . . . . . . . 188
Reflecting on and Tackling Your Tricky Areas . . . . . . . . . . . . . . . . 190
Handling problem situations . . . . . . . . . . . . . . . . . . . . . . . . . . 191
Drawing up a CBT Plan of Action . . . . . . . . . . . . . . . . . . . . . . . . . 195

**Chapter 13: Seeing CBT as a Positive Force in the Workplace** . . . . . **197**

Using CBT in Transition Management . . . . . . . . . . . . . . . . . . . . . . 198
Moving from the individual to the team: Engaging employees . . . . 199
Devising a manager's special . . . . . . . . . . . . . . . . . . . . . . . . . 200
Handling senior staff members' reluctance or opposition . . . . . . 201
Including HR in feedback and evaluation of CBT courses . . . . . . . 203
Offering to enlighten the MD on CBT . . . . . . . . . . . . . . . . . . . 204
Communicating a Consistent Message throughout Your Company . . . . 204
Standardising your company's strategic aims . . . . . . . . . . . . . 206
Appraising the work culture . . . . . . . . . . . . . . . . . . . . . . . . . . 206

Thinking about your company's reputation...................................207
Sustaining your firm's human resources ...............................208
Facing up to Relationship Issues at Work ..................................209
Winning customer respect......................................................210
Maintaining trust in relationships .......................................210
Reacting to broken trust ........................................................211

**Chapter 14: Communicating the Benefits of CBT
to Other People** . . . . . . . . . . . . . . . . . . . . . . . . . . . . . . . . . . . . . . . .**213**
Testifying to CBT by Your Example ............................................214
Acting as an ambassador for acceptable behaviour .................214
Demonstrating rational thinking............................................215
Advocating the Use of CBT at Work............................................218
Sharing CBT with interested colleagues ..............................219
Offering to present your CBT understanding to a group..............220
Handling challenges...............................................................221
Recognising the different levels and depths of CBT ...............222
Using Your CBT Experience to Help Other People's Struggles ............223
Recommending that people seek professional help ....................224
Spotting when colleagues may have a specific
emotional problem..........................................................227

**Chapter 15: Introducing CBT Methods to Your Organisation** . . . . . . .**231**
Including CBT in Your Workplace .............................................232
Seeing How CBT Benefits Your Company's Bottom Line ......................232
Balancing the costs and benefits ........................................234
Leading CBT Workshops and Seminars....................................235
Holding a 3-hour interactive workshop ..............................241
Creating a 5-hour manager-training day in CBT.............................243
Looking at Basic Communication Skills....................................246
Creating a trusting environment...........................................247
Talking in a respectful and professional manner .........................248
Hearing about active listening .............................................248
Reflecting for better communication ...................................249
Probing with questions .........................................................251

*Part V: Next Steps and the Future*.............................. *255*

**Chapter 16: Transferring Your CBT Practice to New Situations** . . . .**257**
Widening the Application of Your CBT Skills................................258
Being flexible in your CBT approach........................................258
Spotting the contextual clues for CBT use ...................................258
Taking confidence into new environments ...................................259
Believing in using your skills and experience .............................260

Making Use of CBT Outside of Work........................................260
Identifying your own working pattern...........................261
Working to live or living to work ..................................262
Using CBT in your personal life .....................................263
Combining your emotional and physical health...........263
Seeking balance through exercise .................................266
Creating an Overall Consistent Way of Being .........................267
Maintaining an awareness of your overall
emotional situation ....................................................267

**Chapter 17: Adapting to the Inevitable Changes at Work..........271**

Accepting the Need to Be Flexible..............................................272
Diagnosing the problem..................................................272
Treating the symptoms with CBT ..................................273
Being Flexible at Work: Transitions, Redundancy and Retirement ......275
Maintaining your skills keeps you confident...............276
Adjusting to transitions at work with CBT ..................276
Retaining a Sense of Who You Are .............................................277
Keeping perspective through changing times .............278
Staying you through thick and thin ..............................280
Affirming your status and sense of worth ...................280

**Chapter 18: Revising and Maximising Your Work Opportunities . . .281**

Assessing Your Thinking about Pressure at Work....................281
Experiencing stress and worry at work .......................282
Using CBT to handle responsibility..............................282
Mapping Your Work Options .......................................................283
Conducting a skills audit on yourself...........................284
Learning from my experience .......................................285
Focusing on the realistic................................................286
Striking Out on Your Own: Self-Employment ...........................287
Weighing the pros and cons of self-employment.........287
Letting CBT show you the way........................................289

**Chapter 19: Exploring Additional Practices for Health
and Wellbeing...............................................291**

Gaining a Perspective on Your Whole Being.............................292
Understanding that CBT is for Life, Not Just for Crises!.........293
Exercising your power to choose additional resources.............294
Becoming more sociable..................................................295
Checking-in with yourself ..............................................298
Rewiring your old brain ..................................................299

## Part VI: The Part of Tens ............................... 301

### Chapter 20: Ten Top Tips to Train You in CBT ...................303
Reminding Yourself of the CBT Basics, Again and Again ......................303
Revising the ABC Toolkit ..............................................................................304
Remembering One Example of CBT in Action............................................306
Using the ABCs: Considering Your Own Examples ...................................306
Reflecting on the Last Week at Work ...........................................................307
Recording Unsettling Work Events ..............................................................307
Carrying out Your Own Self-Assessment on the Workweek ..................308
Applying the CBT Toolkit to Each New Event.............................................308
Working with a CBT Buddy ............................................................................309
Creating Your Own Version of the CBT Toolkit...........................................309

### Chapter 21: Ten Pointers to Maintain Your CBT Practice..........311
Treating Yourself with Patience ...................................................................312
Keeping an Emotions Diary ...........................................................................312
Researching and Evaluating CBT Apps.........................................................313
Choosing Your Method for Recording Your Emotional Life ..................314
Analysing Your Emotional Data....................................................................314
Assessing Your Work Performance................................................................315
Identifying Areas You Want to Improve ......................................................315
Creating a Plan of Action ...............................................................................316
Implementing and Recording Your Goals....................................................316
Making Sure that You Practise, Practise, Practise ....................................317

### Chapter 22: Ten Tips for Maximising Success in the Workplace...319
Developing Enlightened Self-Interest ..........................................................320
Creating a Philosophy for Work ...................................................................320
Being a Fallible Human Being........................................................................321
Keeping a Healthy Perspective ......................................................................321
Laughing at Yourself .......................................................................................321
Exercising Your Mind and Body ...................................................................322
Accepting Yourself ..........................................................................................323
Empathising with Other People....................................................................324
Remembering that Life Isn't a Rehearsal ....................................................324
Prioritising Your Life ......................................................................................325

### Chapter 23: Ten Invaluable Ideas for CBT Resources ............327
Reading Yourself toward Feeling Better ......................................................327
Getting Techy Help..........................................................................................327
Surfing for CBT Websites................................................................................328

Hearing All about CBT..................................................328
Sitting Down with a CBT Movie .................................329
Thinking about Training Courses................................329
Considering Talking to Friends and Family................330
Accessing National Directories..................................330
Staying Local .............................................................330
Employing Mind and Body Resources ........................331

*Index* ............................................................... *333*

# Introduction

· · · · · · · · · · · · · · · · · · · · · · · · · · · · · · · · · · · · · · · · · · · · · · · · · · · · · ·

$C$ognitive Behavioural Therapy, or CBT, is a type of practical helping strategy based upon years of research in the world of psychology. In the search for greater understanding of how you think and behave, CBT has developed into a popular helping tool. Since the early days of Freud and his ideas on the human mind and the many other theories and therapies that have followed, trying to get a clearer picture of the emotional roller coaster of life continues to be a popular topic. CBT seems to appeal to many people both in medical and personal settings. Personal development books rank very highly and continue to be popular. Is this because you are interested in trying to work out what is going on in your head? You may want to find out why you make the decisions you do about life, relationships, and in particular what is going on at work. You spend so much time during your working life dealing with people, issues, events, and interactions and at times you can find yourself struggling to get to grips with all of this. Is it any wonder that you may feel at times that you want to try to stand back and make some sense of it all?

CBT can help you identify what emotions are bubbling up inside you and teach you some practical strategies to help you reduce the negative ones that you could do without. You can apply CBT any time, in any situation that sends you into a spin, but in particular, this book uses examples in the work situation to help you pinpoint common examples of work life imbalances.

Whenever you are feeling worried or anxious about work, you could say it's the warning light that you may want to do something about it to try to reduce the uneasy feelings. You are the only one who really knows how you are feeling. This book gives you an introduction to the ideas of CBT, and explains the practical strategies you can apply to reduce anxieties. There is some of the theory behind CBT included too, to help you put into perspective what makes it stand out from other therapies. You may also want to work with your medical professionals, perhaps a psychotherapist as well at times, but this book will guide you to making choices which are in your best interest.

In all the working situations I have come across in the different jobs I have done, including manufacturing work, education, sales, global financial organisations, central government, prisons, leisure industry and cruise ship lecturing, I found similar problems and difficulties. I encountered problems and emotional upsets both in my own working life and as a psychotherapist working for an international employee assistance H.R. company. All the examples are based on real-life scenarios, across a wide range of employment situations.

I worked for a year in California on a job exchange and first encountered being helped by an Employee Assistance Programme whilst working there.

I returned to the UK and decided I would like to train to be able to work as a Stress Manager and apply the U.S.A. experience to my work as a psychologist in the UK. That was in 1989. Our group was the first to train in a new type of cognitive therapy. Since then, I have used CBT in my work both personally and professionally. This book is the result of wanting to share what I have learnt with as many people as possible, who also find work a struggle sometimes. I know that CBT can be helpful. I have learned this from all the hundreds of clients I have worked with, seeing them work through the difficult times and from the feedback they give saying how useful the CBT has been. I wish CBT had been around when I was in the early years of my career; I would have spent far less time agonising over work problems and decisions, insecurities and sleepless nights. If only I could have applied some CBT to my irrational thinking and understood that worrying and making myself anxious and upset was not going to help. CBT does not suggest that you don't care about life and work, and become some emotionless automaton. CBT helps you to work out your unhealthy negative thinking and change it to a healthy concern that makes a good night's sleep more of a possibility and your work life and career a calmer and rewarding path.

Once you have learned some CBT, you will have that knowledge and a toolkit to apply whenever you start to feel uneasy.

*CBT is for life, not just for crises.*

# *About This Book*

This book is for people who want to find ways to help themselves reduce emotional upsets at work, learn a practical therapy and be able to apply these coping strategies at work and at home. Although the examples are work-based, the suggestions and learning can be equally applied in your personal life. Whatever level of work you are involved in, self employed, team member, management, employer or managing director of an international global organisation, this book is for you. I have worked using CBT techniques with all levels of people in their place of work, written training courses for organisations and provided individual therapy for many who have come for work related issues. This book will also help you to plan for the future, manage your career, provide yourself with coaching to enhance your experiences at work and recognise what sort of work preferences you have and how that fits with your personality. This book covers the following:

The basic ideas of CBT, what the therapy does and how it works

How you can use the CBT techniques to apply to your problems at work

Common emotional upsets with examples from real life

Ways to identify your trouble spots and decide if you want to reduce the anxieties

How to look after yourself at work

Benefits for your workplace as well as yourself

How to deal with difficult people

*CBT is not a quick fix but a helpful tool for life*

All the way through the book, the new ideas presented are backed up by putting them in the context of a situation in the workplace. I have found that clients find the real-life examples give meaning to the CBT and help them to remember how to do it. Like any new skill you learn, you need to understand, learn, apply and go over it again when new situations arise. I didn't learn to ski by just watching the instructor and trying it out once; I needed to go over and over the techniques, try them out, fall over, pick myself up and have a think about what didn't quite work out. The more I was prepared to put myself through the discomfort zone of possibly falling over, and work through it, the more the possibility of a smooth ski run was likely. Skiing eventually became automatic, but there are still times when a wobble reminds me to stay focused and re-apply the techniques.

# *How to Use This Book*

You can use this book to dip in and out of the chapters and subsections. Each chapter is stand alone, and as you scan the contents, you may find that you want to immediately just read the bit that applies to you at this moment. This is fine. The book is designed this way. It is helpful for the beginner and the more experienced who may already have an understanding of what CBT is about. If you decide you really want to have a look at the CBT method and try it out on yourself, then reading Chapter 2 will give you a good introduction to the basic ideas and methods. You do not need to remember all the bits you read in order to move on; you will find you remember the bits that are significant to you anyway. You are the seeker in your own journey of self understanding. You can find your own way and take responsibility for your learning and decide what is useful for you. CBT is exactly that, taking responsibility for your own emotional wellbeing.

There are many stories, anecdotes, case studies, references and descriptions of different types of psychological conditions which can occur. Some of these have their own section or are in grey tinted boxes, called sidebars. These help explain how people feel at times and you can choose which interests you or skip to the ones that are personally relevant. The first section of a self-help book I turned to when I first discovered a book on stress in the 1970s was 'The Symptoms of Depression'. I mentally ticked off 90 per cent of these symptoms. This was the start of understanding that what I was feeling was an actual condition, not a failure on my part to cope.

This book could be a start for you to want to find out more on particular areas. Chapter 23 provides you with information for finding more help, books, downloads, websites, mental health resources, apps and technical help, training resources and opportunities to further your knowledge. There are other *For Dummies* books that expand on some of the topics mentioned in this book. For example, there is a whole book devoted to CBT, another on Mindfulness and a specialist Mindfulness at work.

Within this book, you may note that some web addresses break across two lines of text. If you're reading a hardcopy of this book and want to visit one of these web pages, simply key in the web address exactly as it's noted in the text, pretending as if the line break doesn't exist. If you're reading this as an e-book, you've got it easy – just click the web address to be taken directly to the web page.

# *Foolish Assumptions*

In writing this book, I have made a few assumptions about who you are:

> You are working or are looking for work.
>
> You are looking for ideas and practical suggestions about how to cope with work.
>
> You may have experienced anxieties, insecurity or just general unhappiness in your work life at times.
>
> You want to maximise your opportunities and experiences at work as an investment for your future.
>
> You want to progress your career using logical and well planned strategies.
>
> You have an interest in personal development and in particular how you can apply that to work.
>
> You are interested in finding out how you work and also why others at work behave the way they do.
>
> You have heard people talk about CBT or have read somewhere it is a fairly new form of therapy that has its roots in scientific research and seems to have a high success rate.
>
> You have a friend who has had some CBT treatment and raves about it.
>
> Even though you are feeling pretty much okay about work and your personal life, you are interested in finding out about recent innovations in healthcare.

You are thinking of training to be a psychotherapist and want to look at CBT to compare it with other treatments and counselling.

This book addresses these issues and more besides. It is for anyone who wants to find out about CBT, mental health and work environments. While most employee referrals for CBT therapy are for people over the age of 18, the earlier you can have a greater understanding of yourself and others, the earlier you can start reducing the unsettling emotions in life.

# Icons Used in This Book

There are some icons used in For Dummies books that appear down the side of the page. Here are explanations of the ones used in this book.

This icon encourages you to pay special attention to what's being said.

This icon directs your attention to something to help make things clearer.

This suggests you pay particular attention to help avoid any pitfalls.

This icon suggests you mull something over in your mind to give consideration to the idea.

This icon tells you that the info beside it is a real-world example.

# Beyond the Book

As well as the resources section at the back of the book, listing suggestions for further reading and access to other resources, I have included bonus online material.

There is a brief description of this treasure trove of free digital content and crucially where it's hidden, just for you to discover.

- ✔ **Cheat sheet:** This is a bite size text that lets you know some of the key points contained in *CBT for Work For Dummies* but in an ultra condensed form. The cheat sheet is there to give you the basics. All Dummies books have a cheat sheet, and they enable readers to quickly refer to a fact without having to carry the book around or power up the e-reader. One cheat sheet lists ten tips for the application of CBT when things get tricky. Clients used to tell me that having the cheat sheet helped them focus on what they needed to do when they felt themselves getting upset emotionally. Another sheet contains things to look out for if you feel you might be getting depressed. Cheat sheets are fast, fun and full of useful information, and you can find them at `www.dummies.com/cheatsheets/cbtatwork`.

- ✔ **Dummies online articles:** There is extra information that I think you may find interesting but not contained in the book. One is a true case study of a burned-out employee who had a breakdown and got his life back on track after discovering CBT and applying it to himself. Another is about how people sometimes get the feeling that they are going to be found out that the are no good at their jobs, called "The Imposter Syndrome", and how research has found these feelings are quite common. Another is about how using CBT in your organisation can make a big difference and how many companies are now looking to offer it within their organisations. A fourth online article looks more widely at how including CBT and other strategies can help you achieve a more balanced and happier you. There is so much interesting material to be looked at and add to your wealth of understanding of how you tick. All this extra content can be found at `http://www.dummies/extras/cbtatwork`.

# *Where to Go from Here*

You may have gathered that I am a great advocate of CBT. I do think that even just a little knowledge about how it works and how you can apply it to yourself and become your own therapist for everyday emotional turbulence will help you steer a smoother course in your life. I have worked with thousands of clients and worked in many situations over the years, and CBT has been the most significant addition to all that work. You can choose how much or how little you want to learn. My aim is to share with you the knowledge and experiences I have built up in the hope that some of it will be practically useful to you. I hope you will take away the bits that are relevant to you and encourage others to find out about CBT, too. May you find your great journey of discovery interesting, helpful and even fun!

# Part I

# Getting Started with CBT at Work

Visit www.dummies.com/extras/cbtatwork for great Dummies content online.

# In this part . . .

- ✔ Learn to minimize stress and take control of your emotions at work.

- ✔ Discover the components of CBT and see how you can connect your feelings to your thinking.

- ✔ Change the way you think with the help of a CTB toolkit that you can make.

- ✔ Identify with the struggles you encounter at work to help you make your workplace a healthier environment for you.

# Chapter 1

# Reducing Your Anxieties at Work with CBT

*In This Chapter*

▶ Understanding the pressures of the modern workplace

▶ Diagnosing your work-based emotional difficulties

▶ Tooling up with CBT to survive at work

*T*he modern workplace is often a diverse, fast-paced environment fraught with challenges and potential problems. Your role is to get through each day as best you can and achieve your targets and goals. Considering how much time you spend at work during your lifetime, you'd be unusual if sometimes you didn't wrestle with anxieties, self-doubt, anger, guilt, confusion and a general feeling of unhappiness.

Fortunately, Cognitive Behavioural Therapy (CBT) was developed to help you reduce these sorts of tensions and insecurities. In a sense, CBT guides you to become your own therapist, as you use its techniques to reflect on and tackle your troubling feelings. With CBT, you train yourself to recognise when things are getting tough and affecting your emotional wellbeing. You can then apply the CBT formula to work actively to reduce the intensity of the troubling emotions.

Think of CBT as helping you to be the world's foremost expert on you! Your new internal voice disputes your irrational thinking, allowing you to decide whether you want to make changes in the way you view your job, other people and your employer in order to reduce your worries.

Here I introduce you to the basics of CBT and how it can help you at work. Throughout this chapter, I also provide an overview of the book as a whole, providing cross references to other chapters as appropriate.

# Coping with Changing Roles at Work

The workspace is a constantly changing arena. People have always been concerned about finding ways to survive and coping with the diversification of jobs, whether they're working on the land, in communities and villages or in specialised purpose-built offices.

You may yourself have held many different jobs, needing to adapt and retrain as necessary in order to make yourself eligible for different work roles. In fact, being flexible and having wide-ranging experiences and skills is often seen as an asset these days and not an indication that you can't stick at a job.

The inspiration to write this book comes from my practical experience in working in many different jobs in various settings and recognising the common nature of the problems that people encounter at work.

For example, I've done manual work in a textile factory, taught young children in nurseries and primary schools and worked with emotionally challenged teenagers in the inner city. I've also studied to be a psychotherapist; worked in a ski-chalet in France, cooking and cleaning; managed lectures on a cruise ship; and written courses on change management for international financial organisations and national government.

The great thing about CBT strategies and skills is that you can apply them in all employment situations that people work in today, whether within local communities, in rural locations, towns or cities or in an international setting.

## Stressing out at work

Workplace stress is a pretty familiar phrase in today's marketplace and its negative effects on mental and physical health are well-documented. As a result, developing the skills and attitudes of mind to help you cope is a priority.

External forces, such as changing market economies affecting companies and resulting in redundancies, layoffs and closures, aren't a reflection of your individual performance in a job but of factors outside your control.

## Taking charge of your emotions

You can't control many of the situations you encounter at work, including the bosses and managers you find yourself working under or the people in your team. But you can take control over how you're affected by these factors. Chapter 11 talks more about CBT and work relationships.

Feeling helpless and lapsing into depression can be a response to feeling that you're stuck in a difficult situation. You may start by experiencing feelings of anxiety, butterflies in the stomach and a dread of going into work, and fear progressing to panic. Such anxiety can result in you being more likely to make mistakes and may compound your worries. You can feel like you're on a downward spiral of incompetence, and your self-esteem may plummet too.

The good news is that CBT can help you to train yourself to take charge of your negative emotions and do something about them before you fall into the pit of doom (your GPS won't find it, but it's there, just below the pothole of ruin and nestling behind the shaft of lost hope!). When you implement CBT, you become fully aware of your emotions. You're encouraged to allow yourself to look at what's happening and to use the CBT toolkit from Chapter 3 to work actively on dealing with your negative automatic thoughts (or NATs; see Chapter 8 for details), thus reducing the 'disturbing' emotions to less disruptive and manageable ones.

# Thinking Rationally to Troubleshoot Your Emotions

Of all the counselling methods and therapies I trained in, CBT resonated most strongly with me. I was always a hurry hurry, rush rush type of personality, often working myself up into a state of anxiety and demonstrating low levels of tolerance for frustration. I usually achieved what I set out to do, but the road was fraught with anxiety, self-doubt and, at times, guilt.

Although I agreed with the ideas behind other forms of counselling, I felt that I didn't have the time for weekly sessions and months of therapy. Fortunately, CBT is intended to be short-term therapy that you can apply to your whole life (see Chapters 16 and 19).

Here I lay out the basics of CBT, its practical nature and how the responsibility is on you to tackle your emotional problems and nobody else's.

## Meeting the CBT basics

CBT helps you to discover and prioritise your emotional problems, encouraging you to take responsibility for your emotional development (flip to Chapter 7 for more on these aspects). It uses examples of real-life problems to help you reinforce your learning and become accountable to yourself to work on the issues you identify as needing attention.

You can see CBT as comprising six areas:

✔ Explaining the problems: Here are just a few examples of the long list of emotions and behaviours that may be causing you distress at work:

– Anger

– Anxiety

– Confidence/self-esteem issues

– Depression – withdrawal, feeling sad, loss of enjoyment

– Low frustration tolerance – impatient, angry

– Medicating yourself inappropriately

– Panic – feeling fearful

– Feelings and behaviours as a result of – illness, pain, and incapacity

– Struggles with relationship difficulties

– Unhelpful behaviours – eating, drinking, self harming

✔ Identifying the emotions: You will then be encouraged to work out what emotions you are experiencing which are unsettling or distressing. (Check out Chapter 2 for how to start spotting and naming your negative feelings).

✔ Working out the origin of the reasons for these feelings: There will always be a reason for a 'trigger' which sets you off worrying or feeling anxious, or angry or any other negative emotion. It may not be obvious at first but spending time working out what it is that sets off these feelings is an important step (you may find Chapter 3 helpful here).

✔ Looking at your possible choices and options: You may think you are trapped and have no alternative paths to choose from. This in itself can set off negative thinking and feelings. There are always some choices, even if all of them are unattractive and hard to take. (Chapter 4 talks more about having options and making choices, for good or ill).

✔ Deciding whether you want to work on changing the way you think about what's happening for you: Sometimes you may decide that you are just going to put up with the difficult situations and decide you don't want to change. This is fine, you don't have to do anything. Having a look at the consequences of doing nothing, though, can be useful, as in the long term you may be setting yourself up for an even tougher journey in the future. Taking some time to consider all of this helps you make more informed choices. (Try Chapter 5 to think specifically about your problems in your workplace).

✔ Learning and applying the CBT method of linking the feeling–thinking connection: If you decide you would like to work on reducing some of the negative feelings precipitated by your thinking, then you will need to learn the CBT methods to be able to apply them for yourself. Some people may choose to find a CBT therapist to teach them and others, like you, who is reading this book and is up for teaching yourself and ultimately helping you to be informed about CBT practice. (Chapter 7 is the place to start for using CBT at work).

Choosing to use CBT therapy doesn't involve secrets or magic (no incantations featuring knee of newt or toe of toad!). You just make a conscious decision to learn and apply CBT to your troubles and to take responsibility for your own emotional wellbeing.

In certain situations, you can find that your choices are tough ones to make and you certainly won't like some of the options available at work. But CBT works with you to look at the possible emotional and behavioural consequences of choosing to do nothing and carrying on upsetting yourself.

Often you can choose to ignore what's happening, because it seems too painful or scary to admit the reality of the situation, but CBT helps you to pay attention to it and do something about it.

Seeing your options laid out in front of you, along with the 'logic' behind your irrational thinking and the consequences of continuing to think in a certain way, can be very enlightening.

As the old saying has it: 'procrastination is the thief of time'. How often have you put something off until it becomes so urgent and pressing that the consequences start pushing over into a crisis? But then, after you attend to the task, you find that it wasn't so bad after all and you wish that you hadn't spent so long in a state of anxiety.

## Tackling tough times with CBT

A core belief in CBT is that you can't make changes without pain, which is why some people call it a tough therapy. It involves goals, guidelines, exercises, homework and the constant need to be 'on your own case'. There is no change without pain.

You have to go through the discomfort zones to progress. (I discuss the specific issue of workplace changes in Chapters 13 and 17).

If you want to keep avoiding your problems – living in denial between episodes of distress, surrounded by the crutches of chocolate and hot drinks, and yet aware subconsciously that troubling moments at work lie around the corner – CBT won't work for you. The fact is that you have to make CBT work for you.

CBT guides you through the process, however, because you work out what your unpleasant zones may be in advance of pushing yourself through them. You make the conscious decision to take on the necessary work yourself, in terms of changing your attitudes, and use appropriate coping strategies to see you through.

For example, imagine that your goal is to work alone on your company's reception desk, but that the thought of dealing with members of the public (and their notorious unpredictability) terrifies you. CBT can help you to anticipate what the obstacles may be and how you may feel in advance, as well as to plan experiencing discomfort. No-one can experience the reality of stepping into the scary situation for you, though: you must do that yourself.

# Recognising Problems in the Workplace

You have a core personality, partly determined by your genes, your environment and your upbringing (check out Chapter 9 for more details). Plus, how you present yourself varies in different situations. You may be aware of certain expectations of yourself in different roles, but essentially you remain the same person.

Finding out where you fit in and recognising your own work situation is helpful in identifying recurrent issues and potential struggles.

## Experiencing conflict between your beliefs and actions

In order to be successful in the workplace, you need to be aware of what's expected of you – because you can experience tension when this requirement doesn't fit with who you are. The disquiet arises from a mismatch between what you're thinking and how you're being asked to behave. For example, you may feel angry at having to do some tasks or conform to certain working conditions and think that things just aren't fair. You'd be correct.

But how hard you insist on gripping to your rigid views of how life 'should' be, bemoaning the fact that your work doesn't measure up, is a large influence on how unsettled you feel at work.

CBT helps you to sort out this confusion. You don't lose any sense of your true self and become an emotionless automaton with CBT, but you do find yourself making enlightened choices. I like to call this conscious compliance. You may not agree with something you need to do at work, but you do choose to comply, because ultimately doing so is in your best long-term interests.

## Admitting your struggles

When you allow yourself to admit that things aren't going along too well and that you're struggling, you've made the first step towards doing something about it.

I used to work for a company's Employees Assistance Programme, taking calls on the confidential helpline. I know from experience that the hardest part of the process was for employees to pick up the phone and make the call to say they'd like some help.

Even calling your GP to make an appointment for a physical ailment can be tough, because you may feel that you have some weakness in yourself that you don't want to have to admit. Sometimes, when you've spoken the words, you can feel that it's all too real. But not attending to the warning signs leaves you open to the problem getting worse.

Saying 'I'm struggling a bit here' is perfectly okay. You're likely to judge yourself much more harshly than your friends and co-workers do. When it comes to the crunch, if someone you work with gets a serious illness you often notice people's genuine concern.

Emotional problems can progress into crises and become critical if you leave them unattended for a long time.

## Looking after yourself at work

You have a responsibility to take care of yourself at work. Keeping yourself physically and emotionally healthy isn't only in your best interests, but also in your employer's and workmates' too (as I describe in Chapter 5).

When you drag yourself into work when you aren't feeling well, you're often not met with sympathy and concern. Great relief is felt all round when someone else makes the decision and orders you to go home. Oh, the joy when your boss tells you not to come back until you're better – though these moments are probably quite rare.

CBT can help you develop the confidence to recognise when you need time out to get yourself physically and mentally fit, and the skill to understand and rationalise why doing so is in your long-term best interests.

# Discovering the Benefits of the CBT Problem-Solving Method

This book shows you enough CBT techniques to enable you to go off and apply them to your own situation. For example, Chapter 2 describes CBT's basic principles and practical applications (which come in a handy ABC framework) and Chapter 3 talks you through building your own CBT portable toolkit for fixing your emotional problems. To help convince you of its benefits, I also include real-world stories of how people have used CBT successfully in the workplace. I draw them from my experience of working as a CBT therapist with hundreds of employees in the private and public sectors for more than 20 years.

CBT is an evidence-based theory, using scientific, logical and rational methods to construct, assess and test its effectiveness. It's proved to help people reduce their debilitating emotional states. Many research papers show, for example, that CBT seems to have long-lasting effects in treating anxiety and depression, which may be due in part to the fact that people are encouraged to discover the therapy and help themselves to stay well over time.

Accountability in CBT through confidential assessment and monitoring is a key factor in many health organisations choosing to use CBT as their preferred method of providing emotional support to employees.

## Increasing a company's productivity and positivity

As CBT has gained in popularity, more companies and HR departments are recommending this therapy for their employees.

You can't overestimate the financial advantages of keeping a workforce healthy and happy. Chapters 6 and 13–15 look at some of the benefits to an organisation of adopting strategies that keep stress levels to a minimum and offer support for stress-related issues.

During your work life you're bound to experience struggles in your personal life that may then impact on your professional life. But the great thing about CBT is that knowledge of it is just as helpful for personal issues as work-related ones.

## Being an ambassador for CBT

When you've got the hang of CBT and are actively using it in your life, you may find that work colleagues comment on the change in you: perhaps you seem more relaxed and they want to know how you manage to stay calm during a crisis. Of course, you know that using CBT is an active therapy. You appear calm because underneath you're consciously going through the ABC technique, which I explain in Chapter 2, to be on the alert for feelings of rising panic in yourself. You can then rationalise your thoughts to keep that anxiety in check.

For those moments when co-workers ask you, Chapter 14 encourages you to become a CBT ambassador yourself! I've taught many a colleague some principles of CBT in coffee breaks who tell me that they still apply them years later.

## Selecting the work life you want

One aim of using CBT is to have only a healthy concern for what's happening around you, rather than a debilitating state of anxiety about events.

Work can make many demands on you, some of which may not be to your liking. You may need to fulfil those demands to keep your job, but CBT encourages you never to lose sight of who you are. Even in the harshest of conditions, people have kept their sense of values and personal beliefs. Viktor E Frankl was a survivor of the holocaust who endured terrible conditions. He's quoted as saying:

> *Everything can be taken from a man but one thing: the last of human freedoms – to choose one's attitude in any given set of circumstances, to choose one's own way.*

CBT is about helping you to uncover your beliefs and attitudes and check whether they're helping or hindering you. (Chapter 4 has loads of useful info on the importance of maintaining a healthy attitude at and about work, and Chapter 10 talks about creating your own philosophy on work.) You can always choose your own way (Chapter 12, in particular, shows you how).

# *Becoming balanced professionally and personally*

The issue of striking a healthy work–life balance (which I cover in Chapter 16) is a concern across many countries and cultures. The blurred boundaries between work and personal life can impact heavily on people.

Make sure that your life isn't dominated by work, if that's not what you want. Check out how your life is working every now and again, and use CBT to help identify when you're getting out of balance.

CBT suggests that you work towards an acceptance of some situations and events and not to upset yourself about things beyond your control. When you can truly accept some difficult things, and change the way you view them, you free yourself up to move forward.

> *Once we accept our limits, we go beyond them.*

—Albert Einstein

# Chapter 2

# Discovering How CBT Works

- - - - - - - - - - - - - - - - - - - - - - - - - - - - - - - - - - - - - - - - -

*In This Chapter*
▶ Getting to grips with CBT
▶ Considering the basics
▶ Using CBT to help yourself

- - - - - - - - - - - - - - - - - - - - - - - - - - - - - - - - - - - - - - - - -

*P*eople have visited doctors or healers of some sort for physical illnesses and injuries for centuries. Today, humans know more about their bodies and what to do when things go wrong than ever, and more professionally trained medical personnel are available.

People are also becoming increasingly familiar with the idea of seeking help when life gets to be an emotional struggle. Sometimes people's mental health can become so adversely affected that they have difficulty coping with everyday life, let alone work. But the balance between merely having a tough time and becoming seriously anxious and depressed, resulting in an inability to function properly, varies from individual to individual.

When you experience struggles that affect your emotional state, you can be confused as to where to go for help, and even feel embarrassed – which is where cognitive behavioural therapy (CBT) comes in. In this chapter, I describe CBT's role, the basics of how it works and how it can help you improve your emotional wellbeing.

## Understanding Cognitive Behavioural Therapy

CBT is a practical psychological strategy that takes into account people's thinking, behaviours and emotions. It's designed to help them bring about a change in their emotions, usually from an unsettled and unhelpful state to a calmer and less disturbed one. Healthcare organisations around the world are increasingly recognising and adopting CBT. It's particularly favoured for helping people to address their struggles at work, and for helping them get back to work when they've had to take sickness absences or their performance at work is being affected by distracting emotional states.

As an accredited CBT practitioner offering and implementing CBT in the workplace for individuals and via training courses, I've found that CBT can be an extremely helpful strategy for workers to discover and implement.

A key aspect of CBT is that it shows individuals how to become their own therapist. It's a highly practical therapy that explains and involves the subject. Individuals find out how to work out what's happening for them and why they're feeling the way they are, as well as strategies for reducing unsettling emotions.

Sometimes CBT is referred to as a brief therapy, because it doesn't necessarily require months and years of attending weekly sessions: some people need only a few sessions to get the hang of it and successfully apply it to themselves. On average, depending on the emotional state of the individual, about six CBT sessions can be a good start to gain an understanding of CBT in order to start applying it for yourself. I routinely work with employees who find a couple of sessions helpful enough to redress the mild emotional imbalance they've been experiencing.

This book gives a background explanation of CBT theory and methods. It's not intended to replace medical consultations and advice, which are very important. Emotional imbalances can vary in severity and you should always let your medical practitioner know when you're experiencing troubling thoughts and emotions. This book isn't a substitute for overall healthcare but an informed addition for your wellbeing library. Use it to help you gain more insight into yourself, particularly in the workplace.

## Introducing the components of CBT

CBT is quite simple in concept:

- ✔ Cognitive: How you think.
- ✔ Behaviour: How you act.
- ✔ Therapy: A conscious intention to bring about change.

CBT is about linking your thinking to your behaviours and deciding whether you want to change some unhelpful behaviours. It's extremely effective at challenging everyday problems that affect people in the workplace and looking at ways to help reduce associated negative or 'unhealthy' feelings.

Some frequently occurring such feelings include (in no particular order):

- Anger
- Anxiety
- Depression
- Embarrassment
- Guilt
- Hurt
- Low self-esteem
- Self-doubt
- Shame

People also experience many other feelings daily that come and go without people paying close attention to them.

Human beings are highly efficient information processors and are bombarded with information from the minute they wake up. Just think how many decisions you make automatically: washing, what to wear, what to eat, getting ready for work, and finding your way to work are just a few. If an app were able to monitor your feelings and display an 'emotional graph' at the end of each day, you'd amazed at the gamut of your emotions!

Here's the thing though: only you know what you're feeling – and half the time even you're not sure! Identifying specific feelings can be difficult. You process unconsciously a lot of the time, but that doesn't mean that your information input has no impact on your physiological and psychological systems. Even when you're asleep, your brain is busy and active, sorting out information from the day's events and making links with past ones.

Internal thinking triggered by your own thought processes and past stored memories all have an impact on your emotional state. In order to understand CBT, you have to be aware of all events that impact you.

## *Deciding whether you want to use CBT*

Sometimes you can be so involved in lurching from day to day in order to survive that you don't realise the adverse impact that activities are having. You don't allow yourself to stop and acknowledge that you're struggling, because the primary need to provide for yourself and others means that you can't afford to 'crumble'.

Deciding that you really want to make a change is key to successful CBT. You have to recognise, through your own insight or by another person's prompting, that some of your current behaviours aren't in your best interests.

### Saying 'yes'

The first step in deciding to seek therapy comes when you allow into your consciousness the fact that all isn't well. More often than not, you start experiencing distressing symptoms of anxiety-related behaviours and realise for yourself that things aren't right.

Or, perhaps at work, a friend takes you to one side and expresses his concern for you. This action is a hard thing for anyone to do, because conveying to you that he's worried is difficult for both of you: you may feel as though you're being criticised or judged, and he may worry that he may offend or upset you. Everyone can get defensive in such situations.

Or maybe your manager has a word with you about your performance, which triggers a decision to go to your GP. In some cases, if a person's behaviour prompts concern that he may be a danger to himself, others or to the company, the employer may intervene in the employee's own best interest.

Whatever the way in which you discover that you're struggling, you need to admit it to yourself. The next big step is deciding whether you're going to seek help. Realising that you aren't performing at your best can feel alien and be quite a shock.

### Facing stigmas

In some cultures and situations, particularly at work, people can feel that admitting that they're struggling with emotional distress is a sign of weakness. People fear a professional and social stigma.

For example, people with impeccable work histories, who've worked efficiently, conscientiously and without any previous difficulties, may suddenly find themselves experiencing symptoms of stress. A common coping strategy is to enter a state of denial, which isn't at all helpful.

The most helpful thing you can do for yourself is to allow yourself to accept that you are struggling; it is not a sign of weakness. The next step is to try to tell someone else that you are finding work difficult and that it is affecting your emotional state every day. It is okay to ask for help – you may be surprised at how willing other people are to listen.

## *Realising that you can change if you want*

Most people in full-time work spend approximately 40 hours a week working, with many working a lot longer, depending on their job and the demands made upon them. The all-pervasive use of information technology means that employers can contact many workers 24 hours a day, as well as at weekends and on holidays.

In addition, unless you're self-employed, your job role and requirements are usually externally imposed. You may have some input as to how and when you meet these demands, but your contract with your company is an agreement to fulfil its requirements.

Even if you are your own boss, the management of your own role and the success of your venture is reliant upon you meeting the demands required for the successful completion of projects.

Unsurprisingly, therefore, the issue of work–life balance is a potential source of difficulty and conflict for many people.

One of the major sources of unhappiness and distress is feeling trapped and powerless in a job. Not having control over your workload is a common predictor of workplace stress.

Fortunately, CBT can help you get your job in perspective. It can help you view your job and its demands in a healthy and manageable way so that you concentrate your energies on the things you can control and don't engage in unhelpful worrying about issues and events beyond your control.

# *Meeting the ABCs of CBT*

CBT evolved when psychologists who worked with people with emotional struggles came up with ideas as to why these problems arise (check out the nearby sidebar 'A brief history of CBT' for more).

In the following sections, I introduce you to some essential concepts of CBT, so that you can understand more about what CBT is and how it works, how to investigate your emotional responses, and how to correctly identify your feelings.

The idea that people are upset not by events and people but by how they view those events or people was a new way of viewing mental health or ill-health.

## A brief history of CBT

Even though thousands of years ago the Ancient Greeks recognised that people could become out of sorts emotionally, not a huge amount of research was done into people's moods until the 19th century (when Freud developed his psychoanalysis techniques). Over the following decades, other theories investigated how and why people experience negative and unhealthy emotions.

The 1950s witnessed moves to create theories and therapies that could include people's thinking processes and combine those with the outward behaviours in which the people engaged. This psychological movement was called Cognitive Behavioural Therapy. One of the founding proponents was psychologist Aaron Beck. He noticed that depressed and anxious people seemed to think negatively, beginning a new line of investigation into emotional health.

Even before Beck, a psychoanalyst in New York called Albert Ellis had noticed that people who were upset with events in their lives tended to think in irrational ways: how they viewed themselves, their work and the world in general shared common themes. Ellis proposed that irrational thinking gave rise to unsettled emotions and, in fact, that people were upsetting themselves, and sometimes making themselves unwell.

## *Thinking scientifically*

CBT is an evidence-based theory and therapy. It uses the widely understood and accepted scientific methods employed universally in other sciences. Psychology is still a relatively new science and, although the study of human behaviour isn't the same as studying physics, chemistry or biology, individuals do exhibit common themes and often repeat patterns of behaviour and ways of thinking and acting.

If you do your own detective work and look for themes or patterns of thinking and consequently unhelpful behaviours, you can start to form your own hypothesis as to how you can change.

Think about it this way: if you don't know any math, how can you be expected to work out your personal finances? Similarly, with emotional education: if you've never been taught how to use psychological methods to ease your emotional ill-health, helping yourself is going to be much harder.

## *Simplifying CBT methods*

In general, people aren't upset by what people say and do to them, or what happens at work and elsewhere in their lives; they upset themselves by their own thinking. Bearing this crucial distinction in mind, you can easily learn CBT techniques to help yourself.

### Outlining the ABC framework

Here I describe the ABC model in CBT, which can help you work out accurately why you're feeling unsettled:

- ✔ A: Activating event.
- ✔ B: Beliefs and thinking.
- ✔ C: Emotional consequence.

Notice that B – your processing of the information and what you think about the event – comes between A and C.

### Seeing the framework in action

Here's a practical example to illustrate how people tend to think in this ABC way. Someone makes a round of cups of coffee in your office and leaves you out. Clearly, you feel a bit upset about it.

The activating event (A), no cup for you, is as follows:

- ✔ Ian makes five cups of coffee.
- ✔ Six of you work in the office.
- ✔ He doesn't bring you a cup.

The emotional consequence (C) is that you feel unsettled, perhaps experiencing some of the following feelings: annoyed, confused, defensive, dismissive, hurt, revengeful, surprised.

You jump to the conclusion that Ian caused you to feel unsettled.

But Ian hasn't upset your feelings. You did this to yourself by the way in which you interpreted his actions. Your brain works quickly to process all sorts of incoming information. You decide which information you pay attention to, probably influenced by how significant you perceive it is to you.

You see Ian dishing out the cups and realise that he hasn't given you a drink. But that event (A) doesn't directly cause your hurt (C). Instead, you hold a belief (B), lurking in the background, that people should be fair when they make coffee in the office and everyone, including yourself, should get a cup.

When the evidence proves otherwise, and you don't receive a cup, you see the event as unfair and feel unhappy. As long as you continue to hold onto the belief that you should've received a cup but you haven't got one, you'll continue to upset yourself about it.

Ian didn't upset you by not giving you a cup of coffee; you upset yourself by believing that he should've done. Your cognitive processing and beliefs created the unsettled feelings.

## *Becoming a detective of your emotions*

Most of the time, people are completely unaware of some of the beliefs they hold about themselves, other people and the world in general.

Your beliefs are your unconscious default mode; you carry them round with you all the time. They wreak havoc with your emotions, often without you being consciously aware of it.

But you can help yourself by starting to be your own detective a bit more. Consider this analogy: when your bank sends you a text alert to inform you that you've gone overdrawn, your attention is drawn to that information. You then choose whether you want to ignore it or act on it (ignoring it can have serious repercussions for your financial health).

The same principle applies to your emotional health. If you alert yourself to when you feel 'wobbly', you can choose whether you pay attention or ignore it (and not acting can adversely affect your emotional health).

Identifying the 'wobble' or emotional consequence (the 'C' from the preceding section) is the first port of call when learning about CBT and how to use it in your life to reduce unsettling feelings.

'Wobbly' is a word that seems to resonate with people. You may find that identifying more precisely what sort of 'wobbly' applies to you is helpful in describing your unsettling feelings. Here's a short list of 'wobbles' – I'm sure you can add your own:

- ✔ Wobbly – angry
- ✔ Wobbly – anxious
- ✔ Wobbly – scared
- ✔ Wobbly – tearful
- ✔ Wobbly – unwell

Imagine that you've been physically unwell, perhaps with the flu, and you think after three days off work that you should go back. The work is piling up and you're worrying about it.

You wrap up in warm clothes and head off to work, armed with sachets of cold cures, tissues and vitamin drinks. As soon as you walk in and sit down, you realise you aren't fit. You feel 'wobbly', your head hurts, you feel shivery and the cold preparations have made you feel nauseous. How you feel makes it obvious to you that you're unsettled, physically.

So too with emotional ill-health: your psychological feedback gives you signs and symptoms that all isn't well and that you need to pay attention.

# Your feelings

Recognising when you're feeling unsettled can be hard, and identifying the emotions you're experiencing can be even more difficult. In this section, I encourage you to 'name that feeling'. To do so, you need to understand the interaction of your physical body and your emotions.

### Look! A bear!

People are generally more used to monitoring their physical feelings than their emotional ones. Recognition of physiological changes in their bodies, their biofeedback, is more highly developed. Feelings are a manifestation of what you're thinking and are linked to physiological changes in your body.

People have two basic survival-mode reactions to threats: fight or flight. When you perceive a threat, your body gears up to deal with it. If the threat is a huge grizzly bear about to make you his lunch, you pour adrenalin into your body automatically. This release primes your muscles to stay and fight or run away, the extra adrenalin giving your muscles more potential power.

### Look! An emotional threat that I need to identify!

Although encountering such extreme threats is unusual (if you do meet a grizzly bear while shopping on the high street, I don't suggest fighting it!), you face milder ones every day – and your body still reacts by releasing adrenalin. But when you don't use up this extra energy by running or fighting, you can experience adverse effects from the excessive adrenalin. The degree to which you feel the physical effects varies according to the perceived intensity of the threat, but they include sweating and light-headedness. Psychological effects include anxiety, anger, fear, sadness, depression, frustration, a lack of confidence and negative self-worth.

There are links between the physical symptoms of reactions to threats and the psychological symptoms. This is the effect of the adrenaline released into your body preparing it for action.

How far you're affected by threats in your environment is a result of how you think about them. If you perceive some incoming information as a threat, by how you view it, you're likely to experience negative emotions.

### *Look! A trigger for negative thinking!*

Human beings have a great ability to internalise events and experiences and to be able to retrieve memories in words and pictures. As a result, you can trigger threats simply by your own internal thinking. Recollections can act as internal thinking triggers that produce negative feelings.

To see what I mean, try this simple experiment:

1. Think of an embarrassing, but not traumatic, event from your past.

2. Picture yourself in that situation.

3. Recollect the event and how you felt.

4. See whether you can bring up some of the same feelings that you had at that time.

---

# CBT to the rescue!

A while ago I had to present a workshop to 12 senior managers at a top financial organisation. I'd designed, written and piloted the material months in advance and created the PowerPoint presentation. I'd passed the handbooks to accompany the workshop to my employer's in-house printing department well in advance and they were to be couriered to the company the day before.

The evening before the workshop, a technician said that he had to change my laptop to a different one because he needed to do some work on it. He gave me a different laptop to take to the workshop. At home, I downloaded the presentation and all the necessary resources.

Arriving at the financial organisation's head offices, I was shown to the executive suite where the workshop would take place . . . but no boxes of the workshop handbooks had been delivered!

I felt a flutter of concern. I fired up the laptop presentation, called the office to find out where the handbooks were and prepared to take the group. The senior managers came in, none too happy at having to take time out of their busy day . . . and within ten minutes, the laptop died. The screen went blank.

I was facing the prospect of a three-hour workshop, with no presentation and no back-up handbook resources. After the initial flash of terror, accompanied with sweating and feelings of light-headedness, I decided to implement the best CBT I could:

✔ The activating event was the laptop dying.

✔ The emotion was anxiety.

✔ My thinking was, 'This is terrible, just awful, I must give this presentation. It'll be dreadful if I fail; the firm will lose the contract and it'll all be my fault. I'll be dismissed and never work again. I'm a failure.'

I used CBT techniques in the moment to bring my anxiety levels down. It worked. In Chapter 3, I explore the techniques that you can use to help yourself out of a similar situation.

# Tackling Your Unsettling Feelings

As part of my work training people to become therapists, and when working with clients who come for therapy, I've suggested compiling a feelings vocabulary list that people find helpful as it helps them to name exactly what they are feeling rather than a general feeling of unease.

Learning CBT involves homework. If you really want to make changes, you can't just read a book (great though this one is, of course!) or go to a few CBT sessions and do nothing in between. You need to do hard work to change the thinking habits of a lifetime.

Compile a list of words that describe feelings, positive and negative, to create your own feelings vocabulary.

Here are some to start you off:

- ✔ Positive feelings: Happy; cheerful; optimistic; serene; pleased; calm; spirited; great; inspired; motivated; interested; confident; content; satisfied; energetic

- ✔ Negative feelings: Worried; annoyed; anxious; depressed; fearful; confused; upset; tearful; distrustful; guilty; despairing; uneasy; panicky; alone; terrible; distressed; hopeless; hurt; sad; pessimistic; scared; offended; lonely

Often people use only a simple phrase like 'I am upset about my work' to describe how they are feeling. Trying to be more specific about what type of upset you are feeling helps zoom in on the more specific emotional state you are in: I might ask a client, 'What sort of upset about work are you feeling – upset, angry or upset distressed or panicky or miserable, for example?' I have always found that once I encourage people to try to be more specific about their feelings they quickly pinpoint the specific feelings they are experiencing, and we can start the CBT detective work of focussing on the events leading up to this state.

## Connecting thinking and feelings

Key to understanding CBT is recognising the link between thinking and feeling: thinking gives rise to feelings.

Your body is constantly giving you physiological feedback about, for example, how hot you are, whether you're hungry, if you have a pain or need to go to the bathroom. These feelings are essential to help you survive (or at least in the case of the last item, save you severe embarrassment!).

Your emotional feelings are a result of how you perceive the environment around you, what your internal thoughts are processing and the effects these thoughts have on your body.

When you think about a happy event, you often feel happier. Try picturing an image of a sweet kitten and see whether you feel your mood lifting. If kitties don't do it for you, think of something that you find pleasant: a new technical gadget, a certain car, a painting, song, book or film, a forthcoming holiday plan or maybe a joke you find funny.

When you think about that thing, directing your attention to it, you may find that your mood changes.

Change your thoughts and you can change your mood.

## *Concentrating on what you're thinking*

What you think about in your general awareness has a significant impact on your overall mood, for good or ill.

Concentrate on what you're thinking about. Where/how are you reading this paragraph – from a book, on a device, at home, on a train, sitting on a chair, a sofa? Then stop focusing on your thinking, and try to name your feelings: tired, interested, thoughts drifting, curious, annoyed, anxious, impatient?

Paying attention to your immediate feelings can be called 'being mindful' of what you are doing. This exercise encourages you to practise what being mindful and paying attention in the moment is like. It can help you deal with stress.

The reality is that your thoughts drift in and out constantly. Even when you choose to focus your attention on particular thoughts, in the background other thoughts rumble on as background noise, like programs on your computer.

For example, imagine that you're applying for a loan to make an important purchase. You know that securing the loan is important, and although you're at work trying to focus on the job in hand, thoughts and worries about the loan continue running along in the background.

Understanding just how much these other thoughts impact on your everyday emotional wellbeing is an important aspect of using CBT to help reduce unsettling feelings.

## Discovering what pushes your buttons

Everyone has different concerns running through his or her head all the time and each individual makes different choices about what he or she decides to focus on.

Someone once described to me his annoying condition of feeling generally anxious and jittery all the time as like having a hundred applications running at the same time in his head. He knew he wasn't performing efficiently, and that his functioning at work was slowed because too many things were going on, but he had great difficulty prioritising and focusing on just one thing. As a consequence he was anxious, stressed, unhappy and moving towards feeling depressed. At work, you're mostly given tasks and so are being directed to focus your attention on certain things. At times the demands on you are so many and so varied that you can start to feel overwhelmed.

### Negative stress

Stress in itself isn't necessarily a negative thing. A certain amount can be challenging, motivating and even exciting. The problem is when it tips over into negative stress, which can be upsetting and at times debilitating.

Negative stress is when the perceived demands outweigh your perceived ability to meet those demands. As a result, you feel generally stressed.

Think of your brain as being like a computer: when a data storage system is full, it starts to give warnings that the storage space is running low. Ultimately, if you don't pay attention and carry on adding more data and input, the device stops running.

To use CBT efficiently, allow yourself time and space to investigate what 'applications' are running in your head and to list all the different stressors or triggers impacting on you. If you don't take time to pay attention to the many tasks and demands going on in your life, or heed the warnings of continual unsettling or negative feelings, you start to function less efficiently. You can even make yourself ill by ignoring all the signs of stress.

### Stress tips over into distress

Emotional ill-health is less easy to spot in yourself. It can creep up over a period of time, slowly and consistently, though you may have some warnings along the way. If you choose not to pay attention to them, you can go from mild symptoms to more acute ones, and possibly into an emotional crisis.

Only you know how you're feeling: that's your truth. Don't compare yourself to others, and berate yourself for feeling upset. Accept your feelings and then choose to use CBT to do something about them, if you want.

## Creating a CBT toolkit

When you have the basics of CBT that I describe throughout this chapter under your belt, you can build yourself a CBT toolkit to carry with you at all times. You can then decide when and if you want to use it.

You carry the toolkit around inside your head (and so you don't need any special carrying cases or devices, except perhaps a hat to keep it warm!). It helps you to start recognising the warning signs that suggest using the toolkit would be helpful. Flip to Chapter 3 to find out about building your CBT toolkit.

Applying the CBT toolkit can change your life. After all, like pets, CBT is for life, not just for Christmas – I mean crises!

# Chapter 3

# Using CBT to Change Unhelpful Thinking

*In This Chapter*

▶ Watching yourself at work

▶ Creating your own CBT toolkit

▶ Using your CBT toolkit wisely

*T*he Chinese philosopher Confucius said: 'Choose a job you love and you'll never have to work a day in your life'. So if you happen to like and enjoy your job, consider it a bonus, because some people experience a general feeling of unease about their work situation.

Certainly wanting and needing a job when you're unemployed can be extremely stressful. But even with one, you can feel a sense of trepidation that you need to go to work and stay in your job (unless you're fabulously wealthy, of course!). The fact is that most people face times when they need to take jobs that aren't their preferred work just to make ends meet.

At work and in life in general, people develop their own coping mechanisms for when things get tough. Some of these mechanisms are conscious and others are more hit and miss, with people just entering into a way of being without too much thought. As a result, some ways of coping can be damaging to you, making things worse.

This chapter encourages you to examine your own thoughts and beliefs and start to check whether any of your thinking is unhelpful. If so, you can work on changing this thinking by using the CBT toolkit to minimise the disruption that these unhelpful beliefs are causing you.

# Observing Your Behaviour at Work

Human beings are great at creating habits. Your actions can become automatic and habitual as your thinking habits take shape, becoming embedded in your mind. You need to have some such habits in order to carry out actions automatically to be efficient, but you have a problem when these habits become what psychologists term self-defeating habits of thinking.

If you always do what you always did, you always get what you always got.

Although CBT doesn't involve dwelling on the past – instead, encouraging people to look at and work on what's happening in the present – having a peek at the possible origins of your unhelpful thinking habits can be helpful.

In this section, you get the chance to examine some of your beliefs and thinking habits and to assess how you apply them at work, including how they align (or don't) with those you work with.

## Viewing yourself in terms of your helpful beliefs

Helpful beliefs can assist you in living a productive and happy life. When you apply them consistently, in general they don't pose a problem.

Taking time to consider what your beliefs are is an interesting activity. Often you're unaware of them, because they run quietly along in the background, and yet they influence your every decision and attitude.

Here are some behaviours you may think you demonstrate in the workplace.

- ✔ Commitment
- ✔ Consistency
- ✔ Efficiency
- ✔ High standards and ethics
- ✔ Honesty
- ✔ Openmindedness
- ✔ Optimism
- ✔ Reliability
- ✔ Respectfulness to others

These beliefs are just some of the positive ones that you may have, though many others may apply to you as well.

## *Viewing others in terms of your beliefs*

As well as having your own beliefs you need to have an awareness of others' views and any corporate, social or community values.

Your company is likely to have beliefs about how it tries to operate the organisation and workplace and what it expects of employees. Here are some beliefs and core values for which an organisation may strive:

- ✔ A commitment to sustainability
- ✔ A commitment to environmentally friendly ways of working
- ✔ A commitment to innovation
- ✔ A commitment to philanthropy

These company beliefs would be considered positive values and beliefs. You may not subscribe to these, but if you can accept them, then you are less likely to find yourself in a difficult situation. Other people have their own ways of looking at the world, and we can agree to differ.

## *Identifying helpful and unhelpful beliefs*

You may have developed unhelpful beliefs along the way that turn out to be damaging to your emotional health. You may not even realise that they're unhelpful – until they cause problems for you. The development of such beliefs is highly influenced by other people, including your parents, family, friends and colleagues.

Here's an example of the sort of unhelpful belief you may have.

Markus had an interview for a sales job with a computer company. He was a highly experienced salesperson who'd previously worked in the media. He believed that you should always 'be yourself' and went everywhere with a fold-up bicycle. He was enthusiastic and articulate and interviewed well. The interviewers explained that the company preferred he use a car to visit clients. Markus was asked his view and said that he wasn't prepared to do that because he 'valued his individuality'. Unsurprisingly, Markus wasn't offered the job.

Being totally inflexible about your beliefs means that they may be unhelpful for you as regards what you want to achieve.

## *Seeing damaging beliefs at work*

Everyone has unhelpful beliefs or even prejudices that stop him or her functioning as effectively as possible as work.

Here is a chance to examine some of your thinking habits and how you apply them at work. Check out this example of how someone's old thinking habits and beliefs nearly prevented her from moving on and finding new opportunities. As you read through it, think about the attitudes being displayed and how your assumptions are built up through previous experiences. You cannot know what other people are thinking and you may jump the gun in deciding what they are like.

Serena worked in a college as a lecturer in health and social care. She had a real dislike for the estates manager, whose responsibilities included the health and safety aspects of the college's working environments. She found him abrupt, unhelpful, inflexible and dismissive of other people's views. The estates manager had a background in the naval forces and was very efficient at his job, as well as totally reliable when it came to organising the priorities of his job.

Serena had developed the generalised belief that people with such backgrounds were pre-occupied with their own jobs and unwilling to listen to others' suggestions. Her opinion was influenced by being brought up in a family with a forces background: she often clashed with her father and found him to be unbending of any rules he imposed in the family. This experience coloured her overall viewpoint of people from forces backgrounds.

In terms of the ABCs of CBT that I describe in Chapter 2:

- ✓ A (activating event): The thought of asking the estates manager.
- ✓ B (her belief): 'All people with a forces background are inflexible, unhelpful and even obstructive'.
- ✓ C (emotional consequence): Feelings of anger.

A group of Serena's students wanted to use music and candles to create a conducive learning environment. Serena loved the idea, but (based on her past family experiences) believed that the estates manager would never allow it. She went to see him in low spirits and explained about the request from the students in a single sentence, in a quiet voice. The estates manager's face lit up and he said he thought it was a good idea! He'd need to do a risk assessment and check the details of how many candles and their positioning, but he was amenable to enriching the environment in this way. By the start of the next week, he told Serena she could go ahead!

Serena's belief had been unhelpful and almost stopped her making a request. The estates manager's response surprised her, however, leading her to change her belief and stop it causing a problem in the future. The outcome was constructive and helped her to move on. She no longer believed that all people with forces backgrounds behave in a particular way.

## *Noticing negative thinking at work*

I detail here just some of the many types of work-related negative thinking that you can engage in, sometimes without being fully aware.

Before you even start your day at work, the gremlins of negative thoughts can already be creeping in. The Sunday-night blues of looking at what the coming week has in store can affect you. You know the sort of thoughts:

- ✔ Oh no, Harry's off this week, my workload will be harder.
- ✔ I'm going to have to prepare work at home for Thursday's meeting.
- ✔ I'll have to travel two hours to that meeting in Reading.
- ✔ I'll have to get up at 5 a.m. to miss the traffic.
- ✔ I'll feel awfully tired and annoyed on the journey.
- ✔ I'm so fed up with all the extra work.
- ✔ I'm going to have a rubbish week.

While you're at work, you may find yourself thinking a lot about the niggling details of your work situation. You want to make coffee but someone forgot to bring the milk in. You're too late to go down to the café to buy one. You dread switching on your computer and seeing all the emails that have piled up. You think you'll never get through them all.

The interactions with people at work also impact on you. Colleagues gather round the water cooler and whine about that new project, how their workload is unfair and how they dislike the new manager and want to leave. You feel you have to agree, otherwise you may be unpopular.

You can sometimes feel as if negative thinking is dragging you down into a spiralling pit of despair.

Obviously, being in a negative mood isn't a great place to be. As well as being unpleasant, it damages your work performance, your relationships and even your health.

## *Watching for catastrophising thinking*

*"We're all doomed, I tell yea, doomed!"* — Private Fraser, *Dads' Army*

CBT can help you to recognise when you start winding yourself up with negative thinking that can progress into catastrophising.

Thinking the worst, stressing yourself out with increasingly disastrous thoughts and coming to the conclusion that everything's hopeless is an all too common way of thinking. You're not alone if you find yourself obsessing about things at work, focusing on the terrible event that could happen and deciding that you're hopeless and worthless.

You can fall easily into this chain of thinking, moving from a seemingly simple blip in your work to a disastrous outcome. Check out the nearby sidebar 'Maybe I'm a fool' for an example.

An academic I worked with used to say that people have a natural predisposition to think irrationally. He'd met many clients with the same tendency to catastrophise their thinking and turn themselves into shivering wrecks with anxiety and guilt, beating themselves over the head with imaginary sticks.

### 'Maybe I'm a fool'

Catastrophic thoughts can spiral away from you. Imagine that you're a newly promoted junior manager expected at an important meeting a couple of miles away to discuss office finances. You arrive in reception, with your notes and spreadsheets at the ready, and are told that the meeting's at another location.

Your anxiety level rockets and your thinking spirals out of control:

'I'm such an idiot. I'm in the wrong building. It'll take me ages to go back to the other one. I'll be late. The Finance Director will be so angry that I'm not there . . . she'll think

I'm not coming. All the people at the meeting will think I'm a fool too. This is terrible. If I don't give my report on time, I may be downgraded to a different role for being incompetent. If I'm downgraded I'll get less money. How will I pay my mortgage? My family will think I've let them down and think I'm hopeless too. My wife may go off on me and turn to another man who's more reliable. She'll want a divorce and I'll be left on my own. I couldn't bear to be on my own, but it'll be nothing less than I deserve. I'm a worthless person.'

## Deciding if some of your beliefs need changing

Working out whether some of your beliefs are at odds with the beliefs of your work colleagues is helpful in trying to understand your unease or conflict. You're unlikely to work somewhere where everyone has the same views and everything is totally harmonious. More often than not, people with all sorts of different views are thrown together in the workplace. Rigid beliefs and trying to impose them on others leads to conflict. We are not all the same, but there may be times when we need to recognise and accept these differences.

Having different views isn't bad in itself, but can be at the root of differences of opinion. Accepting that helps you to enjoy a calmer emotional work climate.

# Building Yourself a CBT Toolkit

Making up a packed lunch to take to work is an efficient and cost-saving way to look after your physical needs. Making a toolkit to look after your emotional needs makes sense too! You don't even need a special plastic box or paper bag, because you carry your CBT toolkit around in your head, to use whenever you spot negative thoughts arising.

## Tooling up to take control

Here's what you need in your CBT toolkit:

- ✔ A space in your head to step back from the immediate situation
- ✔ A trigger button to recognise when you are being affected by events
- ✔ A negative-thinking alarm that monitors unsettling feelings
- ✔ An uncomfortable-feeling strategy – a holding pattern plan to help avoid panic

The first thing is to decide how you're going to recognise when the negative thinking starts. If you wait too long, the thoughts can start spiralling and increasing in intensity. You may have difficulty regaining a sense of composure if you ignore the warning signs for too long.

### Spotting the warning signs

People experience the warning signs in different ways. Here are just a few common symptoms of starting to feel uneasy:

- Anxiousness
- Fearfulness
- Feeling hot and sweaty
- Feeling 'wobbly' (refer to Chapter 2 for more on this)
- Light-headedness
- Starting to shake
- Tearfulness

These are just a few of reported symptoms of starting to feel uneasy.

### Activating the alert button

You may want to be more aware of how you are feeling and be prepared with a holding pattern strategy to help avoid the spiral and descent into panic.

Decide for yourself which feelings indicate that things are getting tricky and be on the alert for them.

When I start feeling wobbly, I say to myself, 'Why am I feeling wobbly? What's happening around me, or in my head, that's the trigger for these uncomfortable feelings?' I then tell myself a few times, 'I don't want to upset myself'. This helps me focus on the uncomfortable feelings and gives me time to hold the thinking and to prevent the feelings from escalating. Once I am aware of the feelings, I might say to myself: 'I do not want to panic, I will breathe normally and give myself time to deal with it'. I may not have to time now to think it all through, but I know that I have the ability to work it out.

I then apply the CBT toolkit based on the ABC framework from Chapter 2:

- Identify what started it off: the A (Activating trigger).
- Then identify the B: the Belief or thinking about the trigger.
- Identify the unsettling emotional Consequence. This is the C in ABC.

You sit down to work, open your emails and find one from your line manager asking you to attend a meeting that morning, without specifying what the meeting is about:

- A: You recognise that the trigger is the email, calling you to a meeting.
- B: Your thinking is negative: 'I must've done something wrong'.

✔ C: You start to feel anxious. You tremble, stumble over your typing, make mistakes, feel hot, have trouble focusing on the screen and feel a bit light-headed.

You start to have catastrophic thoughts:

> *What have I done wrong? Was it because I had to go to the dentist in work time last week? What must she have thought of me . . . probably that I can't organise my personal life as well as my work life. This is terrible. She's going to tell me I'm underperforming and the dentist appointment was the final straw. People have been talking of redundancies. I'm probably on the list now. I'll be made redundant and not even given a good reference to get another job. I'm done for.*

You then apply your CBT toolkit:

1. Apply your holding pattern strategy – 'I won't upset myself.' 'I do not want to panic, I will breathe normally and give myself time to deal with it'. 'I may not have to time now to think it all through, but I know that I have the ability to work it out.

2. Take time to challenge your thinking and beliefs. My belief that I should never take time off for something like a dental appointment is not helpful.

3. Work hard on changing the irrational thinking to rational thinking – 'I would prefer not to be in trouble, but if I am, I can deal with it', and bring your anxiety levels down.

You keep repeating the new rational thinking to yourself to help change your thinking from unhealthy negative thoughts to healthy ones.

## *Keeping your CBT toolkit prepared*

Storing your toolkit is easy and user-friendly. You don't need to buy a steel toolbox, install a row of hooks in your garage or even buy a special shed. You keep your CBT toolkit in your head and so it's very discreet. No one at work can see it. Only you know it's there, ready for when you need to use it.

Do use it regularly, though, when troubling feelings arise, so that it doesn't get forgotten and covered in dust.

The brain is like any other device. The more often you use it, the more the 'cookies' pick up that it's a favourite and the more accessible it becomes.

# Choosing to Use Your CBT Toolkit

You're most likely used to thinking, interpreting and reacting to events at work as you always have over your whole lifetime. But when you decide that you want to minimise the unsettling feeling that work is bringing up, you can feel liberated. No one else can do this for you.

## Getting smarter at using your CBT toolkit

The more you get used to the idea that you're in charge of your emotions, the smarter you get, though it takes a lot of practice. You will have been used to thinking and interpreting events in the same ways for your whole lifetime, so far.

Imagine this scenario. You're at work and notice a few people congregating around the water cooler. They're talking quietly, almost in hushed whispers. A couple of them keep looking over at you and then returning to the chatting. You start to feel anxious. You convince yourself that they're talking about you. The company is rumoured to be in trouble and you wonder whether they know something you don't.

You remember the ABCs of your CBT toolkit (see the earlier section 'Activating the alert button') and put it into action:

- ✓ Situation (or Activating event, A): People looking at you from the water cooler group.
- ✓ Beliefs (B): Your thinking around the situation.
- ✓ Consequence (C): You feel worried; this is the trigger for you to bring out the toolkit.

Your thinking is along the following lines:

> *Oh no, they keep looking at me. They must be talking about me. That's awful; they may be discussing that I'm next to be made redundant. That would be terrible. I couldn't stand it. What would I do without a job? I feel sick. They mustn't make me redundant.*

But you use the holding pattern strategy (that I describe in this chapter and in Chapter 2) to hold back that thinking and not let it escalate:

> *I'm feeling anxious. I don't want to upset myself. I'm going to allow myself to rationalise my thinking using CBT. I'm going to change the should, ought and must thinking to preference thinking.*

(I discuss should, ought and must thinking in Chapter 5.)

Your thinking shifts to the following:

> *I'd prefer that I'm not made redundant. I wouldn't like it, it would be most inconvenient, but if it did happen, I could stand it. It wouldn't be the end of the world. I'd struggle, but I could cope.*

In the meantime, how is keeping my strong belief that I absolutely must not be made redundant helping me? It's not. I'm winding myself up into a state of high anxiety by interpreting the water cooler talk as a fact that the worst scenario is going to happen.

> *I've been having catastrophic thoughts. There's no evidence that they're talking about redundancies. Even if it were true, I could cope.*

> *I'm going to calm myself down by changing my irrational thinking to rational thinking, settling down and getting on with my work.*

Ahhhhh. Peace.

By the way, they were discussing buying a cake for your upcoming birthday.

## *Exercising your brain muscles*

Your brain is a muscle and, like all muscles, the more you use it, the stronger it becomes.

The brain's nerve endings (synapses) are like electrical connections in your body. They're responsible for sending messages and instructions for what your muscles need to do. For example, if you decide to go running, you send messages to your leg muscles, the synapses fire up the neurons to the muscles and off you go.

The same applies emotionally. If you decide that the unsettling feelings you're experiencing need to move in a different direction, you can use your CBT toolkit to send messages to your brain to change the direction of your thinking and have a workout to instruct more rational thinking.

## *Checking your alerting strategies*

You need to become the expert on yourself for when the 'wobbly' feelings start (see the earlier section 'Spotting the warning signs' for more details). Your toolkit can help you check which practical strategies for alerting yourself to your unpleasant emotions work for you. You need to become the expert on yourself when the wobbly feelings start.

The type of holding technique you employ will be individual to you.

You can use devices and apps that monitor your stress. They give you feedback such as blood pressure, heart rate, sweat output and skin temperature, because all these change when you're stressed.

Some people wear mood rings or bio dots (small sticky heat sensitive paper dots that change colour to indicate changes in skin temperature), which can then be interpreted as changes in stress levels. There are also apps for smartphones that do the same. When you're stressed, your skin temperature at your body extremities can go down due to the 'fight or flight' mechanism (refer to Chapter 2). Blood drains to the core of the body to prime the big muscles to be prepared to fight off threats. You will know when your body changes as you start to feel different, but some people like their phones, or other indicators, to confirm this.

For most people, working on increasing their own awareness naturally, through practice, is enough to help increase their awareness.

## Deciding when to implement your CBT toolkit

You decide when to bring your toolkit into action. You experience many emotions during the day and not all unsettling feelings are troublesome enough to need your special attention.

Also, you may not have time in the moment to apply the toolkit, but just being aware and making a conscious decision to employ your holding pattern strategy may be sufficient to stop an escalation into unmanageable feelings. You can then work on analysing what's going on and what the ABCs are, and trying to change the irrational thinking to more rational thinking, when you have time to pay your full attention to it.

Writing down all that went on, particularly into the ABC framework, can really help with this.

## Practising the routines

Being prepared for future emotional disruptions is very helpful. Practising the CBT approach when you're calm and comfortable is a great way to prepare yourself for any future turbulence. After all, difficult situations are going to arise in your life at work and at home.

CBT isn't a one-off type of therapy, where you have a few lessons and then forget about it. You become the primary expert on yourself with practice.

When you're developing your CBT skills, looking at examples and case studies of how to apply it can be useful. The more you familiarise yourself with the theory and practice, the more you're able to become your own therapist. See the back of this book for references and resources.

## Demanding more of yourself in a helpful way

Some people see making demands as a negative idea, interpreting the word to mean impositions and insistence, with arrogance thrown in.

A more productive way of viewing demands is making pleas or requests to yourself that are in your own best interests. Instead of making unrealistic and irrational demands such as 'I must finish all these reports before I go home even though they aren't due yet', you can use your toolkit to correct your thinking, and make a helpful request to yourself that you'll work consistently and to the best of your ability.

The latter is a more helpful demand that you can acknowledge and strive to achieve – and, crucially, it's possible to achieve!

## Using your toolkit to gain a little peace

You can have more control over how you work when you increase your awareness of your preferred working conditions. For example, your work environment may be fast-paced, with lots of background noise. You can make decisions to find some space in your head to allow a bit of peace from the frantic working pace.

Taking breaks is important as well, to avoid finding yourself effectively chained to your desk or other place of work, with little chance to get away. You have to be responsible for prioritising your needs for regular breaks (check out Chapter 5 for more on taking responsibility for your wellbeing).

Plan for how best to use your time away from the immediate demands of the job. Very often the talk between colleagues on breaks centres on work, and soon the worries and conflicts become a focus of conversation. If you like spending a break this way, fine. But if you prefer a bit of peace in your busy day, use your CBT toolkit to support that you don't have to spend your breaks with other people. Taking yourself away from the workplace is okay, too.

Getting caught up with discussions of office politics, and the gripes and negative feedback from other people, can impact on you and perhaps start to suck you into a downward spiral of negative thinking.

# Chapter 4

# Working in Healthy Ways

## In This Chapter

▶ Considering your work conditions

▶ Working out your own attitudes to work

▶ Aiming to work in the optimum conditions

The day-to-day conditions in which you work have a large influence on your physical and emotional wellbeing. People have to work inside buildings with varying environments. Some workplaces are purpose-built, providing optimum conditions for comfort and efficiency to maximise the potential output of the employees. But others are conversions of existing buildings whose original purpose may differ from the intended current use.

As a result, you can encounter common conditions and potential difficulties associated with your working environment. The amount of space you have available to work in, temperature, daylight, furniture, equipment and provision for comfort breaks influence your overall perception of your job and your work performance.

The more you can identify with the struggles you encounter at work and see how CBT has helped people, the easier it becomes to train yourself to manage your current problems to maximise the chances of reducing your anxiety and worry.

I design this chapter to encourage you to take a wider view of your environment, and then to hone in on the specific physical surroundings and the more subtle psychological cultures that are around you at work. This type of exercise leads you to look more closely at the attitudes of others and, more specifically, gives you a chance to discover your own views about work. This 'view from above' provides you with greater perspective, which often reduces some of the tensions and underlying anxiety.

I walk you through your own work environment, how you think about and relate to it, and suggest ways in which you can make it healthier and more conducive to a relaxed but productive work and home life.

# Discovering Your Environment at Work

In order to work in a healthy way, physically and psychologically, you need to assess your own situation. When you take time to examine the conditions of your workplace, including areas of potential conflict, you become more aware of the multifaceted influences on you in your everyday life at work.

Take some time now to consider your place of work:

- ✔ How do you get to work: What method of transport do you use and how long does it take?

- ✔ What area is your workplace situated in: Urban or rural, shops nearby, isolated?

- ✔ What's the architecture surrounding your workplace like: Old or new?

- ✔ How do you feel when you walk through the door of the building: Positive or negative, enthused or weary?

Don't forget to consider your commute. The journey to work can become automatic as familiarity with your job takes place over the weeks and months. The journey time can be an important factor in setting your mood for the day, with commuting times taking up to four hours a day.

The sacrifice of time spent at home may be weighed up against the opportunities and monetary rewards the job offers. The impact of some of your choices may not be felt for years but pushed back into your subconscious.

## Looking at your physical surroundings

You may find yourself working in a number of different workplaces during your working life. Check out these common industries and associated working environments:

- ✔ Agriculture: Farms, dairies, factory farms and wind farms

- ✔ Building: Housing, retail, public buildings, schools, hospitals, roads and infrastructure

- ✔ Creative industries: Theatre, orchestra, dance companies, fashion companies, home offices or studios (for writers and artists)

- ✔ Factories: Warehouses, production lines, design and technology offices and product testing

- ✔ Food and drink: Restaurants, cafés, pubs, coffee shops, chains, franchises and festivals

- ✔ Gardening: Sole-trader businesses, larger companies, councils, National Trust homes and gardens, public spaces and private estates

✔ Leisure: Sports teams, sports arenas, gyms, spas, entertainment venues, nightclubs, airlines and hotels

✔ Media: Newspaper offices, social media companies, publishing companies and virtual offices

✔ Office work: Office buildings, reception areas and call centres

✔ Public services: Schools, preschools, playgroups, hospitals, prisons, social services, local and national government offices, emergency services, cleaning services, and maintenance services

✔ Sales and marketing: Office buildings, events and conferences, sales areas and virtual offices

✔ Transport: Airports, train services, delivery companies, green travel services, bike sales and repair, and car sales and repair

At work, you're constantly influenced by your surroundings. You don't often get a choice in which office, classroom, factory floor or public space you're assigned to. In fact, the efficient use of available space means that many offices favour an open-plan layout. As a result, the noise levels can be higher than in a small office and the constant interactions of employees in the space can create a dynamic atmosphere.

All people have preferences for their personal space. Your personality may favour one preferred way of working over another and so you may need to carry out varying amounts of adaptation to realise your optimum working conditions. Just as animals have evolved to adapt to their surroundings for their survival, so humans have adapted to their working environments to be successful.

Your workspace is a crucial factor in both your physical and mental health. Some people are quite happy with a smaller amount of space to work in whereas others may find it a problem. But studies do show that when people work in cramped conditions, they can experience anxiety and stress that affects their work performance. Plus, the décor and lighting of your surroundings have an impact on you. Availability of fresh air or regular circulation of temperature-controlled air can affect your energy levels and psychological wellbeing, too.

You need enough space for yourself and your equipment to be able to function efficiently and feel that you have sufficient security and support. The type of furniture you sit on, how long you spend sitting down, and whether you have the opportunity to personalise your space all affect you.

If you have any medical problems that can be aggravated by sitting for long periods of time, take these into consideration where possible and try and plan for this problem by using more suitable furniture that you can adapt to your needs. For example, a correctly positioned chair and computer, which allows you to work with a straight back and without bending or kneeling, makes your work life a whole lot more pleasant.

Depending on your employer's size and situation, you may not always be able to get your needs met at first. But recognising potential obstacles to maximising your comfort, and in turn efficiency, is an important first step.

## Describing the psychological environment

A sense of wellbeing when you're at work is integral to helping you maximise your work performance. When you arrive at work each day, you're already experiencing a certain level of wellbeing – influenced by events happening in your personal life, your journey to work and outstanding issues occupying your mind.

When you walk into your workplace, you may leave these thoughts and concerns behind and find work a sanctuary from concerns – or you may find that entering the workplace raises work-specific worries that impact directly on how you feel. You can find yourself worrying before you even arrive for work, feeling drained before the day even properly begins. Work meetings and appointments ('Am I prepared?'), home problems ('The boiler's broken again!') and social engagements ('I must get Amanda's gift to her today – she hates late birthday presents!') bubble around your mind in a soupy mess.

On the positive side, however, certain aspects of your working environment can also impact on your sense of wellbeing in a favourable way.

Where do you fit in? Do you look forward to going to work or do you dread it? Understanding your feelings is a great start to addressing work-related issues.

How you view going to work is likely to vary along a continuum: you can expect to feel slightly different each day. For an example, check out the nearby sidebar 'The Sunday-night blues'.

---

### The Sunday-night blues

The 'Sunday-evening school-night' feeling is common and quite normal: people know exactly what you mean when you use the phrase to refer to the week at work starting again after a weekend (put bluntly, it's a downer!). If you don't work shifts, having two clear days away from work, with time to choose which activities you want to do instead of having an externally imposed list of chores, can be liberating. But then some people find going back to work on a Monday a relief if home and personal life is hectic and fraught with its own problems.

Either way, you usually experience a change in your emotional climate before going back into work at the beginning of the week.

---

## Assessing your feelings about work

How do you feel about going into work?

- ✔ Anticipation
- ✔ Awareness
- ✔ Alertness
- ✔ Some positive feelings
- ✔ Looking forward to seeing work colleagues raises your spirits
- ✔ Having things in common with your workmates stimulates creativity
- ✔ Forming relationships and friendships enhances a sense of inclusion
- ✔ Extending the boundaries to discuss your personal life and using break times to share events is a valuable source of support
- ✔ Being in a well-functioning, co-operative team can promote energy
- ✔ Enjoying a positive relationship with your manager, with mutual respect, is affirming

## Looking on the bright side

Describe the positive things you like about work:

- ✔ Consider some of the people at work you like and get along well with, and describe their qualities and attributes.
- ✔ Focus on the structure of your working environment and the aspects that you find appealing.
- ✔ Reflect on some of the best times at work.
- ✔ Write a list of the most enjoyable things about work.
- ✔ Add other ideas to help enhance your sense of wellbeing at work.

## Being realistic about the negatives

Think about some negative feelings. Allowing yourself to write down lists of things you don't like about work can be helpful psychologically. Here are some areas to consider:

- ✔ Anticipated workload
- ✔ Your perceived ability to meet the demands of the job
- ✔ Your lack of current skills to complete work tasks
- ✔ Anticipated amount of time available to be able to work successfully
- ✔ Concerns about the ability of others to meet the demands of the job, which impact on you

- ✔ Unhelpful and possibly obstructive team members
- ✔ Uninteresting and tedious work tasks
- ✔ Difficult and complicated work demands
- ✔ Constantly changing tasks within the job
- ✔ Boundary changes within the job that cause insecurity and anxiety
- ✔ Unhelpful managers and bosses
- ✔ Negative things you don't like about workplaces

Sometimes you're generally aware in your subconscious that all isn't well with work. This feeling can have other effects on your wellbeing, but the necessity of keeping your job, paying the bills and everyday living sometimes means that you struggle on with a generalised feeling of anxiety.

If you don't allow yourself opportunities to recognise and take steps to release some of these tensions, the long-term effects can increase. The following exercise deepens your knowledge about your work experience:

1. What are some of the aspects of the job you don't like?

2. Describe those aspects and the feelings you experience when you think of each of them.

3. Think about the limitations your current job brings.

4. List some of the people you work with that you find:

   – Annoying

   – Frustrating

   – Inefficient

   – Intimidating

   – Unpleasant

   – Unproductive

Taking time to list the irritations of work can help you focus on potential sources of conflict and start to process them.

Anticipation is the first point of enlightenment for you. The CBT method shows that you can allow into your consciousness what you're really thinking, but may not be aware of. It can also help you plan for potential sources of conflict that activate the unsettling feelings and create tensions.

### Digging deeper into your work experience

Think about some aspects of your current job in terms of these five categories:

- ✔ Professionally: How you see your career

- ✔ Personally: You as a person in work

- ✔ Socially: How you interact at work with your colleagues, workmates, managers and bosses in a more relaxed way outside of the work environment

- ✔ Emotionally: The feelings that you have at work

- ✔ Intellectually: Your thinking around your work

Viewing your job in these different categories is helpful, especially when a problem arises: it can help you identify which area of your job is most affected. For example, you can easily have differing points of view around a professional work issue with a colleague but still like the person, as a friend. Seeing these boundaries clearly can provide a rational perspective in work.

## *Recognising conflicting influences*

Allowing yourself to recognise that you have potential conflicting influences about work, which can conspire to shake your emotional wellbeing, is the first step in doing something about them. After all, to work in as healthy a way as possible, you need to give yourself the best chances possible.

In this context, you can see conflict as meaning 'to come into variance, disagreement or collision. To be in opposition or to clash'. But not all conflict necessarily has negative outcomes – identifying changes that need to be made can be helpful to move on in a preferable way. But conflict that results in fighting (mental or physical), discord, antagonism or unwanted interference that impedes or inhibits your progress forward can result in negative, unhealthy feelings.

In the work situation, conflict can have serious implications for you as an employee and a person whose emotional wellbeing is adversely affected. Unresolved conflicts and the fallout from disputes can cause problems with job and career prospects.

Here are some of the fallout feelings you can experience (what I call sinking pit feelings): hopelessness, unhappiness, withdrawal of communication, dissatisfaction and depression, which in turn can affect physical wellbeing. Illness and absenteeism often occur as a result of unresolved conflict, which is a high cost to pay both for employee and employer.

In the rest of this section, I describe some of the influencing factors to watch out for that can lead to conflicts.

### *Job description*

Vaguely defined job roles and responsibilities can be a root of conflict. Unclear boundaries mean that people can 'tread on others' toes' (ouch!) by overstepping their own responsibilities and taking over other people's jobs. The reverse can also occur. Individuals whom you rely on to do their roles may not shape up, with a consequence that you're prevented from doing your job in a timely and efficient way, which has negative consequences for you as an employee.

### *Conflicts of interest*

Different categories of goals exist in the work situation:

- ✔ Your employer's company goals
- ✔ Your department and team goals
- ✔ Your individual work goals

These goals are often imposed from above and pre-decided. At times, you're highly likely to experience conflicting interests between the three levels. But open communication, democratic working parties and meetings to discuss current situations, and opportunities for constructive feedback at all levels are more likely to lead to harmony and a level of general consensus. In this situation, the opportunity for unhealthy conflict is reduced.

But unless you own the means of production in your job and have control over the finances of the company, issues such as pay, working hours, schedules, job roles, expectations and productivity are more likely to be out of your control.

### *Locus of control*

The locus of control (the perceived level of control you feel you have over your job) is a major factor in how you view and interact at work. It affects, for good or ill, the relationship between job demands or workload and wellbeing.

Psychological studies into people's locus of control and the incidence of depression reveal it to be a major factor in emotional wellbeing. Researchers found that those jobs with the most negative impact on health had high demands and low control. Nothing is intrinsically bad about high demands, because some people thrive on high-pressured jobs, and at times most jobs involve short bursts of high pressure. But the key factor is how much control people perceive they have in the job and how helpless they feel.

As you can see, this is all very much linked to the attitudes you have towards your work. How you view your work, your beliefs about work, what's fair and what's unfair, reasonable or unreasonable, is directly linked to your feelings at work. Check out Chapter 1, where I define CBT and how attitudes and beliefs give rise to feelings.

### Availability of resources

The amount, availability and allocation of resources is always a potential hot spot for conflict at work. Money, space, time, supplies, human resources, bonuses and perks are all competing within departments and the company, and are also subject to external demands. The sense of a 'lack of fair play' gives rise to many conflicts. At times people can pour excessive amounts of energy into obsessing around issues of injustice and unfairness.

No one said it would be fair.

### Lack of clear communication

This problem can spark many a lively conflict. The company grapevine can spread a 'chain of whispers' in a few minutes, where someone saying that 'the CEO lost at squash' quickly becomes 'we're all losing our jobs'!

In the hierarchy of a larger company, with many different interfaces, the following inter- and intrapersonal relationships have the potential for dynamic exchanges:

- ✔ Employee to employee
- ✔ Employee to line manager
- ✔ HR to management to employees
- ✔ Line manager to senior manager
- ✔ Sales team to outside contacts
- ✔ Senior manager to Board of Directors

Clashes of goals, values, expectations and perceptions can all give rise to conflict.

Use CBT to reduce unhelpful conflict at work. You can achieve conflict resolution, or at least reduction, by deciding to implement some CBT techniques (check out the next section).

# Changing Your Attitudes in the Workplace

In this section, I show you how to concentrate on yourself in order to minimise the impact of conflicts in the workplace (the sort I describe in the preceding section). Examining your attitudes helps to clarify what you expect in work.

Unsettling situations are bound to arise frequently. But in classic CBT terms, although you can't change the situation you can change your attitude to it.

# Recognising the importance of attitudes

Attitudes are your in-built viewpoints. They're shaped by your experiences from being a child through to adulthood. You aren't always aware of what attitudes you hold because they can be implicit.

Just as CBT highlights the need to be aware of your beliefs that are causing negative feelings (so that you can work on pinpointing the trigger and changing the thinking), so an awareness of your own attitudes at work helps you to be more logical and rational to minimise the triggers for conflict.

You need to understand your attitudes to work in order to start working on tackling unhelpful ones. Therefore, examining what your attitudes comprise is a useful exercise.

Answer the following questions to discover your points of view about work:

- ✔ Why do you work?
- ✔ What do you think work should provide for you?
- ✔ What expectations do you hold regarding your working environment?
- ✔ What sort of values and ethics do you think your work should recognise?

Your thinking influences your everyday life constantly. Attitudes are a way of thinking. Your attitudes influence how you relate to the world of work.

Psychologists and sociologists break down attitudes into the following three components:

- ✔ Cognitive: Your thoughts, beliefs and ideas about your environment, such as, 'I believe that people should wash up their own coffee cups'.
- ✔ Affective: Feelings that result from a generalised view about events, such as, 'I can't stand people who don't wash up their coffee cups at work'.
- ✔ Conative: Apparent as you express a behavioural intent resulting from your attitude, such as, 'I'm going to hide all their dirty cups'.

These components of your attitudes interact together and affect how you are at work.

Cognitive dissonance is when a mismatch exists between what you're thinking and how you're behaving: it can make you feel extremely tense.

For example, you may be aware that the photocopier requires toner, because the warning light is flashing madly, but you carry on feeding it your sheets of paper to make copies. Your underlying thinking is 'I should change the toner', but your outward behaviour is to keep feeding, feeding, feeding. The result is a mismatch between thinking and behaviour – and stress.

You feel frustrated and annoyed because you know that you're putting off a task that will need doing soon. Also, the quality of your copies are poor. The next person using the photocopier is sure to be annoyed that you didn't attend to the problem and may well hold negative thoughts about you.

All these thoughts (and more) are whirling about in your mind while you continue feeding paper into the photocopier.

A conscious or unconscious refusal to acknowledge your thinking and attitudes, and continue to behave in ways that are, ultimately, self-defeating, results in unsettling feelings and tension. Plus, if you need more encouragement to bite the bullet and change the toner, just imagine your co-worker's angry, grimacing, frustrated expression!

## Challenging your expectations of comfortable conditions

Most people need to work in order to provide themselves with shelter and food. When those essentials are in place, and with a certain level of security, how you use your financial resources is influenced by your personal choices.

Generally, people go through life trying to make a comfortable life for themselves. Having attended to the basics of air, shelter, food and sex (which Abraham Maslow identifies as the basic survival needs), people make decisions and choices to try to improve their basic life needs. After safety and security, social needs, friendship and family, people attend to self-esteem, confidence and achievement. The highest level, the pinnacle, is self-actualisation.

Your personality also influences how far you're willing to venture outside of your comfort zone. More introverted people often prefer to try to maintain their comfort zones, whereas the more extroverted may strive to find challenges and step outside of their comfort zones.

In the earlier section 'Discovering Your Environment at Work', I encourage you to consider your own situation. Identifying areas of conflict between what you want or expect in the workplace and what you're actually experiencing, can provide an opportunity for you to use CBT strategies to start to rationalise your thinking.

The key trigger for negative conflict is implicit in how much control you feel you have over your job, which is linked to your attitudes. When your work surroundings don't match up to your expectations (your attitudes), you may regularly feel uncomfortable and unsettled. The next two sections discuss changing your attitudes.

## Identifying your preferred way of working

CBT makes it clear that you can't always change a tense situation, but you can change the way you view it. Therefore, you can work on changing your attitudes in the workplace when you find yourself unwittingly outside your comfort zone (as I describe in the preceding section).

Working styles often develop as a combination of your basic personality traits and your conscious choices of selecting different types of jobs.

Identify your preferred working styles. You can also see this exercise as finding out about your flexibility in the workplace. Consider the following working style points:

- How I prefer to work
- Types of jobs I do and don't enjoy
- Looking back at the jobs I liked most
- Which aspects of those jobs were especially appealing
- My working style: the ways I work best and the ways I don't enjoy working
- Working alone on projects or being part of a team
- Leading projects or working on projects managed by others
- Managing others or avoiding management roles
- What are my strengths
- Obstacles that I feel impede my optimum way of working

Take some time to reflect on your working practices, and see whether you can identify areas in the past and now with a mismatch to your preferred job and working style.

## Exploring new attitudes

When you've identified some of your attitudes to work (refer to the preceding section), you have a chance to consider changing some of them that may be getting in the way of having a steady emotional outlook at work.

Here's how:

- ✔ Scan your attitudes for unhelpful ones: Identify those attitudes you hold that may be at odds with your actual experiences at work currently.

- ✔ Classify your attitudes into the cognitive, affective and conative (refer to the earlier section 'Recognising the importance of attitudes' for details): Look at each attitude and identify the associated negative feelings.

- ✔ Take time to consider whether you want to explore new attitudes: Changing attitudes requires hard work.

- ✔ Decide which attitudes you want to work on: Make the task manageable. Changing your way of thinking and viewing your work differently is no easy task.

- ✔ Decide on one attitude you want to change: Bring in the ABC model from Chapter 3 and start to identify the feelings, the trigger and the actual belief.

- ✔ Start the process of cognitive restructuring using CBT.

## *Creating the best outcomes*

You can start to sort out the troubling issues in your working life by making a conscious effort to increase the amount of control you have over your job (your locus of control; see the earlier section, 'Locus of control', for more on this). You can then start to create the best outcome for your current situation.

Feelings of helplessness are a root cause of feeling low and depressed. Often people get depressed by work because they think that they're trapped and can do nothing to change the difficult position they're in. CBT helps you to see that you do have options. They may be tough, but investigating where the mismatches lie (between how you want your working life and practices to be and the reality) is the first step to doing something about it.

# *Using CBT to Adjust Your Workplace Emotions*

Your CBT toolkit is on hand 24/7: you can bring it into your consciousness and use it to implement changes in your thinking and attitudes. It allows you to become your own technician for adjusting your emotional barometer.

The pressures at work (and internally) that you create with your thinking increase and decrease according to the changing work situation. Even if you can't use your toolkit in the immediate situation, when you recognise the feelings associated with a clash or conflict you can decide to enter a holding pattern until you have more time to work through the incident.

## Implementing healthy work routines

When you start to become truly aware of the environment in which you work, you can plan and make changes when you want to create the healthiest surroundings you possibly can – in the current circumstances.

You can be proactive in working to maximise your own health and wellbeing, professionally and personally. I doubt very much that your job ticks all the boxes for being an exemplary model for employee satisfaction: some aspects can always be improved. Certain companies do, however, pride themselves on implementing the optimum strategies to enhance their employees' wellbeing (awards and published charts measure and list them).

But the reality may well be that you experience struggles in your working conditions: you can either focus on the negative aspects and upset yourself constantly by thinking about them, or you can choose to work to reduce some of this negative thinking (check out Chapter 2).

## Dealing with obstacles

The big question to ask yourself when you decide you want to work to change your unhelpful attitudes is, 'What will prevent me from doing this?' Your past experiences at work are likely to provide you with lots of examples of when you tried to make some changes and then obstacles appeared. How you view these obstacles and setbacks is an important factor in how likely you are to be successful at change.

CBT implementation is a continual process and every tricky situation needs hard work. CBT can show you how to refigure what's happening and provides you with a helpful toolkit. Expect obstacles along the way – anything else is unrealistic – but trust CBT to show you how to deal with them and move on.

# Part II
# Benefits, Bonuses and Added Value for All

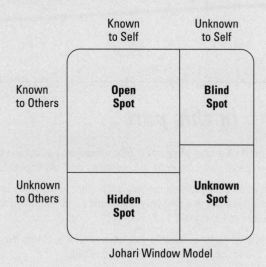

Johari Window Model

Part II
Benefits, Bonuses and
Added Value for All

## *In this part . . .*

- ✔ Learn to take care of yourself; otherwise you can leave yourself open to experiencing negative emotions and physical ill-health.

- ✔ Reflect on your professional integrity, what you believe in and how sometimes you find yourself at odds with what you're required to do at work.

- ✔ Identify what areas trouble you, admit that a problem exists and use the various ways in which CBT can help.

# Chapter 5

# Looking after Yourself at Work

· · · · · · · · · · · · · · · · · · · · · · · · · · · · · · · · · · · · · · · · · · · · · · ·

*In This Chapter*

▶ Putting yourself first

▶ Being responsible for your own wellbeing

▶ Staying healthy

· · · · · · · · · · · · · · · · · · · · · · · · · · · · · · · · · · · · · · · · · · · · · · ·

*O*ften you're so busy responding to the demands of work, colleagues, targets, planning, organising, meeting deadlines and generally racing about like a headless chicken that you don't find time to prioritise yourself.

A central premise of CBT is that you're responsible for your own wellbeing. If you don't take care of yourself, you can leave yourself open to experiencing negative emotions and physical ill-health.

Part of this responsibility is to assess what sort of person you are and what you expect from work in order to get the best out of yourself. Doing so helps you to clarify what you find acceptable and what you struggle with.

In this chapter, I discuss the importance of developing an enlightened self-interest, taking responsibility for your own life and looking after your health. I suggest that instead of always worrying about the effect you have on others, you make sure that you take some time for yourself as well.

# Allowing Yourself to Be Number One

I wonder what you think of this saying:

> *The only person who is really responsible for your happiness is yourself.*

Some people think that the statement is a bit harsh. But when you think about it, although other people can be helpful and considerate – adding to your happiness and enhancing your everyday life – the decisions and actions are all your own. (I'm not denying of course that other people can also negatively impact on your life, especially at work, and create stressful situations.)

## Replacing selfishness with enlightened self-interest

In CBT, the emphasis is on working out what you can do to make life the best you can for yourself. You're bound to encounter difficult situations and times when you struggle. But you can help yourself to deal and cope with these difficult times when you allow yourself to stand back – what is known as cognitive distancing to see the whole picture. Putting yourself first can be considered 'selfish'. In this case, the interpretation of the word is negative, along the lines of this definition:

> *Lacking consideration for other people; concerned chiefly with one's own personal profit or pleasure.*

That all sounds negative and inconsiderate of others. There is another way of looking at the idea of putting your interests first: the Buddhists call it *enlightened self-interest*.

Looking at the issue using this phrase can be helpful in finding your place at work and in the world generally, and helps to make accusations of selfishness redundant.

After all, when you look after yourself, taking responsibility for your health and wellbeing, your work and family also benefit. Plus, if you have a good idea of what's best for you and work to achieve your goals, society benefits as well. If you're not feeling 100 per cent at work, through stress or ill-health made worse by unhealthy coping strategies, you can't give your best to any of these areas.

In case you're thinking, 'great, I don't need to think about other people any more', hold on there! Nobody who lives with a total disregard for other people is going to be happy. You need to take into account the needs of others too. Having other people like you and hold you in positive regard not only helps you along the way (and makes for a happier and fun life), but also together you're encouraging each other to help contribute to the development and survival of society. But first of all, you may need to work out how you would like to be and how you want to live your life.

## Viewing yourself honestly

Taking a look at yourself, your beliefs and behaviours can be interesting . . . and a bit scary. You may find it easier to comply with what you think is expected of you. Behaviours outside the norm always feels uncomfortable.

So most people bundle along, responding to outside influences, taking onboard what society expects and most times conforming and behaving nicely. Some people consider that society ticks along better when people agree to conform to the usual standards and norms – the established standards of behaviour expected in society. Being true to yourself may be a challenge but more meaningful to you in the long term and reduce internal conflicts. Here are some examples of norms you may have come across:

- ✔ Wash your hands before dinner.
- ✔ Pay for your train ticket.
- ✔ Work the hours agreed on your contract.
- ✔ Complete your work in time.
- ✔ No singing in the workplace.
- ✔ Respect your colleagues and bosses.
- ✔ Don't lie on your CV.

Many of these may be seen as essential for the smooth running of society or for your own health and safety, but you do have a choice; there are consequences if you take another path. CBT encourages you to actively look at the pros and cons of the decisions and choices you are making. For example, if you choose to be disrespectful to your colleagues and bosses, there will be consequences that may not be in your best interests.

Take some time to look at yourself honestly. No one is here to judge you! Your thoughts will remain a secret, between you and this book.

## *Reflecting on your behaviours*

If you carried a video camera around with you one day at work, what do you think you'd see when you played back the recording? What sort of impression do you give to others?

For example, on my first teaching practice, I was told that I looked fierce and didn't smile much. This made me think about the impression I was giving. I learnt that when I am anxious, my face looks very serious. This was helpful feedback. Here are some pointers as to how to measure your image and your impression management:

- ✔ What sort of expression do you have when you get to work?
- ✔ How do you interact with your workmates?

    ✔ Do you settle down to work quickly?

    ✔ Does your day include moving around?

    ✔ What's your overall demeanour?

    ✔ How do you think others see you?

Very often, you find that you're almost acting a role at work. You may be very different at home and out socially than in the workplace, perhaps because your work managers have expectations of how they expect you to behave.

You can sometimes locate a source of unhappiness at work in the mismatch between how you are when relaxed and how you need to be at work. Consider whether you can detect marked differences between the 'work you' and you as a person outside work. If you do, CBT can help you to minimise the discomfort that you're experiencing (see Chapter 8). Also, check out the later section in this chapter on 'Placing yourself in context' for more on understanding your workplace persona.

Look out for shoulds, oughts and musts:

    ✔ I must be like this at work.

    ✔ I shouldn't say what I'm really thinking at work.

    ✔ I ought to behave impeccably at all times at work.

If you find them, apply your CBT toolkit (refer to Chapter 3 for more) to examine your thinking. Are you being too hard on yourself? Are the expectations and demands you place on yourself unreasonable?

## Valuing yourself

Valuing yourself is important for your wellbeing in work and in your personal life too.

Think of someone at work whom you like and admire. How do you treat her? Maybe you speak respectfully to her, and you're patient, considerate and kind to her. If something awful happened (say, she had a sick child and had to take some time off work), you'd be understanding and do all you can to help her at work. When she gets stressed out and upset at work, you'd do what you can to support her with compassion.

Now think about how you treat yourself. Are you as considerate to yourself as you are to other people? Very often you find that you're harder on yourself.

Valuing yourself is important for your wellbeing in work and in your personal life too. Treat yourself as you treat others. It may be an old saying, but that doesn't make it any less true.

## *Treating yourself with respect*

Confucius is quoted as saying: 'Respect yourself and others will respect you'. Sometimes you can concentrate your attention so much on behaving in order to treat others with respect that you neglect yourself in the process.

Many factors influence how highly or otherwise you regard yourself. As you develop from childhood, a sense of self emerges, though this takes time and often changes at different points in your life. You may emerge as confident, insecure, unsure or full of self doubts depending on your past and current experiences. Here are some other words that describe respect for you to think about:

- ✔ Admiration
- ✔ Appreciation
- ✔ Approval
- ✔ Esteem
- ✔ Praise
- ✔ Recognition
- ✔ Regard

Take each word in turn and place yourself on a sliding scale of 0–10 in relation to it, where zero is a low score and 10 a high score. A score of 5 indicates an average score of how you rate yourself. Anything under 5 may indicate that you don't rate yourself so highly. If you find this for yourself, spend some time thinking why you have such a low self-esteem score at the moment.

# *Taking Responsibility for Yourself*

When you're a child, other people take most of the responsibility for you. Caregivers provide your basic needs and school teachers monitor your intellectual development. As you develop greater intellectual skills, your brain starts to think in more abstract terms. You're able to reason and judge what you consider best for yourself, such as what things you choose to learn and how you want your life to be.

Alongside this cognitive development, you're able to create your own code of ethics and sense of responsibility. A definition of self-responsibility can include the idea of being accountable for what's within your power, control or management.

A great leap forward is when you realise that you want to learn something, as opposed to having to go to school and do the homework to avoid getting into trouble.

Self-motivation and taking responsibility for your own learning and development is something that you take to work with you.

## Recognising the need to take care of yourself

When you've developed to the point that you have the thinking capacity to make your own choices, you really are responsible for yourself.

CBT stresses that personal responsibility for your thinking, choices and structuring of your life is a key factor in maximising emotional wellbeing.

If you constantly look to others to make choices for you, or rely on other people to direct you in life and work, you can find yourself on a life course with which you're uncomfortable. A side effect of relying on others is that when things go wrong, you tend to blame everyone except yourself. This reaction may be convenient in the short term, but in the long term you're setting yourself up for future emotional turbulence.

Eventually people may get annoyed by constantly having to organise your life and also for getting the blame when things don't suit you! The balance of power in a relationship, whether at work or in your personal life, can be a dynamic and sensitive area.

## Rationalising why you're important

Often you can develop the habit of putting other people's needs and considerations before your own. Perhaps, culturally, you were taught to always think of others before yourself.

Although a noble and laudable philosophy to have, if you take it too far and too often, the consequences can be that you don't help yourself to live in the most emotionally healthy and desirable way.

Deciding the holiday rota at work is a good example of where, if you always put others first, you're also not looking adequately after yourself. Perhaps you stand back when the holiday rota is up for grabs, thinking:

*Oh, Kevin has a young family, he should have priority when he takes his holiday. Mandy has an ageing parent to take care of, she should have the whole of Christmas off. Eric works so hard at managing the team, he must go on his foreign holiday to relax. I can manage the office while they're out. I live on my own, I only have to sort myself out.*

This sort of thinking means that you probably reduce your chances of going to places you'd like to visit, at the times that suit you, to find company and relaxation.

You're important and need a break like anyone else, and when you want it too, if possible. Continually putting yourself last, over time, erodes your self-confidence and sense of self-esteem.

## *Needing to earn a living*

You may be thinking that what I say in the preceding sections is all well and good in an ideal world, but the job you have isn't exactly your dream job, and while you have bills to pay, you don't have much choice. You can often feel discontented, trapped by your circumstances, and that life is pretty unfair.

But what's that appearing over the horizon, riding to your rescue? It's CBT, reminding you that you do have a choice over the way you feel, and that you can choose to view things in a different light when your feelings are troubling you.

Perhaps you start by thinking:

*I'm really unhappy in this job. I have to come to work and I shouldn't have to do a job I don't like and it makes me miserable.*

But using your CBT toolkit (for more, refer to Chapter 3), you can aim to change your viewpoint to the following:

*I'd rather I didn't have to work in this job, it's just a stop-gap really until I can find a job I'd enjoy. It's unfortunate that I need to earn money, but that's just the way it is. How is upsetting myself every day and dwelling on all the negative aspects helping me? It's not. I'm just making myself miserable if I think like that. I'll accept that this is the way life is just now, and I'm concerned and a bit annoyed, but I'm not going to let that way of thinking invade my whole life.*

## Considering how much work means to you

The current ratio of time spent at leisure and at work (or working at home) is weighted heavily on the work side. With the advent of the computer and other technology, your workplace can now contact you at any time of the day or night and even when you're on holiday. A huge pressure exists to be constantly in touch with work. Plus, the high levels of unemployment in some countries mean that people in work are increasingly anxious to be flexible and available to maximise their contributions. The notion of presenteeism, when people stay at work for longer hours, taking work home and checking emails at the weekend, is a word that only came into the Collins dictionary in 1979. That dictionary describes presenteeism as: the practice of persistently working longer hours and taking fewer holidays than the terms of one's employment demand, especially as a result of fear of losing one's job.

In itself, nothing's wrong with working long hours. But if you'd prefer not to do so, and your personal life is being affected negatively, you may want to consider investigating your work–life balance.

Working hard and long hours in the short term may be an exciting challenge and a way of achieving success, which enhances your promotion prospects as well as gives you a sense of achievement. But if it means that you're making yourself ill, you may want to evaluate what's most important to you.

Use the CBT toolkit from Chapter 3 to weigh up the pros and cons of excessive working practices and rationalise preferable ones that are in your best interests.

## Being responsible for your own happiness

Deciding that you're going to take charge of how your life goes, as far as is possible and within your control, is a major factor in taking responsibility for yourself.

Protecting and cultivating an environment to maximise your chances of good health and emotional wellbeing are within your control. When you've worked out what you need, you can start to assert yourself and communicate these needs to others in your life. How you are in the relationships in your life at work and at home has a large influence on how your life progresses.

If you have difficulty asserting yourself and conveying clearly what you're willing to do at work, you need to keep practising and stay focused. Make a start by considering the following list of considerations:

✔ Make a list of your strengths, talents and positive attributes.

✔ Recognise that you're an adult and your decisions decide your future.

✔ Accept that you choose the direction for your own life.

✔ Understand that how you view your work affects what you feel.

✔ Work out time-management structures.

✔ Educate yourself to be alert to the dangers of stress (Chapter 3).

# Being Your Own Best Friend

Having a loyal, attentive, caring best friend, who listens to your problems and shares your burdens, is a huge benefit to anyone. If you have such a friend on your side, great! But even if you don't, remember that you can fulfil that role yourself!

Treating yourself as your own best friend is a great asset, because people often treat others with much more consideration and respect than they do themselves. Some of the things you think and say to yourself you'd never say to another person. You can sometimes see friends working themselves so hard that they have no time to socialise, they hardly have time for their partner and their children see them only at the weekends. You may even become concerned for their wellbeing.

Yet, interestingly, you may be treating yourself in just the same way, but somehow you just accept it and struggle on.

## Assessing whether your work habits are healthy

Taking some time to look at your priorities may reveal lifestyle habits that have developed, often across communities and cultures, that have crept in as the new normal without any deliberate decision.

Ask yourself the following questions to gain insight into how much your work life impacts on your whole life:

✔ Do I put work above everything else?

✔ Have I cancelled arrangements in my personal life because of work pressure?

✔ Do I go into work when I'm feeling ill?

✔ Is taking work home part of my routine?

✔ Does checking emails outside of work time feature highly in my life?

✔ Do I spend more time communicating with work contacts than others?

✔ Am I welded to my phone and laptop?

✔ Do I sometimes forget to eat during the day?

✔ Is my holiday location dictated by Wi-Fi connections?

✔ Are my conversations mostly about work?

✔ Do I want to have more sleep?

If you answer 'yes' to quite a few of the above questions, you need to take a serious look at your own work habits.

What would a good friend say to you about your habits and priorities? Some people thrive on and enjoy a work-dominated lifestyle. Writing down a list may help you identify areas of conflict and reveal patterns that may have developed over years of which you are unaware.

When you don't give yourself the same regard as you would give others, or you put yourself bottom of the list of priorities in terms of your work demands, you aren't taking good care of yourself. Sit down with yourself (as your new best friend!) and make a list of how you want your work life to be. Even allowing yourself the luxury of thinking about yourself is a good start.

## *Realising others don't always care*

Sometimes you can experience that sad realisation that not everyone else at work has your best interests at heart, even when you've helped co-workers. You ask for some help from colleagues and they turn their heads away. Or perhaps, in virtual terms, they don't respond to your emailed plea. You may have gone out of your way to help them and expect the same in return, but often this assistance isn't forthcoming.

The old saying about asking a busy person to do something because he's more likely to get it done often seems particularly true in work. You may have found yourself running round like a headless chicken to get your work done and help others in times of crisis, only to find everyone disappears when you need help.

Upsetting yourself on these sorts of occasions is self-defeating. Use CBT to rationalise that, yes, it's unfortunate and disappointing, but it's a lesson learnt. Consider the advice of your best friend (you!) and decide how you'll behave in the future. Perhaps you tell yourself, 'I don't always need to help others out if it's not in my best interests. If it means I get stressed out with the extra work, saying no is okay'.

# Investing in Your Overall Health

Your health comprises many different aspects. Your health is a combination of your mind and body. Generally you are described as healthy when you are free from illness, injury or pain. The World Health Organization (WHO) describes good health as follows:

A state of complete physical, mental and social wellbeing and not merely the absence of disease or infirmity.

In other words, your health is a combination of your mind and body. Generally you're healthy when you're free from illness, injury or pain.

When you look at the influences of work on your wellbeing, you start to see that work is only one of many things having an influence on your health. I talk a lot more about physical and emotional health concerns at work in Chapter 4.

## Placing yourself in context

When considering work and health in your life, you may find that you're a different person at work than at home or in your personal life. Flexibility to be able to conform to the general expectations at work is helpful in settling into your work role, but for some people it can be a source of conflict. Watch out for tensions that can arise as you change your persona to fit in.

Sociologist Erving Goffman wrote an interesting book in 1959 called *The Presentation of Self in Everyday Life* (Anchor). His stated aim was to 'consider the way in which the individual in ordinary work situations presents himself and his activity to others'. Goffman discovered that the more able people are to adjust their presentation of self in different situations, the more likely they are to be successful.

In the work setting, he concludes that the most successful people are the most proficient at doing so. He likens it to employing acting skills, in order to maximise your chances of getting on in life. He calls it the art of impression management.

Some people say that if you have to change yourself to fit in at work you're not being true to yourself. Although an interesting point for discussion, my concern in this book is to focus on what you can do practically, using CBT techniques, to help overcome uncomfortable feelings you experience at work.

## Dressing for business

Jamie is an IT business analyst with responsibility for customer-facing meetings to ascertain the business needs of companies. At home, he favours jeans and t-shirts, and his interests include music and going to heavy-rock concerts. He has strong business ethics. He chooses to wear dark business suits at work, because he discovered that it makes a positive impression with customers.

Although he'd prefer to dress casually for work, he knows that it's in his best interests to conform to the business dress code. He rationalised, using CBT, that accepting the conforming dress code serves his interests.

If you find a mismatch between who you 'really are' (whatever that may mean for you) and what work expects you to be, implementing the CBT toolkit (check out Chapter 3 for details) helps you to identify the feelings and pinpoint the trigger. You can then work on what about your thinking and attitude to work is in conflict with how you want work to be.

## *Replacing your bad work habits and routines*

Old habits die hard. People can become so entrenched in doing things a certain way that they inadvertently shut themselves off from new, better ways of working and often negatively affect their health as well.

If you fall prey to this behaviour, you don't only make life harder for yourself than is necessary, but also you may be limiting your progress at work.

Everyone has some less than perfect habits at work. Check out the following common ones and see how many apply to you:

- ✔ Constantly checking your emails
- ✔ Writing and sending emails too hastily
- ✔ Not planning your day and prioritising, but just jumping in
- ✔ Always saying 'yes' to people's demands
- ✔ Finding yourself repeatedly overloaded

✔ Spending a lot of time involved in office politics.

✔ Taking work home with you.

✔ Having ill-defined boundaries of work and home.

✔ Working until late at night and getting up early to work.

✔ Not taking holidays and breaks.

✔ Finding yourself moaning frequently about work.

✔ Having constantly to change childcare provision to fit in with work.

✔ Cancelling social arrangements because of work.

Log and analyse your work habits, looking at what you do and how much time you spend on various activities. Then make a list of your personal 'bad' working habits, ones that get in the way of you functioning at optimum levels in an all-round capacity. Think carefully about them and use them to help you focus on making some changes for the better.

## Making efforts to assist your health

Making changes in your life isn't easy. You're bound to find some level of discomfort as you start to change your habits and routines. The fact is, however, that you rarely experience these personal gains without a degree of discomfort.

Changes in behaviour mostly come from people thinking about what they want to do and acting on those thoughts and decisions.

Some things you do on autopilot. Maybe you have the same food for breakfast, buy the same brand of shoes, get the same bus to work each day or try to stick to a routine for the family. If you didn't include some habits and routines in your daily life, you'd have to rethink every decision and behaviour and probably take two hours to get out of the house in the morning! But if you find that a routine or habit is getting in the way of achieving your work goals and therefore becoming a problem, consider re-evaluating your behaviours.

Extreme rigidity and adherence to some patterns of behaviours and also thinking patterns can tip over into obsessive compulsive disorder (OCD). I don't have space to go into such behaviours in this book, but they may warrant some specialist help. If you have concerns in this area, check out *Managing OCD with CBT For Dummies* by Rob Willson (Wiley). When you decide consciously to change your thinking in order to correct any unhelpful behaviour, or to work towards new, more helpful ways of behaving, you may quite naturally get flutters of nervousness. A little release of adrenalin into your bloodstream as you think about acting on these new ways of thinking is your body's way of preparing you for new territory.

You'll find that as you repeat your new thinking and consequently your new ways of behaving, the nervous feelings becomes less and less until you don't even think about them.

Katharine decided to go on a training course to learn how to use some software to create a website for her new business. The day course was fast-paced and the group was large so she didn't get a lot of chance to ask questions. She took a manual home with her and faced a deadline of two weeks to launch her website (she'd booked a stand at a local business enterprise exhibition day).

She felt very nervous about starting to build the website and found every reason possible to do other things rather than get on with it. She complained to her partner that the course had been too crowded, her computer was slow, she thought she had a cold coming on and she suddenly decided she needed to visit her sister. I'm sure you've done the same type of things, pre-varicating when a stressful job needs doing.

Her anxiety at the thought of sitting down and making a start was preventing her from carrying out the task.

Then Katharine remembered a bit about CBT she'd been taught at an evening class. She found the CBT book and turned to the section on procrastination. She realised that her thinking about how hard and difficult she thought the task was going to be was getting in the way of her doing anything construc-tive to achieve her goal.

Using the ABC framework method (from Chapter 2) she identified:

- ✔ **The emotional consequence:** Feeling anxious.
- ✔ **The activating event:** The thought of getting started.
- ✔ **Her negative beliefs and thinking:** Creating this website must be so hard. Katharine worked on changing her thinking from the 'must' demands to the 'prefer' type of thinking.

Her new thinking was:

*I'd prefer that making this website wasn't too hard but if it is, tough. I can either insist that it's hard, and not get on with it, or I can change my demanding thinking to a preferred way of thinking, such as although it may be tricky, I'll give it a try.*

Katharine decided to sit down at 10 a.m. and work for 30 minutes, no matter what. She started reading the manual and trying it out on the computer. She felt a bit jittery, but not so anxious that it prevented her from starting work.

She was still sitting there three hours later, having become totally engrossed in the task and created the first version of her website. The sound of internal cheering resounded inside her head!

Too often you may be quick to criticise yourself and your faults and overlook self-congratulation when you're happy with your work. Don't forget to give yourself a pat on the back when you achieve something.

Although too often you may be quick to criticise yourself and out your faults and overlook self-congratulation when you are happy with your work, other people noticing and acknowledging your achievements is rewarding. View their approval as not necessary but just an added bonus (see Chapter 7 for more). After all, as I describe earlier in the section 'Being Your Own Best Friend', you're now your new, best, most supportive pal, aren't you?

# Chapter 6

# Impressing Employers with Your Professional Integrity

*In This Chapter*

▶ Presenting yourself as a great potential employee

▶ Taking control of yourself as a worker

▶ Being an asset to your organisation

**D**iscovering how you can use CBT and its methods at work is an investment for yourself and for your employer. When thinking about how you fit in with the organisation you work for, you need to consider how you can match up the firm with your preferred ways of working and your values and ethics at work.

I see this aspect of work life as your professional integrity. It fits in with the CBT way of thinking that you can't change the situation you work in, but you can be in control of how you view work and how you can hold on to what you believe in, even if sometimes that doesn't match up to your experiences.

When you spend some time reflecting on your professional integrity, what you believe in and how sometimes you find yourself at odds with what you're required to do at work, you can bring stability into your whole life.

In this chapter, I cover using CBT while you're looking for a job, as well as benefitting yourself as an employee and your employer.

## CBT working at work!

A knowledge and understanding of CBT techniques and strategies can benefit all sorts of organisations and companies. For example, a client requested me to write some courses to help employees manage changes at work. I used CBT as an underlying management tool, which underpinned all the courses. The main theme of the three- and five-hour workshops was 'Transition Management', with other titles created according to the company's briefs, such as:

✔ The Science of Happiness at Work

✔ Managing Stress at Work

✔ Managing Change

✔ Redundancy, Redeployment and Reorganising

✔ Ship In or Ship Out: Decision-Making

The courses were piloted and rolled out to many other organisations, including international financial, IT, HR and government departments, manufacturing companies, and pharmaceutical and food industry businesses. Thinking in terms of the organisation you work for, and how you fit in with your preferred ways of working and your views about values and ethics at work, you may want to take some time to see how you can match them up. You could call this way of being at work your 'professional integrity'.

# *Ensuring Your Firm Hires a Responsible Person – You!*

Before you can worry about using CBT at work, you need to have a job! The process of looking for work can be incredibly stressful, with the inevitable setbacks and all the pressure of being 'judged' by other people.

Many unsettling emotions can surface when you're searching and applying for work. Thoughts can start running through your head, such as 'Am I good enough to apply?', 'They'll never consider me', 'There's no point applying' and 'Why would they give me a job?'

Although understandable, this sort of negative thinking is counterproductive. The more you think that you're not good enough and fill your head with self-doubt, the more likely that chain of thinking is to inhibit you from even applying. But one thing's for sure: if you don't apply for jobs, you're very unlikely to ever get one!

CBT can be a great help throughout all aspects of job-hunting. In this section, I discuss making sure that you prepare and present the best of yourself when looking for a job.

## Preparing for work

The process of searching for work is often a hit and miss affair. The sources available to seek work are varied:

- ✔ Agencies
- ✔ Consultancies
- ✔ Job centres
- ✔ Journals
- ✔ Newspapers
- ✔ Websites
- ✔ Word of mouth

Applying for jobs is certainly a lot easier now that you can do so online for many applications, but it still requires concentrated thought and attention to detail.

One of my CBT therapy teachers had been to America to study and qualify as a CBT therapist. With masses of experience and a string of qualifications, he returned to the UK to find work: he had over 70 applications, some interviews and no job. But it didn't stop him from applying for more jobs. Eventually, one interview led to being offered a position at a university and some years later he was made the first Professor of Counselling in the UK. Persistence paid off!

His experience made a big impact on me. I used to moan and whine about having to go through the laborious task of filling in applications, only to get an interview and then perhaps not be offered the job. I thought it all very unfair. Injustice had always been a major theme in my thinking processes. But following the CBT training, I realised how self-defeating it was to think and behave in those ways.

CBT helped me to see that blaming the system wasn't helping me at all. Instead, if I changed my views to accept that, yes, it was tough, but that moaning was limiting my applications and inhibiting my quest for a job, I'd be more likely to keep applying for jobs and increase my chances of finding or changing my employment.

## Analysing a job description

When applying for jobs, you may find a job description attached to the advert or a more detailed description on the application form. Generally the description outlines the roles and responsibilities of a job, contracted hours requirements, relationships and line management in the organisation, as well as those all-important salary and benefits details.

Some job descriptions are quite flexible, in anticipation of rapidly changing markets and technological advances. For some management jobs, the flexibility may reflect the nature of the role to allow for creativity and developments.

When considering different jobs, bear in mind that, at work, the changing expectations and boundaries of the role can cause anxiety and inner conflict. The necessity for flexible thinking and the ability to change your own way of working and adapt to new circumstances can be a key factor in your emotional stability at work. Therefore, it's something you need to prepare for.

## Recognising your skills and abilities

Carrying out a skills audit on yourself is an interesting and useful exercise when considering the type of work and job you'd like to do. Analysing your skills and attributes helps your self-confidence and attitude to gaining employment.

Although some companies and agencies can give you careers coaching and include questionnaires to focus your attention on your current skills situation, you can start to do this yourself.

Make lists of your qualifications, experiences at work and other experiences from school, voluntary work, part-time jobs and past employments.

Avoid labelling yourself and limiting or minimising your current status. For example, describing yourself as 'just' a teacher, personal assistant or parent doesn't help you to acknowledge your past experiences and future potential. Check out Table 6-1, where I itemise some sample skills you may want to include on your list. In the second column, add specific examples from your experience to back up your claims in the first column.

| Table 6-1 | Sample Skills in Your Personal Evaluation List |
|---|---|
| *Skills* | *Evidence* |
| Organisation | |
| Time/Financial management | |
| Tolerance | |
| Social | |

| Skills | Evidence |
|---|---|
| Ethical | |
| Professional | |
| Management | |
| Creative | |
| IT literate | |
| Flexible | |
| Progressive | |
| Open to new ideas | |
| Reliable | |
| Responsible | |

In rapidly changing world and work cultures, flexibility, and a willingness to update your skills and adjust your attitudes according to new challenges, are of great importance.

Get testimonials from people you work with or have worked with to give you a different insight into yourself. Doing so helps to give you a greater perspective on yourself and increases your confidence as you gain a wide understanding of your strengths.

## Facing the fear of being found out

Feeling that you're not worthy of applying for jobs – and that if you do get offered a job, worrying that you may be 'found out' as unsuitable – is a commonly held belief.

Unfortunately, just at the time you need to be at your most confident, your self-confidence may be at an all time low when you're applying for jobs or promotions; such feelings of insecurity are natural during times of transition. You can feel particularly vulnerable when out of work or desperate to change your current job.

Doing the skills audit in the preceding section can help you to reaffirm your inventory of current talents and experiences. Quite possibly, you have more qualities than you give yourself credit for!

Simply being aware that you have self-doubts about your real abilities helps you to reduce irrational thoughts, because it allows these feelings into your consciousness. You can then use the ABC model (from Chapter 2) to pinpoint the emotional consequence, identify the trigger (the job application) and work with the irrational beliefs about yourself, applying the CBT techniques to help you to reduce anxiety and worry.

## Succeeding at interviews with CBT

Going for a job interview can be a nerve-racking experience. Getting over-anxious about the interview works against you because you don't show your best side. CBT can help you to calm down and rationalise the process of the job interview in order to maximise your chances of getting the job you want. Also, because interviewers are trying to assess your suitability to work in their company, as well as your qualifications and experience, it benefits your potential employer too because it gets to see more of the 'real' you.

Often the overall perspective of the fringe benefits for your employer when you are more in control of your emotions in an interview is that the inter-viewer will see more of the real you. You can feel that you need to act in a certain way for every different interview, to play to your particular strengths for the position on offer, only to find that you lose a sense of yourself. But the person the people are interviewing needs to be in balance with your real self and aspirations. When you rationalise the interview situation, fully accept that there may be a conflict between your real self and the role you are being asked to adopt, so that the person and the job match up only partially but everyone's happy and you accept this.

## Negotiating your pay

Frequently, you may find that the topic of what you're going to be paid is an uncomfortable one. The job specification may include an idea of the salary or an hourly rate, but you may want to know more specifically what the com-pany is going to offer you. Negotiating pay and benefits can bring up unset-tling emotions and a lack of self-confidence and self-worth.

An American Psychological Association study looked at 51 countries and found that when women bargain on behalf of another person, they're better at negotiating than men. But when women negotiate on behalf of themselves, their own team or their own company, they aren't as good. The researchers concluded that women feel social pressure to display some gender-consistent behaviour, such as accommodation or co-operation, as if they'd face criticism and disapproval if they behaved contrary to what society expects from them.

Getting some training in negotiating pay can certainly help to redress the balance. Many of the CBT techniques and tips I provide in this book are particularly useful for improving your self-confidence and self-acceptance.

# Taking Responsibility for Yourself as a Dynamic Employee

Looking at your own commitment to being a responsible employee is a vitally important step in taking control of your work life.

Considering what's needed to be an efficient and productive employee is a two-way process. Your employer will have ideas about how it wants you to work and what's required of you. Clarifying in your own mind your preferred way of working can be helpful so that you can monitor whether the two expectations are complementing each other. Sometimes, especially when struggling in other areas of your life, you may not be able to give the absolute commitment you'd want to work and your personal life.

You need to take responsibility for your health, your relationships and your domestic arrangements as well as work. At certain points in your personal life you'll experience conflicts in terms of obligations and demands. You aren't helped if you place extra unrealistic demands on yourself, trying to meet all work requirements and changing home circumstances perfectly.

CBT helps you to see that all people are fallible human beings who can't possibly always be the top person at work. If this disappoints you, help yourself to reduce some of your workplace tensions using the CBT technique of rationalising your thinking so that you can work on changing the unrealistic demands you put upon yourself.

In this section, I show you that the more you're in charge of yourself at work, the more helpful you are to the organisation.

Work is often a hectic, fast-paced environment – your line managers and bosses are probably so engrossed in delivering on their own job demands that they have little time to notice your struggles or to help you out when you need support. People want their own problems solved and they rarely go looking for extra ones.

## Assessing the situation

Being fully aware of the overall situation at work can only benefit the way you work and the organisation as a whole. To see new opportunities and future development in your professional life, you need to be open to new experiences. Finding out that you focus only on your individual work schedule and tasks is sure to disadvantage you as a company employee.

Don't get into the habit of closeting yourself away at work. Although concentrating solely on your particular role may feel comfortable and create a security blanket around yourself, it may not be in your best long-term interests. To see new opportunities and future development in your professional life, you will need to be open to new experiences.

## Prioritising the work

Within your own job role, with its many demands, deadlines and different projects, you need to develop the skill of prioritising your work effectively in order not to feel overwhelmed and swamped by work.

You may find this definition of stress helpful:

> *When the perceived demand outweighs the ability to meet those demands*

The majority of clients I see who refer themselves from their workplace for counselling are experiencing stress. Many people have great past work records, haven't experienced problems at work in the past and have enjoyed their jobs. But something changes and they find that as time goes by, the extra work they're given becomes more and more onerous. They've been struggling quietly for a long time until they start experiencing emotional disturbances and physical symptoms of stress.

Developing the skill of prioritising is vital. When you recognise the feeling of being overwhelmed by the tasks and situations in front of you, you can take steps to change things. Allowing yourself to pay attention to upsetting feelings – that is, recognising that all is not well – is the all-important 'C' in the CBT toolkit from Chapter 2.

Writing down the tasks that are needed to be done enables you to start prioritising the order in which they are done, and review if they are all essential at this point in time.

## Meeting expectations

Your perception of the expectations that the company has of you is the basis for your emotional good health. You may discover that you develop your own rigid view of the expectations and what you feel is required of you. If you find that you aren't meeting these expectations, you can be setting yourself up to start feeling uneasy. This is not made easier by changes in company demands, and individual managers requiring different things from you. You need to stay attuned to this moving pattern.

This is important during a period of rapid change when company management itself might change, or in a merger/acquisition scenario. The only thing you have control of in these circumstances is your attitude to what is going on around you.

You can only do your best, even when others may have another expectation of this.

The harder you work to fulfill these expectations and the longer you find that you're failing, the more extreme your feelings of unease become.

## Becoming aware of your weaknesses

To bring out the best in yourself at work and make a significant contribution, you may want to work on your weak spots. Being able and willing to look at yourself, assess how you work and be open to constructive feedback is a surefire way of initiating the process. Working hard at implementing changes when you've identified the areas for progress is a vital and necessary prerequisite.

You're bound to be unaware of certain aspects of yourself at work. Becoming more aware of characteristics and behaviours that are as yet unknown to you increases your self-knowledge. For example, you may not realise that you have a loud telephone voice or that you present reports full of typos and inaccurate punctuation. If you never ask for constructive feedback, being unaware can be a real hindrance.

The Johari window is a technique created in 1955 by two American psychologists, Joseph Luft (1916–2014) and Harrington Ingham (1914–1995). It's used to help people better understand their relationship with themselves and others.

Use the simple Johari window diagram in Figure 6-1 to reflect on how you fit in at work.

Taking opportunities to discover your weaknesses is advantageous for your employment, now and in the future.

## Going beyond the boundaries

Checking out the boundaries of your job is a useful exercise. Very often these boundaries get blurred in practice and over time. Tensions emerge as rules change and you lose control of your work–life balance, and what is preferable for you.

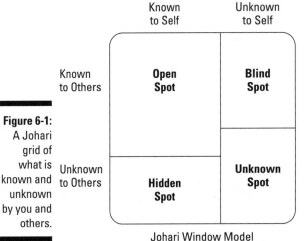

**Figure 6-1:**
A Johari
grid of
what is
known and
unknown
by you and
others.

Johari Window Model

Devote some time to reflecting on what you think your job is:

- ✔ Where does your job start?
- ✔ What are the primary responsibilities of your job?
- ✔ Are the boundaries of your job clear?
- ✔ How far does achieving the aims of your job depend on others?
- ✔ What helps you to keep within the boundaries of your job?
- ✔ What hinders you from staying within the boundaries of your job?
- ✔ Do your boundaries of work and play get blurred?

Setting boundaries is aided by making your own rules about how you work (as far as is possible).

Try to keep work and play-times separate. Drawing up boundaries can be easier than adhering to them, but try to keep work and play-times, as well as personal time separate. What can seem like a valid reason to change the boundaries, such as an urgent project or crisis at work, can be the start of the boundary edges becoming blurred.

Technology has freed people up in many respects to work flexibly, but it also brings the potential for a tyranny of work seeping into all aspects of your life. The Internet, laptops, tablets and mobile phones mean that work can reach you at all times, unless you switch the power off and shut down the appliance. Having a phone dedicated only to work can help in that, because (in theory at least) you can switch it off outside of office hours. In reality, you may find that 'switching off' is difficult. Job insecurity and unemployment may add to the pressure of feeling the need to be connected to work and becoming a slave to the company.

The notion of being addicted to work is an ever-present threat. Sometimes you may use the necessity of being in touch constantly as an excuse to get out of social situations or avoid other pressing tasks. Although nothing is inherently wrong with wanting to stay in contact with work, when you find that it's affecting your personal life and relationships detrimentally, taking a look at your work–life balance habits is worthwhile.

## *Being bold and audacious in your job*

Engaging with your work and making a significant contribution to the company is within your control. How confident you're feeling influences the extent to which you want to put forward your points of view about your own job, how it sits in the team and in the context of the whole organisation. Some people are more assertive than others, and of course your personality has a big effect on your levels of assertion.

You want to match your personality and preferences with an appropriate job, if you're to succeed at work. Studies show that different personality types are found all over the world and seem to be influenced by the genetic makeup of each person. Some people are naturally more extrovert and outgoing than others and appear more confident. A person who tends more towards the introvert type may be more hesitant and less forthcoming, especially in public situations.

In Chapter 9, I encourage you to assess what sort of personality type you are in order to get the best out of yourself.

### *Taking the initiative*

Taking the initiative implies being encouraging, seizing control and supplying leadership, perhaps with enthusiasm and drive. It also hints at the ability to work under your own steam and boldly go forward with projects – and perhaps even be creative and offer up new ideas.

In the work culture (see the later section 'Influencing the work culture'), some environments positively reward initiative whereas other workplaces require a certain steadiness in the job, and don't see inventiveness and resourcefulness as a necessary skill. Your enjoyment or otherwise of the job is sure to be influenced by such factors. If you enjoy a challenge and the opportunity to work independently and creatively and your job doesn't require these talents, you can find you becoming bored or even depressed over time.

In CBT terms, the situation (not you) is the fundamental source of the tension. In such cases, try and get a perspective on the mismatch between the job and yourself. Look to change how you view the job in order to start reducing your tension and anxiety.

### Finding your locus of control

How far you feel in control of your job and yourself is connected to your locus of control (refer to Chapter 4):

- **Internal locus of control:** You feel that most of what happens is down to you. People with an internal locus of control believe that they have more control over their lives. This tendency reflects their sense of personal responsibility, which impacts on their health, attitudes at work, productivity and leadership tendencies.

- **External locus of control:** You feel that most things are out of your control and decided by outside factors. People with this tendency may not pay as much attention to detail, sometimes feel powerless and are more likely to blame others and the world for their misfortunes. They can lapse into a state of inactivity and inertia because they believe that they can do nothing to help themselves.

Your locus of control varies in different situations and times in your life, but when you reflect on past events you may discover a specific, repeated response of behaviours when facing adversity. Changing your locus of control is difficult but possible, with a concerted effort to implement CBT practices to move towards more personal responsibility and less tension.

Psychology studies show that people with a more internal locus of control tend to be happier and less stressed than those with an external one. The latter people may be more susceptible to depression and often seem to stay in situations where they feel out of control, which exacerbates the feelings of helplessness and uncomfortableness. CBT training, and maybe some social skills training as well, can help these people considerably to move towards a change where they feel more in control.

### Going beyond what's required

Discovering CBT – and how to change your outlook to make the most of your time at work with least discomfort – benefits you and, in the long run, your organisation. Think of it as working for the greater good.

Allowing yourself to look beyond only yourself at work and extending your thinking about the wider picture is part of creating your own philosophy in work and life in general. Chapter 10 looks at this issue in more detail.

### *Exceeding your own expectations*

Having an idea about what sort of person you are comes from feedback from others during your life. Experiences at school, and evidence from school reports, may leave you believing that you're a certain type of person. The words can be positive and negative, according to different subjects and situations.

See which of the following common descriptions you've heard about yourself:

- ✔ Concentrates well/inability to pay attention
- ✔ Conscientious and hard-working/lazy
- ✔ Diligent/careless
- ✔ Enthusiastic/half-hearted
- ✔ Helpful/disruptive
- ✔ Independent
- ✔ Natural leader
- ✔ Patient
- ✔ Resilient
- ✔ Risk-taker
- ✔ Uses initiative

Growing up with positive and negative feedback influences your sense of self. It can have a big impact on how you view yourself and encourage or discourage you in the areas of choosing work, careers and making forward progress.

A self-fulfilling prophecy is when something is believed so strongly that it pre-determines what you do. It can limit you so that you don't try things because you believe you're not capable. Having a pre-decided view of yourself inhibits you.

CBT can help you work out what you're really capable of, based on your own honest judgements, and help you start to believe in yourself rather that what you've been told by others. CBT helps you overcome the negative views that you may hold about yourself and exceed your own previous expectations.

# *Benefitting the Organisation*

Finding a sense of place and purpose where you work is an excellent starting point for generating future feelings of security and contentment for yourself. But organisations also want happy, productive and motivated workers, and so any strategies and training that can enhance your sense of wellbeing and diminish discontentment in the workplace are of great benefit to your employer as well.

## Working out where you stand

You live and work in many different communities. Your immediate community is your personal living situation, your family, friends, social groups and work. Discovering where you're placed in these differing settings is important to your sense of wellbeing, because people are much more efficient at getting on with their lives when they have a secure base to operate from. Feelings of insecurity are generally not helpful or conducive to progressing in life.

Your working life probably includes many phases and changes as you make your way: for example, being the 'newbie' in a job is guaranteed to cause unsettling feelings. No matter how old you are or however many jobs you've had, feeling nervous and insecure when starting a new job is pretty much expected and totally natural, so don't beat yourself up about it.

In biological terms, if you didn't approach new situations with some level of apprehension, and treat each new 'threat' with some degree of caution, you'd be exposing yourself to an unsafe situation without due regard. A certain level of caution fires up your senses and makes you more alert. Human beings are efficient information-processors, inveterate seekers and habitually curious, and they progress best when one threat is dealt with before another is addressed. When familiarity sets in, the level of alertness reduces and those energies can be used for the next 'threat' or project. Human beings are very efficient information processors, they are seekers and curious. Progress is made as one threat is dealt with before another is addressed.

## Valuing your place at work

How you view yourself at work is a key factor in contributing to your sense of ease at work and subsequent wellbeing. The work for which you're responsible may bring its own pressures and stresses, but it may also bring the possibility of unsettling feelings from tensions in your professional relationships – 'office politics' can often dominate a workplace. Chapter 13 has more on office politics and relationships in the workplace.

Unless you work for yourself as a sole trader, a hierarchy forms as soon as you get two or more people in a work situation. Who's the 'boss' and who's the 'employee' depends on a number of factors, some obvious but many less so:

- ✔ Who owns the company
- ✔ Who's the managing director
- ✔ Who's the 'boss' in your line management
- ✔ How you feel within your own team
- ✔ Your level of autonomy within your role
- ✔ How you view yourself within the social hierarchy at work

The important thing is to value your role, whatever it is.

## Influencing the work culture

A general definition of culture is a group of people who recognise some shared values, beliefs, underlying assumptions, attitudes and behaviours. A work culture is the result of this group coming together with a general set of behaviours and rules, which are unspoken and unwritten.

Culture is a powerful element that shapes your work enjoyment, your work relationships and your work processes. But because culture is something that you can't see, you make your own interpretations from what you witness and experience around you at work.

Whether you like it or not, you're part of the work culture! You bring your own personality, skill sets and talents.

### Appraising your job

Constantly be on the alert to check out what your job entails and how you're getting along with it. You may find that, when in a new job and after the first few weeks of getting to grips with the situation and demands of the role, you start to relax a bit and get into a familiar routine. Being aware of your own performance over the weeks and months, and monitoring how you're doing, can assist you to be focused and give your best in the job.

Some companies have appraisal systems built into the review process and you may be aware that you'll have yearly appraisals, but many people just get along with their job with no formal feedback. But getting constructive feedback at regular intervals can be motivating, and how well you perform at work is influenced by how you feel in the job.

Having a system of financial incentives – such as bonuses, commissions, performance-related pay, promotions and incremental pay increases that recognise longevity at the same company – or extra qualifications is fine. But psychologically you may find that other, more individual and personal recognition of your hard work is just as meaningful. Just a supportive word from the boss can mean quite a lot.

### Managing your boss

Whatever job you have, you're likely to have a boss and this person potentially has a huge impact on how you view your work. Strictly speaking, the person is just responsible for judging you on the quantity and quality of your work, but in reality you know that the interpersonal communication between you plays an influential part in your experiences at work.

How you handle your boss is a key factor in your overall wellbeing at work. Many people struggle with some relationships in the work hierarchy. You can think that you want to change your job because of your boss's behaviour, only to find that similar themes and patterns of managing occur in your next job. In my career coaching and counselling employees, the most common difficulty is between the client's boss and line management.

You can't change the reality of the situation, but you can change how you view it. Use CBT to find ways to change your viewpoints at work so that you can accept the situation. You don't necessarily have to like it, but you can discover ways to reduce your upsetting feelings about your boss, which allows you to do the best job you can in the circumstances and work on new constructive behaviour for yourself (check out Chapter 7 for some ideas on working with awkward people).

### Handling disputes

Getting into disputes and conflicts in the workplace is upsetting and unsettling. Most clashes stem from differences of opinions. There is nothing wrong with having a different view, but sometimes you may decide to agree to differ and accept that this person sees things differently. It is not right or wrong – just different. You may be annoyed, which is appropriate, but not unhealthily angry.

You and your work colleagues are all different people, thrown together with the common goal of getting tasks done for the overall benefit of the organisation. To be honest, you should consider it a bonus if you find that you like some people and enjoy their company and you make friends at work.

Just because you're working together, don't assume that you share the same values and attitudes about work and life in general. Dealing with people you can't stand is a real skill that you can develop using CBT methods; it's an investment that stands you in good stead generally, not just in the workplace. Chapter 7 helps you to do just that, reinforcing the basic CBT strategies in Chapter 2.

### Dealing with aggression

Continuing differences of opinion in communication can range from mere irritation with other people to genuine tension in the workplace. It can even escalate into aggression with levels of hostility and anger.

This type of situation can trigger the flight or flight reaction (which I describe in Chapter 2). When you're on the receiving end of, say, a verbal attack, you can start to feel threatened and your anxiety levels rise. Use your CBT strategies to recognise, acknowledge and make a conscious effort to rationalise what's happening. Doing so helps you to stop your response escalating to a point where you may end up 'losing it' and behaving in ways that aren't in your own best interest.

# Chapter 7

# Putting CBT to Work . . . at Work!

## In This Chapter

▶ Spotting your troubling work areas

▶ Admitting to yourself that you're struggling

▶ Using CBT techniques to help you cope

*T*hroughout this book, I describe all sorts of CBT techniques that you can use to look out for signs that you're starting to struggle. When you've gained an understanding of them, you can choose whether you want to help yourself to minimise the disruptions of this unhappy state of mind when you experience them at work.

In effect, you start to become the detective of your unsettling emotions. You're looking for evidence that all isn't well in your world of work and to do something before it goes critical and possibly makes you ill.

In this chapter, I discuss identifying what areas trouble you, admitting that a problem exists and using the various ways in which CBT can help.

## Identifying Problem Areas at Work

Here you get to become a seeker of truth and insight into your emotional climate at work. So don your Sherlock Holmes hat (checking in the mirror that you look suitably snazzy!) and have your magnifying glass at the ready: you're going to scour your work environment and scan yourself for signs of emotional disruption.

Monitoring your actions and feelings as follows can help you in your detective work:

1. **Stop:** When you feel 'wobbly' – that is, when you notice you're feeling upset.

2. **Feel:** Name the feeling you're experiencing.

3. Acknowledge it: Ask, 'What am I thinking?' To help, look for the destructive 'should, ought and must' types of thinking. (For a reminder of these types of thinking, turn to Chapter 5.)

4. Hold: Pause for moment.

5. Identify your thinking: Think through the ABC model.

6. Investigate: Ask, 'How logical is my thinking?'

You learn CBT best when you apply it to real-life examples and then see how to use it.

In this section, I cover all sorts of work-related issues, from experiencing anger and bullying to feeling fearful and neglected. (Later in this chapter, in the section 'Implementing CBT Techniques for Work-Related Problems', I also look at some more in-depth strategies for using CBT techniques to manage work-related issues.)

## Dealing with anger at work

Experiences at work can often make you feel angry.

You open an email with the next year's holiday rota on it. You read that you have to cover the period between Christmas and New Year . . . again. You feel a flash of anger. But, remembering your CBT training, you react as follows:

1. Stop: 'In the name of love'!

2. Feel: Name that feeling as anger.

3. Acknowledge it: 'I'm feeling angry'.

4. Hold: Enter a holding pattern.

5. Identify your thinking: 'They shouldn't make me do the holiday'.

6. Investigate: 'Is my thinking logical?'

7. Challenge: Your thoughts.

Here's how your chain of thoughts may go:

> *Just because I think they shouldn't make me do the holiday again doesn't mean they'll listen to me.*
>
> *If I keep insisting to myself that they shouldn't have done that and yet the rota shows me that they have, I'm just going to keep upsetting myself.*
>
> *Is my thinking logical? Sadly, no.*
>
> *Mmm, what can I do about this?*

*I can put my thinking into a holding pattern until I get home and have a think about what I can do.*

*What's within my control?*

Imagine a little monkey on your shoulder having a conversation with you. You have your irrational thinking cap on and your other voice, Bubbles the monkey, is wearing a rational thinking cap.

*You – They mustn't give me the holiday shift to work.*

*Bubbles – Is it logical for you to insist absolutely that they're fair and treat you with respect and not give you that shift?*

*You – Well, not really, because if a Law of the Universe of fairness stated that nothing unfair would ever happen to me then no unfairness would exist.*

*Bubbles – But evidence shows you that many unfair things do happen that are out of your control, don't they? If you categorically insist that everyone should treat you fairly, and if you choose to hang on to that belief, then you're going to upset yourself.*

*You – Why so?*

*Bubbles – Because unfair things will happen; you can see that from the holiday rota.*

*You – True.*

*Bubbles – You'll just keep winding yourself up into a state of anxiety or anger or some other unhealthy negative emotion if you hang on to your irrational belief that they shouldn't put you on the rota, because they can and they have.*

*You – So what can I do?*

*Bubbles – Change your thinking beliefs to a preferred preference way of thinking along the following lines: 'I'd prefer that they didn't give me the holiday shift, but the evidence (the rota) shows that they have'.*

*You – But am I not giving in to unfairness? That can't be right.*

*Bubbles – No, you're simply accepting that things can be unfair. You don't like it, but such is life.*

*You – It's hard to change to that way of thinking.*

*Bubbles – It works though. You'll feel annoyed but not all wound up. Remember that changing your thinking is within your control. Changing the rota isn't immediately within your control.*

*You – You're one smart monkey.*

*Bubbles – I know. I did a CBT course.*

Yes, you've read it before and you will again: you can only deal with what's within your control! Use CBT to change your irrational and disruptive thinking and beliefs to a logical way of thinking.

## Handling anxiety about work

Many people often experience anxiety about work.

Anxiety in itself isn't a bad thing. You can work at your best up to a certain level of anxiety and increased alertness. Plus, heightened awareness can give you an edge to focus more carefully on projects and it increases some people's creativity. But your personality has a big influence on how levels of anxiety influence your work. Chapter 9 looks at different types of personalities and your basic personality type is an important factor in your preferred way of working and your reactions to anxiety and stress.

That's not to say that you're landed with certain characteristics that always work against you. But if you find that you struggle in certain situations at work, adapting and changing may be harder for you. CBT can show you how to make these changes work for you.

## Feeling depressed about work

Like everyone, you're going to experience many mood swings during a week at work. Daily changes in work schedules and demands are sure to impact on your moods. You can't always dissociate from demands and changes in your home and personal life and work: they interact with each other.

Feeling a bit blue every now and again is natural and to be expected. The warning signal for you is when you find that you're constantly in a low mood and negative feelings are persisting. For details about slipping into depression, check out Chapters 2 and 9, or take a look at *Managing Depression with CBT for Dummies,* by Brian Thomson and Matt Broadway-Horner (Wiley).

If you think that you may be at risk of experiencing or heading towards depression, let your GP know. Your doctor can do a full examination of your symptoms and make decisions as to your emotional wellbeing. The earlier you get professional help, the better the prognosis for the length and depth of the illness. And yes, being clinically depressed is an illness. The many contributing factors and symptoms can include changes in mood, behaviour and thinking, as well as physical factors.

## Lacking self-confidence at work

Lacking confidence in yourself at work and more generally in life is a common condition that you may try to hide. Feelings of not being good enough, lacking skills and talents, and struggling with work responsibilities can lead to underlying anxiety.

## Wondering whether you belong here

In 1978, researchers Pauline Clance and Suzanne Imes used the term imposter syndrome to describe the psychological state of high-achieving women who tended not to believe that they were intelligent and thought other people overrated their real abilities.

The term was later expanded to describe people who consider themselves to be frauds with their work and worry that they'll be 'found out'. Even Albert Einstein – one of the 20th century's greatest thinkers – had these feelings and considered himself to be an 'involuntary swindler'.

As you go about your job, you may have a string of thoughts whirring away in the background telling you that you aren't good enough and you can't do your job; this can cause worries about being 'found out'. A frequently voiced fear in work is privately believing that you're an 'impostor' (see the nearby sidebar 'Wondering whether you belong here').

CBT can be especially helpful for people who experience self-confidence issues. Generally, people associate self-confidence and low self-esteem as similar problems. CBT therapy can help you see ways to examine how you view yourself, challenge your negative and irrational thinking, and help you work towards self-acceptance. Check out the later 'Replacing low self-worth with self-acceptance' section.

Wanting other people's approval is a natural and important part of life, but when you place too much emphasis on what others think of you, to the point that it's causing anxiety, consider using CBT to help you rationalise your irrational views of yourself.

## *Being neglected at work*

Feeling isolated, and at times even lonely, in work can create feelings of anxiety, frustration and even guilt. Events such as being passed over for some types of work, being refused promotions and not receiving constructive, or in fact any, feedback can cause negative thoughts. Extended periods of little interaction with others, especially if you're the type of person who finds interpersonal communication motivating, can also lead to these feelings of isolation and even depression.

Talk therapy (talking either to others or yourself) can be useful to help you recognise the feelings you're experiencing and clarify your thoughts so that you can make sense of the situation. Working through your thoughts with CBT helps you move forward to new, more constructive behaviour – perhaps even in a direction you didn't realise you wanted to go.

## Facing bullying at work

Bullying is a real problem in the workplace and sometimes you may not even realise that you're feeling bullied. An event as seemingly trivial as being left out of the drinks run to the local coffee shop can be a significant factor in how you feel you're treated at work.

A colleague constantly criticising your work, or piling on what you think are excessive workloads, may seem more obvious routes to feeling singled out for unreasonable treatment, but often the more subtle difference in how you feel you're being treated in comparison to others may have an accumulative effect, which starts to tip you into the discomfort zone.

Spend a moment or two considering this definition of bullying:

> *Behaviours used to assert dominance in what's perceived to be an unreasonable manner.*

Bullying can include the impression of an imbalance of power, resulting in feelings of persecution and powerlessness. The sources can be emotional, verbal and nonverbal, and physical or virtual (cyber-bullying).

Feelings to look out for when you're on the receiving end of bullying include emotional and physical symptoms. Fear, sickness, headaches, anxiety, depression, absenteeism, reduced performance, anger and withdrawal (both socially and physically) can all be possible outcomes for the person who feels bullied.

Any feelings of being bullied are real to you, so if they are causing distress, it is important to write down the incidents and situations as they occur. You may decide to have a meeting with your manager; you can then clearly evidence through the diary when you felt bullied. At some level you may start to blame yourself for the situation. CBT can help you rationalise that you cannot be responsible for other people's behaviour. Other people can and will behave in unfair and undesirable ways. You will not like it, but upsetting yourself will not help. If you can accept the unfortunate situation and move on to consider constructive ways to deal with the possibility of any further attempts to undermine your confidence by using your CBT toolkit, you will be more prepared.

If someone is being mean to you, and she can see it having no impact on you, she may stop doing it. Either way, use your CBT to change any feelings of hurt, shame, anger and embarrassment to ones of healthy concern, but not over-riding distress. Easy to say, but it takes a lot of practice to change such beliefs.

# Replacing low self-worth with self-acceptance

Good news! CBT can banish feelings of low self-esteem. Take the problem words out of your vocabulary and replace them with 'self-acceptance'.

Putting too much energy into monitoring self-esteem can lead you to be constantly rating yourself each day according to what happens and how you view yourself in different situations and events. This behaviour can become exhausting. If you can accept yourself as basically a good person, going about your life with the best intent, you will have more stability in how you view yourself, irrespective of what is going on around you.

Instead of judging yourself differently every day, decide permanently to accept yourself as an okay person. Of course, sometimes you'll make a mistake or not perform as well as you could, but on the whole you view yourself as a pretty acceptable person. Accept yourself as a person with skills and talents, including some strengths and some lesser developed aspects, but who generally goes through life with the best intentions.

You can't get everyone's approval – that's impossible. Some people will always not like all your behaviours or judge you negatively . . . that's life. You can only do your best.

Of course, sometimes you may not do your best, and I bet that you're pretty good at mentally beating yourself up about things you do that didn't have the best outcome. Plenty of other people are ready to give you negative feedback, but making yourself unhappy about those things doesn't help you. Instead, accept that you're a human being who sometimes makes mistakes (flip to the later section 'Making mistakes in work').

You don't have to like your less helpful behaviours, and by all means strive to improve any damaging behaviour on your part, but certainly don't jump on the bandwagon of judging yourself harshly.

Change your irrational thinking from 'I must do everything well and have everyone's approval' to 'I'd prefer to do well at most things, but if I don't and some people judge me negatively, although I don't like it, I can accept it. In future I'll try to do some things differently to minimise messing up. That's my new constructive behaviour'.

## Suffering from scared feelings at work

Many people experience feelings of apprehension and dread about work, perhaps as strong as: 'I wake up every morning feeling scared to go to work'. Some people have a generalised feeling of being frightened and others feel physically sick and shaky at the thought of going to work.

Perhaps you have a boss you're afraid of or you worry you can't do your job effectively. Experiencing low self-confidence, putting off doing difficult work, and avoiding reading emails or answering the phone can pile up until you start avoiding as much as you can. Unfortunately, simply taking time off, and delaying asking for help and getting to the root of the problem may just make you feel worse.

But these feelings are rooted in anxiety and so you can apply the same CBT strategies used for anxiety, depression and self-esteem issues to the situation of feeling scared to go into work and being frightened while you're there.

## Having guilty feelings

Repetitive thoughts going round and round in your head, worrying and feeling guilty about things you have or haven't done in work . . . all these thoughts are distressing and potentially harmful to your emotional health.

Studies show that feeling guilty for a length of time can also have a serious effect on your body chemistry and lower your immune system, making you more susceptible to illness. In other words, guilt can make you ill, because you're more likely to pick up colds, viruses and other conditions.

Ask yourself: 'How is worrying and feeling guilty about something going to help me?' You know the answer: it's not. Instead, use CBT to acknowledge what's happening, remember that feeling guilty may be natural, but also acknowledge that upsetting yourself won't change what has happened. Accept that something bad has happened and work on rationalising your thinking. What have you learned from the experience? How might you do things differently in the future to avoid making mistakes or being inconsiderate? You are a fallible human being and will make mistakes.

## Thinking twice before going to work ill

Dragging yourself into work when you're feeling physically ill is a debilitating feeling. You know that you'd prefer to be at home resting and giving yourself a chance to recover, but you feel the pressure of your job weighing down on you. Perhaps you have a job where you're actively in charge of groups of others, such as teaching, nursing and social work, and you know that getting colleagues to cover your work will be very difficult; plus, you may worry about the people for whom you're responsible.

Don't fall into the trap of presenteeism (spending more time at work than is strictly required, including when sick; refer to Chapter 5). Only you can be the judge of making that decision, but you do need to take responsibility for your own physical wellbeing. You may use CBT to work out what is in your best interest in the current situation – you may need to put those extra hours in at this time – but rationalise that in the long term you need to avoid overwork and becoming ill.

Sometimes people get so ill that their work colleagues or managers have to intervene and tell them to go home until they feel better. You're not doing anyone any favours by going into work with infectious viruses and spreading it round the workplace, so that ultimately more people are affected.

You have a duty of care to your own physical health and emotional health. If you constantly battle on when you've been experiencing many symptoms of stress, including anxiety, sleeping problems, feelings of depression, panic attacks, feeling angry and increases in negative coping strategies, you eventually make yourself ill to the point that your work is affected anyway. You may then be requested to seek help or you even find yourself at the end of your tether and totally unable to function.

## Dying to hide away! Embarrassment and shame at work

Overcoming feelings of shame or embarrassment about yourself, your performance in work or how you behave among your colleagues is linked to feelings of low self-worth (see the earlier section 'Replacing low self-worth with self-acceptance'). You can experience painful feelings linked to believing that you acted in a foolish way, engaged in wrongful behaviour or made mistakes.

Shame and embarrassment tend to result from the fear of not having approval, including self-approval as well as approval from others. You may want to hide your work away or be reluctant to start or finish a piece of work. You may avoid interpersonal relationships, because you rate yourself so low on the scale of being a worthy colleague that you withdraw from social interactions.

Feeling embarrassed can cause a range of emotions: awkwardness, discomfort, uneasiness and excessive self-consciousness. Some people blush when they feel embarrassed. Rashes, itching, sweating and blushing are all outward signs that you're under stress. The source of your stress in many embarrassing situations is your own internal thinking about yourself and how you should be behaving. Don't forget that your thoughts are pretty strong triggers!

Use CBT to work on identifying those irrational thoughts about yourself 'not being good enough' and check out the earlier section 'Replacing low self-worth with self-acceptance'.

## *Making mistakes in work*

Focusing on your work and giving it your best concentration in order to produce the best results can be affected by different factors. For example, your physical condition, in terms of your overall health, impacts on performance. Feeling under the weather, headaches, aches and pains can detract your attention from the job in hand. Whether you find the nature of the job itself interesting, challenging, boring or difficult may also affect the way you work.

Continually making mistakes is a sign that unless you take time to ascertain the reasons behind your negative performance, your job security can be at risk. Studies in performance at work indicate that making the odd mistake shows that you're human, because no one expects you to be perfect (except, possibly yourself), but repeatedly making mistakes may lead your bosses to conclude incompetence. So get in first by using the detective skills of CBT.

Emotional distress has a significant impact on your ability to perform well on a task. The heightened fight-or-flight physical response when under threat impairs judgement and reduces your ability to think straight. When you feel anxious or nervous, the extra adrenalin in your bloodstream causes side effects such as shaking, sweating, rapid breathing and even dizziness, which certainly don't help you to complete tasks effectively.

## *Defusing frustration at work*

Frustration results when you experience tensions from struggling with a task you can't achieve or when other people annoy you. On a scale of increasing irritation, frustration can be the precursor that builds up to full-blown anger (which I discuss in the earlier section 'Dealing with anger at work'). Conflict, opposition, disappointment, unresolved issues and dissatisfaction can all be associated with describing your feelings as frustrated.

The longer the frustration goes on, the more likely you are to get increasingly anxious and possibly even depressed. You continually use up mental energy as you come up against the same frustrating situations day after day, until you feel low, sad and demotivated.

By acknowledging your feelings and allowing yourself to identify the situation or behaviours that trigger your frustration, you can start to work out why you're feeling that way. Somewhere in that soup of despair you're hanging on to some thoughts and beliefs about how things should be; as long as your experiences don't match up to reality and these inherent beliefs, the frustration continues.

## Crying at work

The ultimate in expressing your emotions visually is with the outpouring of tears. Crying is universal: it's seen in all cultures and isn't restricted to any particular group. You may find sometimes that work gets too much and you cry at home, when you finally get away from the source of frustration and distress. Or you may break down at work.

Either way, crying is a well-known stress relief method for frustrating experiences. It's also an expression associated with pain, sadness, joy, laughter, relief and surprise. Interestingly, analyses of the chemical composition of tears triggered by different situations vary. Tears of joy have a different chemical composition than tears of pain or grief, for example.

Take time to find out what has been upsetting for you. Accept that it is okay to cry as an outlet for tension. You are human and have limits on your ability to cope with stress. Use CBT rules to accept that you have reached this point, but it doesn't make you any less a person – just someone who cried today.

# Targeting Unsettling Emotions

When you accept that your emotions naturally ebb and flow throughout the day, as you experience different events and interact with other people, you can more easily make yourself aware of your emotional state. If you then notice that unsettling emotions are popping up more frequently than you're comfortable with, you can decide to take action to reduce them.

The key is making yourself aware of these negative feelings.

The following sections explore the importance of accepting difficult emotions, and consider whom you can talk to if you need a friendly, helpful ear.

## *Allowing yourself to accept the difficult emotions*

Being strong in the face of adversity is a fine sentiment and may help you achieve certain goals against the odds, but at what price? Only you know how you're feeling. Other people can make a guess at your mood based on your observable behaviours, but no one really knows your inner feelings. You may be good at hiding your feelings, not only from others but also from yourself!

Finding a healthy balance between not paying any attention to your emotions and becoming preoccupied with your emotional health is a fine line. You can decide to ignore the warning signs of impending distress or you can find that you constantly self-monitor your physical sensations and emotions to the point of becoming totally preoccupied with yourself.

If either extreme becomes a source of anxiety for you or starts to interfere with your ability to pay attention to your work, take some time to look at what's happening to you. Use CBT to discover your individual tipping point of emotional imbalance. Only you can know at what point you start to feel anxious; for myself, my tipping point is when I start to feel what I call 'wobbly'. I find it hard to concentrate, start to feel lightheaded and feel like I am heading towards being tearful. When things start piling up and I feel overwhelmed, the physical feelings kick in. That is the point at which I try to stop and allow myself some time out to reassess the situation.

When working with clients, I find that one of the hardest things is for them to open up to themselves and make that first step to see that all isn't well.

But if you wait until your colleagues and family need to tell you that 'you don't seem yourself', you may well be further down the line of distress than you think. You may even believe that admitting that something is wrong is a sign of weakness. Wrong! It's the essential first step.

## *Telling another person of your struggle*

When you become aware that you're struggling, you can do something to help yourself. Making moves to give yourself permission to accept that you're having a hard time and suffering because of it shows that you're taking responsibility for your wellbeing. No one else can do this for you.

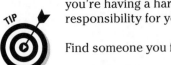

Find someone you feel you can tell that you're having a hard time.

Your friends and family can support you in many ways and they're a valuable and important source of help, but helping you when you're anxious or depressed is difficult. They worry about you and don't always know how to help or even recognise that you may be depressed. How you're feeling and behaving always impacts on them too. (For this reason, counsellors and therapists learn when training that they can't counsel their family or friends. They're too involved because they already have relationships with these people and so can never really be objective.)

Therefore, when you decide to receive help from an uninvolved professional, it can often be quite a relief for family and friends – taking some of the responsibility away from them. When you share your predicament with experienced and trained people, you can only move forward.

### Visiting a physician

Do yourself and your family and friends (and work) a favour – get some professional advice. Don't try to struggle through on your own. Make an appointment to see your GP.

Picking up the phone and booking that appointment can be the hardest first step. Be prepared to perhaps feel tearful when you speak to the receptionist who books your appointment. Admitting that you'd like some help is a huge positive step.

Before you go to the doctor, prepare yourself. You may ask someone to go with you but, either way, make a list of all the changes in your emotions and behaviours that have been occurring. Making an assessment of what's going on helps you and your GP; also, if you get emotional in the consultation and have difficulty speaking, you can hand the list to the doctor. Having a friend with you means that she can read the list out. Doctors and health workers are used to seeing people in distress; it feels alien to you, but health professionals are trained to identify and give help for emotional distress as well as physical ailments.

Here are some of the things that you may have been experiencing and want to put on your list:

- ✔ Feeling very tired, not been sleeping well for a while
- ✔ Feeling tense and edgy, anxious or nervous
- ✔ Getting irritated and sometimes angry quite a lot
- ✔ Feeling like crying or actually bursting into tears
- ✔ Lacking any enthusiasm
- ✔ Feeling worthless and unhappy with yourself
- ✔ Having panic attacks
- ✔ Thinking about problems constantly

- Feeling isolated and lonely
- Withdrawing from family and friends
- Changing eating and drinking habits, and self-medicating
- Thinking the future is bleak and seeing no end to the difficulties
- Withdrawing from life, feeling low all the time
- Feeling that everything is pointless

Your doctor knows what to look for in your emotional state that can be a warning sign of anxiety and depression. Let her be the judge of your distress – provide as much information about your struggles as possible so that she's able to make some suggestions to help.

If you feel embarrassed or awkward about going to your doctor for emotional ill health, perhaps you can open your conversation by saying, 'I haven't been feeling good for a while now and my friend/partner/work colleague/mother thought it may be a good idea to just let you know'.

### Talking freely

You may think that a stigma is attached to admitting to emotional struggles and that you'll be judged negatively, but modern-day healthcare is much more inclusive than even a few decades ago. Plus, your work wants as many workers to be as healthy as possible in order to do a good job – a healthy workforce makes financial sense – and so you're doing your employer a favour.

In fact, your employer has a responsibility for your physical and emotional wellbeing at work. As a result, some workplaces even have a system whereby employees can ring a confidential helpline and get advice and support on issues, whether professional or personal. The helpline can assess your needs and often set up some practical help.

Life and work can get tough. No one said it would be easy. Accept that fact, deal with it and move on!

# Implementing CBT Techniques for Work-Related Problems

In this section, I lay out the process for improving your emotional life at work. I run through an illustrative example and talk you through tackling your own personal problem, whatever that may be.

## *Addressing your discomfort*

## *one step at a time*

When you find yourself struggling at work, here's what to do:

1. Use the CBT toolkit from Chapters 2 and 3 to rationalise what's happening to you.

2. Allow yourself to accept that you don't feel too well.

3. Name those feelings.

4. Recognise that your thoughts are giving rise to the upsetting feelings.

5. Realise that the situation is triggering the thoughts in your head.

6. Understand that the thoughts precipitate the feelings.

7. Accept that by hanging on to 'should, ought and must' thinking, you continue to wind yourself up.

8. Start working on changing your thinking.

This task can be hard work: you've probably had years of repeating your thinking patterns and beliefs. But you can change how you think.

CBT takes practice and repeated revisiting of the basics to make a serious cognitive shift, as you move from getting the hang of the ideas to really changing your set-in-your-ways beliefs. You know when you've achieved the transition because you genuinely feel less upset.

Just as you learn a new skill by practising it, you can get better and better at CBT until it becomes automatic.

Consider this situation as an example. Using CBT to implement new procedures and ways of thinking is similar to learning a new skill. Old unhelpful patterns of thinking eventually, with lots of concerted effort to change them, become new ways of thinking with more efficient outcomes.

A new photocopier arrives at work, complete with instruction manual. Now you dread going to get copies done because getting to grips with all the new procedures will take ages. You feel frustrated and quite annoyed. With all the time it'll take, keeping the old one would've been much easier: although it was unreliable at times and created problems, you felt comfortable with it.

What can you do? You can ignore getting the copies done – but this will have worse consequences. You can put off doing the copies until the end of the day – but procrastination can create anxieties because the job is still there, hanging over you. Or you can bite the bullet, decide at a certain time to go down and read the manual, and get stuck in.

You choose the latter route. In other words, you decide to act – you make a concerted effort to find out how to use the devil machine!

You struggle a bit at first and have to keep rereading some of the instructions, but eventually you produce all the copies, which turns out to be more efficient and will save you loads of time in the future.

## *Finding an example where CBT could've helped*

Now it's your turn. Take an example from your past and have a go at using CBT to see how you could've helped yourself not to get so anxious:

1. Find an example of when you felt anxious about something at work.

2. Visualise yourself at work when you felt this anxiety.

3. Remember the situation you were in.

4. Identify the trigger: was it something someone said, something that happened (say, reading an email) or something you suddenly thought about?

## *Applying the technique to your problem*

Taking that example, apply the ABC technique from Chapter 2.

You're thinking is likely to be along the following lines:

> *I was feeling anxious. I thought that this shouldn't be happening but the evidence showed that it was happening.*

> *I realise now that as long as I was thinking it shouldn't be happening and how awful it was and how it would make my life difficult, I was making myself upset. If I could've put the brakes on my runaway thinking, and put my thinking in a holding pattern, I could've given myself some time to stop the anxiety escalating.*

> *I could then have worked on my irrational thinking. Instead of thinking 'this must not be happening', I could've changed my thinking to: I'd prefer that*

*this hadn't happened, but it has. I don't want to upset myself. I'm going to accept the situation. I don't like it, but how does it help me upsetting myself about it? I'm going to leave it for now, and think some more about it when I get home, and see what's within my power to change for the future'.*

# Maintaining vigilance for your emotional outlook

Quite possibly, CBT is starting to make sense; you may even be thinking that it's just common sense. Perhaps you decide to close the book, thinking that you have the hang of CBT now. That's great if you have. Many people do get the basic ideas and methods of CBT pretty quickly. I've found that even two sessions can really help clients to kick-start tackling their problems.

On the other hand, don't be too hasty. Instilling a permanent change in your thinking habits takes a lot of practice and reminding yourself. Understanding the ideas intellectually is one thing; putting them into practice and achieving a deep, lasting transformation is quite another. I hope you can stick with me a little longer!

Discovering how to use CBT isn't a one-off read. Similarly, you can't carry out the ABC exercise for your problem once and expect the negative thinking to vanish and everything to be hunky-dory from then on.

Imagine that you read how to make a Lemon Drizzle cake for someone's birthday at work. You study the recipe, reread bits that need particular attention and transform the ingredients into something that at least resembles and tastes like a cake. But if you want to make that cake a month later, chances are you need to look up the recipe and the instructions again, though some of the procedures are more automatic because you've done it before. Eventually, after making quite a few of this type of cake, you get to the point where you don't need the recipe because you remember it all in your head.

Applying CBT to issues in your life is similar. No short-cuts exist to replace paying attention and consciously applying the 'recipe' for tackling a problem. In time, with more practice, you become efficient at using CBT. Only instead of a cake being the outcome, the result is a calmer emotional life (I know, I know, you want the cake; but don't worry, you can have both!):

- ✔ **Be aware of negative thinking:** Keeping a weather eye open for negative thinking helps you identify potential trouble spots.

- ✔ **Take the wobbles out of your life:** As you become more vigilant at alerting yourself to unsettling and uncomfortable feelings, and doing something about them, you experience less emotional disruption.

✔ **Stay aware of lifelong habit-changing:** If you hang on to old ways of thinking and beliefs about how you, other people and the world in general should be, you always get those same old feelings. But if you decide to work at changing your outlook regarding how you prefer things to be, you can make a choice about how you deal with it.

✔ **Form your vigilante group of one:** Don't worry, I don't expect you to go all Charles Bronson – this group's friendly! I simply mean that no-one else can monitor your feelings for you, because only you know how events and people affect you. Take responsibility for yourself. You know it makes sense.

# Part III
# Working with CBT (Work and You)

## *The Top Five Ways that Work Affects Your Whole Life*

It's easy to let work dictate your life. And while hard work is admirable, letting it overtake other parts of your life puts you in an imbalanced lifestyle. Do any of the following apply to you?

1. Putting work above everything else in your life

2. Going into work when you're feeling ill

3. Obsessively checking work email while you're away from your office and on your own time

4. Talking about work and work situations more than discussing social topics with family and friends

5. Taking work home on a regular basis

Visit www.dummies.com/extras/cbtatwork for great Dummies content online.

## In this part . . .

- ✔ Learn to take care of yourself; otherwise you can leave yourself open to experiencing negative emotions and physical ill-health.

- ✔ Reflect on your professional integrity, what you believe in and how sometimes you find yourself at odds with what you're required to do at work.

- ✔ Identify what areas trouble you, admit that a problem exists and use the various ways in which CBT can help.

# Chapter 8

# Feeling Positive about Your Work

**In This Chapter**
▶ Increasing positive thoughts and relationships
▶ Seeing the bigger picture and gaining perspective
▶ Creating a 'luckier' you

*T*he more you think positively, the more apparent luck and good fortune will come your way. The more outward looking your attitude, the more positive encounters you will have in your life. The reverse is true, too. If you are easily put off by obstacles – for example, if you have an interview for a job and you discover, when putting on the interview suit, that a button flies off your trousers, you burn your shirt with the iron, and the dog jumps on your jacket and rips the sleeve – you have choices. You can either fling your arms in the air and give up, or make do with another outfit . . . which isn't your first choice, but will get you to the interview. Having the interview means you may get the job; staying at home crying in a pile of clothes certainly reduces your life chances. If you rely only on being reactive at work and consider yourself fortunate if just some days are good, you minimise your opportunities for beneficial experiences. In this chapter, I describe how you can become pro-active at helping to make your experiences and relationships at work more rewarding. Enjoy your life – you (probably!) only get the one.

## 'Keeping It on the Sunny Side!' Working at Optimistic Thinking

Being an optimistic thinker comes naturally for some people, because having a sunny disposition is strongly influenced by your genetic makeup. Some people seem born to see the best in situations and make the most of difficult ones. In Chapter 9, you find more information about how your genes largely influence your personality and what you can do if you are naturally more pessimistic and life is a struggle for you.

As I demonstrate in this section, studies show that the effort is well worth your while. So see this section as being one of encouragement that you can move towards a more positive outlook on work and life.

I really believe that reading this chapter and implementing its insights is going to improve your work life – I wouldn't be writing this book unless I was positive!

## Expecting the best outcome

Research shows that having an optimistic outlook brings about more positive experiences, which in turn enhances your wellbeing. A study by Professor Richard Wiseman of Hertfordshire University called 'The Luck Factor' found that optimistic people are 'luckier' than those who tend to view the world more pessimistically.

The fact is that how you view your job and the expectations you hold about it influence what you experience. If you expect the worst, guess what? You're more likely to experience negativity. Conversely, if you adopt a positive attitude, you're more likely to encounter constructive and productive experiences.

These two statements aren't just hearsay and sweeping generalisations; they're backed up by research into positive psychology and personality studies.

## Squashing NATs – like the bugs they are!

Unfortunately, getting into bad habits is all too easy. Negative automatic thoughts (NATs) describe the process of habitually repeating negative thinking. The brain is like any other muscle: the more you use and repeat some actions, the more likely those actions are to become automatic.

To see what I mean, consider when you first used a computer to learn, say, a word processing package. You had to concentrate on how to use all the different parts of the software, and with time and practice it became automatic. You don't even think about it now. You switch on the computer and away you go, writing all sorts of documents. Your brain has developed a well-used circuit to use that computer package so that it becomes automatic.

The same applies with your thinking at work. When you get used to viewing things negatively and expecting the worst to happen, doing so becomes a habit. Fortunately, CBT can help you to recognise what you're doing and help you change that way of thinking.

## Drinking from the negative water cooler!

I worked with a company that was going through many transitions, including downsizing and outsourcing. It was a tough time for the employees, who were experiencing a lot of insecurity.

When I arrived in the morning and walked to the training room, I noticed a group of people often clustered round the water cooler; they looked very down and some were talking avidly but in hushed tones. In the debriefing sessions I held, a few employees voiced their concerns that although they knew that change was going to happen, they felt worse when joining in with this negative talk. They felt that if they didn't join in they might be ostracised, but that listening to the endless complaining was getting them down more than the thought of the reorganisation. Nothing being discussed was very positive, and there were no constructive outcomes from the discussions.

One person said that it felt like being sucked into a downward spiral of negativity towards a dark pit. That old saying 'misery loves company' has a ring of truth in it. If you're around people who are constantly negative, it can impact on you.

## *Implementing positive body language*

Much of the time you're probably unaware of how you appear to others. You may occasionally pay attention to your appearance in terms of clothes, hair and so on, but unless you're constantly taking selfies (you aren't, are you?), most of the time you can be unaware of how you move around, interact and indeed communicate in a nonverbal way.

Yet your body language (how you present yourself, the way you stand, your posture and, most importantly, your facial expressions) has a huge impact on your work colleagues and everyone you meet. So much so that some customer service training specifically encourages people to be aware of body language and to manipulate it to give the best possible impression to customers.

When I worked on cruise ships, one company had a policy of employee training that spelled out in detail how staff members' actions impact on guests. I watched all the training videos in my cabin and decided to implement some of the recommended procedures. A very simple one was always to smile and say 'good morning/evening' when entering a public space from the behind-the-scenes offices on the ship.

It took a lot of effort and seemed quite alien for me: my natural expression is rather serious, especially if I'm preoccupied. But I received a great reaction from the passengers. I can't ever remember anyone not returning my smile and most echoed the greeting.

One byproduct of this action I hadn't expected was that I felt happier too and I felt my spirits rise a little. I shouldn't have been surprised though, because psychology research backs up that being proactive and initiating positive behaviour raises your sense of wellbeing.

## Playing the 'glad' game

Central to developing a more positive outlook is to want to change your thinking and interpretation of events so that you can reduce your emotional disturbances at work.

When I was a child I watched the film *Pollyanna*. She'd experienced loss and hardship in her young life but was determined always to try to find something to be cheerful or glad about in order to see the good side of even the worst situations. She called it playing the 'glad game'. Even when she was laid up one summer with a broken leg she said she was glad, because her special friends spent time visiting her and she got to know them better.

I used to think that this idea was unlikely and slightly saccharine. But as an adult psychologist, I've discovered that adopting this attitude of trying to find something useful or positive, even when faced with adversity, can help reduce the emotional negative impact of events.

Here's an example of how someone changed around his disappointing experience and made the most of the situation to his own benefit.

A business trader who sold handmade clothes had applied to have a stand at a music festival. When he reached the festival traders' entrance, he was told that his application hadn't been correctly processed and he wouldn't be allowed in. The news was devastating. He and his partner had spent nine months preparing for this three-day event and were relying on their sales to live.

He decided that it was too late to head home and so he camped for the night outside the festival. In the morning, some people offered him breakfast and started chatting; it turned out they had a shop and needed supplies. They also introduced him to a network of independent traders that kicked off several business opportunities. If the trader had got frustrated and angry and stormed off home the night before, he'd never have found these opportunities.

Unless you really like being angry (!), CBT encourages you to say to yourself: 'How's getting angry going to help me?' Insisting that everything goes right for you is irrational and unhelpful. But how you deal with the more unfortunate incidents in life has a big impact on you and your relationships. Anger brings out a fear reaction in others. No-one wants to stay around angry people, so work on calming yourself down; who knows what opportunities may present themselves.

## Counting your blessings

People who are consciously aware of the good things that happen in their life are on the whole happier than those who tend to focus on the negative events.

The aptly named Professor Wiseman from the University of Hertforshire organised a public experiment with 26,000 people, which was designed to lift the nation's spirit. It was called 'The Science of Happiness Study'. Participants were asked to reflect on a positive experience: perhaps something that happened during the day, a film or television programme they enjoyed, an event that went well at work – or any happy memories.

The results were very interesting: smiling, counting your blessings and reliving positive memories raised people's spirits. More specifically, thinking of a positive thing that happened the day before was by far the most effective way for people to cheer themselves up.

## Reflecting at the end of the day

Reflecting on a positive or good experience from your workday just before you go to bed at night (such as a delicious drink or a chance for a walk at lunchtime) can have an accumulative positive effect on your overall sense of wellbeing. In fact, The Science of Happiness study showed that this activity had a significant impact on people and seemed to give an additional boost of 15 per cent in happiness, as measured by the before and after questionnaires.

These results are in line with findings that people report a feeling of calm and increased sense of wellbeing when they meditate and focus on the positive things in their lives. I look at this idea of including simple meditation routines in your life in more detail in Chapter 19, where I introduce using holistic practices alongside CBT techniques.

# Increasing Favourable Interactions at Work

Work is clearly more enjoyable and less stressful when you get on with the people you're working alongside. Here I talk about a couple of approaches to help your own and your colleagues' work lives go smoothly. At work, you will naturally gravitate more to some people more than to others. You may have more in common and share more values with some of your colleagues. There are, however, some specific strategies that you can use to help expand favourable interactions at work.

## Engaging with other people

In the 1930s, a businessman called Dale Carnegie wrote a book about how to win friends and influence people, which became a huge bestseller internationally. You may have heard of it – it was called, er, *How to Win Friends and Influence People!*

He lists six ways to engage with others that can be helpful in influencing positive exchanges in work:

- ✔ Smile when you meet people.
- ✔ Use their names.
- ✔ Make them feel important.
- ✔ Listen attentively to them.
- ✔ Take an interest in their interests.
- ✔ Be genuinely interested in them as individuals.

Do all the above genuinely. Human beings are very good at picking up on microexpressions, which can give away your true feelings. If you're just going through the motions and not really interested, people can tell.

## Nodding and smiling to give you a breather

When you're confronted with a tricky situation at work – say, a potential source of conflict, anger or discomfort – you don't have to respond straightaway.

In true CBT style, when you recognise that flash of emotional discomfort arising within you, put yourself into holding patterns (I introduce these in Chapter 3) to give yourself a breather before you respond. Even simply nodding and smiling can give you a moment before acting.

Obviously, different types of smiling exist. Employing a sneering type of smile is likely to inflame the situation, whereas a pondering smile can be quite neutral.

You don't have to say anything, but you can also use one of the following expressions as part of your holding strategy:

- ✔ 'Mmm, that's interesting, I'll have a think about that'.
- ✔ 'That seems to mean a lot to you'.
- ✔ 'I hadn't thought of it that way'.
- ✔ 'Let me get back to you on that one'.

# Putting Your Job into Perspective

Finding a happy balance between the time you devote to your job and choosing how you spend your time otherwise can be a struggle. If you love your job, home and work life can merge into one. Nothing's wrong in itself with working long hours and taking work home, but it can be a problem when you find that you don't have a personal life and enough time for significant relationships and the social activities you'd like to pursue.

In this section, I lay out some ideas to regain a healthy balance between work and the rest of your life.

## Dividing your time

Make a conscious effort to review your working practices every so often to help ensure that you don't get swamped by work; it stops you ploughing on until your physical or mental health starts giving you warning signs of burnout.

Standing back from your job and reflecting on how it's going, or even making an advantage and disadvantages list of your working life and recording it in a diary form or a review file, encourages you to be aware of how you're getting along.

## Prioritising your day

Take some time to plan your working day to try to include some aspects in which you do have some say or that can help you feel that you have control in your life.

Here are some examples to give you an idea of what I mean:

- ✔ Pay attention to the here and now of your work journey. Be aware of your surroundings: nature, architecture, urban art, interesting design of transport, signage, billboards, shop displays.

- ✔ Load up your favourite music to listen to on your commute. If appropriate, download some reading material or take a book on the train.

- ✔ Prepare some lovely food for your lunch, or plan to meet up with a friend.

- ✔ Prioritise taking a break during the workday, perhaps visiting a friendly coffee bar or café.

Making a conscious effort to be in the present and aware of your surroundings is called mindfulness. Many cultures have practised forms of mindfulness for centuries as a way of calming the brain and helping to bring an inner tranquillity. You always have this opportunity within yourself if you choose to use it. I talk more about how you can discover and practise mindfulness and other relaxation techniques in Chapter 19.

## Letting time heal your wounds

You can help to get your job into perspective and minimise disruptions you encounter at work by applying the time frame exercise. It helps you to see that although the current problem is all-encompassing at the moment, in time it usually fades.

The exercise is very simple. Just ask yourself: 'How will this work problem feel in two weeks' time, a month's time, in six months and even in a year?' I've seen many clients with work-related problems, such as a general accumulation of stress or a particular immediate difficulty. After they've been coming for a few weeks and practised some work using CBT to help minimise the disturbances, they find that the original problem has reduced in severity and their new ways of thinking are helping them to restructure their view of work. By doing the exercise while they are in the middle of the struggles and using CBT to consider how work might be in the future, they can see that actively working on the problem now will boost their chances of a better outcome.

## Gaining perspective on the grand scheme

As part of gaining perspective on your work situation (that is, changing your irrational thoughts to more rational and less upsetting ways of viewing events), ask yourself: 'In the grand scheme of things, how is upsetting myself about this work problem helping me at the moment?'

Answer – it's not. Instead, think philosophically about it to try to put it into a wider perspective (check out Chapter 10 for more on how CBT encourages you to become your own philosopher).

Giving time to learning and applying CBT involves some rethinking of your life and priorities in order to create the best you can for yourself in different circumstances. Thinking about how you prefer to live your life, what your beliefs and values are, and how you view yourself and the world, is the beginning of creating your own philosophy for life.

Children can be natural philosophers. The world often seems much simpler to them. Their beliefs and values are quite logical and rational to their way of thinking. Life just gets more complicated as they grow older and start to worry and make things complicated for themselves.

CBT doesn't dwell on the past. Of course, your experiences and life 'story' impact on you today, perhaps making some of your beliefs and ways of thinking unhelpful. But CBT helps you unlearn the negative attitudes and move towards more rational, self-helpful thinking.

Remember your 'inner child', the one who had carefree fun, was free of fear of judgement, and had a passion and energy for life? Maybe that person will resurface when you allow yourself time to reflect and move on. Laughter is a great stress release. You can't frown and be worried at the same time as laughing. Chapter 19 includes fun facts and suggestions to increase your sense of wellbeing and deal with the effects of stress by incorporating more holistic types of strategies.

# *Taking in the Wider View to Catch Important Opportunities*

After you feel as if you're getting your work life into perspective (see the preceding section), try to free yourself up to look at the bigger picture. Doing so allows you to spot and make the most of opportunities that come your way.

You can see this activity as containing two aspects:

- ✔ Appraising your current job: How is your immediate employer positioned in the industry and what career opportunities exist for you?

- ✔ Allowing yourself to see your place in the world: How do you fit into the world in general? What other interests and aspirations do you have?

The following sections consider how you can keep yourself open to new experiences – and how you may just increase your good fortune along the way!

## *Being open to experience*

Some interesting research shows that the more people are open to new experiences, the more chance opportunities come their way and so their 'luck' increases.

When you free your mind, you're more likely to start thinking creatively. If you go around almost as if you have blinkers on that restrict your view to what's only in front of you, you also limit your ability to see opportunities, solutions and innovative thinking. Although this ability to focus narrowly is a necessary skill for some types of work (and highly skilled people who can work in this way are extremely valued members of society), you can fall into the trap of not allowing yourself to switch off.

Give yourself a break! Make sure that you have some downtime to allow your brain to wander freely and be open to new experiences. To change to this way of thinking takes concerted effort and planning if it's not your natural default mode. But whatever your basic personality characteristics, you can work at employing different ways of behaving.

## *Increasing your luck and fortune*

Studies into luck and fortune by Richard Wiseman, using scientific methods, found that people who consider themselves lucky seem to be employing four basic principles. As I was studying this research, I discerned links to the CBT methods for encouraging people to reduce emotional discomfort. Certainly, your attitude to life strongly influences your life chances; indeed, in a sense you make your own 'luck'!

Richard summarises the four main principles that so-called lucky people use:

- ✔ Maximise chance opportunities: Includes having a more relaxed attitude to life, taking opportunities such as networking, trying new things, not necessarily judging people straightaway but listening to what they have to say, and being open to experiences.

- ✔ Listen to their hunches: Includes your intuition and going with your initial gut feelings. The British Psychological Society held a conference about intuition and decided that it's not some superstitious, plucked out of the sky phenomena, but the net result of all your past experiences and wisdom coming to the fore in some situations. When you go with your intuition, you're probably making a well-informed judgement.

'Lucky' people were also more likely to include activities in their lives that actively boost their intuitive powers. Taking time out to clear your mind, relaxing and perhaps meditating or practising mindfulness (see Chapter 19) all help to make your mind more open to increased creativity and intuition.

✔ Expect good fortune: Appears to link to the idea of being optimistic and expecting good things to happen (refer to the earlier section "Keeping It on the Sunny Side!' Working at Optimistic Thinking'). Positive people who seek to find some good in every situation and persist in difficult times are more likely, overall, to have positive outcomes.

This self-fulfilling prophecy isn't magic. People whom others consider 'lucky' aren't passive human beings with good fortune pouring out of the sky onto them. Instead, their actions, behaviours and attitudes lead them to engage in activities that are more likely to increase their own fortune.

You can always choose the easier, more comfortable options in your life if you want. But, as with CBT, you need to go through some discomfort zones to progress.

✔ Turn bad luck into good: The 'Pollyanna' effect I mention in the earlier section 'Playing the 'glad' game'. 'Lucky' people find ways to cope with difficult events and even turn them around to benefit from the ill-fortune they encounter. They seem to employ the similar CBT technique of recognising that 'it could've been worse'. So-called fortunate people don't spend time dwelling on the negative events, but seek to find what they can do to take control and move forward.

## Not losing the plot

I was very fortunate to work with the wonderful crime writer PD James, when she was in her 80s and lecturing on a ship. I was managing the onboard lectures and general welfare of guest speakers. One evening she said that she never turned down invitations, because she saw them as opportunities and she believed that you should always seize every opportunity because you never know how it will impact on your life, usually in a positive way. Her own life had included many hardships and loss but she managed to bring up a family, be the prime breadwinner and became a world-class author.

She related an example. One windy, cold and rainy night she was sitting by her fire in Oxford considering not going to a dinner she'd been invited to in the Law Court Chambers in London. She thought they'd excuse an 80 year old not turning up, and so she decided to stay by the fire. Those thoughts lasted all of two minutes! She chided herself, got organised, dressed in her finery and headed off in the taxi. And she learnt some vital information that night regarding the layout of the London Law Courts, which stopped the plot and denouement of the book she was writing from being totally unbelievable.

## Reading your palm

People are sometimes surprised that I give lectures on palm reading. I expressly point out that I'm not a palm reader, but I have learnt some interesting aspects of palm reading from a US attorney, Kathryn Harwig, which impressed me greatly. As you read this sidebar, you can see that her ideas echo those of CBT: you're the only one truly responsible for yourself; listen to your intuition and emotional flows; when you sense changes and warnings that your equilibrium is becoming unstable, take action to help yourself.

Kathryn explains that your palm lines change throughout life: children's palms only have three basic lines at first and the finer, meshing lines appear later in life. Apparently, your body's physiology changes internally and responding to external events can be expressed as changes in lines on your palm, including stress. In short, internal disturbances in your biochemical makeup can cause effects in your palm.

Kathryn tells of her illnesses as a youngster and later in life, and how she got back in touch with her intuitive side because of long periods of immobilisation. She notes that one of the lines on her hand was quite short and that some people consider that an indication of your length of life. Whether you believe that or not, she had a major medical trauma in her 30s and a long period of recuperation. When fully recovered, the line extended far longer, right down her hand.

She wasn't saying that the short life line was telling her to have surgery, just that she paid attention to it being short and later in her life noted the change in length of the line. Her conclusion that lines change over time was confirmed, but this is not to say that it is indicative of lifespan – just her interest in what happened.

She discusses palm reading with a strong disclaimer that I want to echo: no-one can ever tell your future and don't ever 'hand your palm over' to someone else to dictate your life for you. But by using your intuition and being alert to signs of physiological changes and distress, you can help yourself to take action to maximise your health and wellbeing.

# Optimising Your Chances of a Positive Work Climate

Perhaps you've been resigned to considering yourself a bit unlucky in the past and that negative things always seem to happen to you. You know the type of thoughts: 'I'll never get that job/promotion and so what's the point applying. I'm no good at interviews. It's pointless'.

Guess what? You're highly unlikely to get any job or promotion if you don't even give yourself a chance. Maybe you'll apply for 90 jobs and get three interviews before you succeed, but remember, you stopped after the 90th application because you got the job! By staying positive and not being put off by the other rejections, continue to apply until you get a job. For some people this could be after 3 applications; for others, 90 applications. Persistence, being proactive, and a positive attitude will bring rewards.

Only you can change your 'bad luck'. Yes, life is uncomfortable and at times disappointing and potentially dispiriting, but you limit your own opportunities by your own behaviour.

Make your activities and goals realistic. Don't apply to be a brain surgeon if you haven't even got a medical qualification or a footballer if you have two left feet!

## Studying optimism

Find out as much as you can about optimism and how you can try to engage in more optimistic behaviours and adopt more helpful attitudes at and about your work. Doing so definitely helps to increase your chances of positive outcomes.

If you're quite happy being more pessimistic, you may prefer to accept that that's your way of being and it's not a problem; fair enough. No-one's judging you and saying you must change.

Only you can decide that things aren't as good as you want them to be and decide to do something about it. Therefore, if you'd prefer to be more optimistic, train to be so.

## Hedging your bets at work

Having an open mind at work and not limiting yourself to one particular way of working or supporting only one project or colleague helps you to maximise your opportunities. A closed mind may make an instant decision about something and not be willing to contemplate anyone else's viewpoint or projects.

Dale Carnegie also lists suggestions for the most useful ways of dealing with others at work in order to maximise your positive interactions. These activities include being open to others' views, not criticising, showing respect, trying honestly to see things from the other person's point of view and showing empathy for others' ideas and desires.

High on his list too, as with CBT, is to be the first to admit when you're wrong or have made a mistake, as well as showing a willingness to learn from it. This means, for example, accepting that sometimes you make mistakes rather than arguing out of a sense of misplaced pride, sulking or dwelling on hurt feelings. It is this 'I must always be right' irrational belief that sneaks in.

## *Brightening your work future with CBT*

When through CBT you gain some insight into yourself, your preferred ways of working, your default thinking modes and the influence of your basic personality, you can be more proactive in your future.

The more you take charge and control of your life, with positive steps to maximise your opportunities, the more you get out of life. Self-education and self-help are lifelong processes, though. The more you understand, the more aware you become. And after you raise your awareness, no-one can take that from you.

Even if you become less vigilante at implementing new ways of thinking and behaving, regular checking in with yourself, especially if you get warning signs of imbalance, gives you the option of revisiting what you need to do.

# Chapter 9

# Matching Your Personality to Your Job

### In This Chapter

▶ Discovering your personality type

▶ Sorting out the best jobs for you

▶ Using CBT to get the best out of yourself

*L*ife sometimes seems to pass in a whirl, as if you're racing through the stages: growing up and progressing through school and family life; getting jobs; making friends; forming partnerships; and experiencing significant events. It can all go past so quickly without you stopping to consider what sort of person you are. Plus, although you may get feedback on this from family and school, you probably receive less as you enter the world of work.

In this chapter, I look into the issue of personality types and how they relate to work. I help you discern your strengths and weaknesses and show how this knowledge can assist you in finding a niche for yourself at work within which you can flourish.

## Considering the Personality Types

Psychology research into personality suggests that, like everybody else, you're born with your basic personality. Observations of how people behave as babies and through their lives seem to indicate that some of the characteristics they exhibit as young as eight months old, such as extrovert and introvert types, endure throughout their lives.

Much debate exists about the origin of your personality, but experts do agree that your experiences as you grow up and the different opportunities you have influence how your personality develops. Studies of identical twins brought up separately seem to show that they grow up to have similar personalities, but with differences due to the different environments they experience.

Whatever your own view about the origin of your personality, my concern here is how you fare in the world of work and how you can struggle in some environments. So read this section to discover the theories of different personality types, how to discern them and some of their limitations.

## Looking inwards or outwards

The more you can discover about yourself, the better equipped you are to take control of your life, make changes and adapt to varying conditions.

I imagine an Ancient Greek conversation going, 'I feel really positive today'. 'That'll be your liver talking'. Oh that human moods were that simple! I provide a brief discussion here of one highly influential theory of personality, that of psychologist Carl Jung (who studied with Sigmund Freud). But many other ideas and interpretations of personality also exist (check out the nearby sidebar 'My bile's playing up again' for what the Ancients thought about this subject).

One of Jung's theories is that people are either introvert or extrovert. He suggested placing people's personalities along a continuum, from the predominantly quiet, reflective and solitary introvert to the naturally more outgoing extrovert, who craves stimulation and excitement and prefers the company of other people:

- ✔ Introverts: More focused on their inner world; typically shy; concerned with inner feelings, ambitions, fantasies and their own behaviour.

- ✔ Extroverts: More focused on the outside world; typically influenced by their environment; more objective.

---

### My bile's playing up again

The study of personality goes back as far as the Ancient Greeks. Hippocrates and Galen put forward a theory of personality based on body types, classifying people into four types: irritable (or choleric), depressed (or melancholic), optimistic (or sanguine) and calm (or phlegmatic).

These philosophers believed that the body contains four body fluids: yellow bile, black bile, blood and phlegm, produced respectively in the spleen, gall bladder, liver and lungs. They theorised that imbalances in these fluids affect people's temperaments: too much of any of the four fluids meant that your personality was affected and showed up as your mood.

Jung considered that introverts and extroverts function in different ways, at different levels and to varying degrees. Having some understanding of where you lie on this continuum can give some insight into your own patterns of behaviour.

# Analysing your personality's origins

Over the years, psychology researchers have come up with theories and studies based on observing people. Although human behaviour is hard to analyse scientifically (and of course, many forms of experimenting on people would be unethical), over the years psychology has become more refined at developing helpful methods for testing human behaviour. The use of more sophisticated scientific apparatus such as MRI scans to pinpoint the changes in the brain under different circumstances, and the analysis of biochemical changes and their subsequent effect on human behaviour, have helped to start to understand and explain some changes in people's behaviours.

I take a quick look now at how science has helped the study of personality.

### Causes of depression

The reduction of levels of the serotonin hormone in your blood system can produce depression-type symptoms. This is an example of internal changes in your body. External events can also impact on your feelings and a combination of both can contribute to depression-type symptoms.

Two main origins of depression exist:

- Exogenous depression: Events around you impact on you over time and eventually you fall into a depression.

- Endogenous depression: Chemical changes occur inside your body with no obvious circumstantial influences and you become depressed.

   Seasonal Affective Disorder (SAD) is one such case. When the levels of natural light decrease owing to seasonal fluctuations, some people start experiencing depressive symptoms. Medical science pinpoints the cause as reduced levels of serotonin arising from the lack of stimulation in the pineal gland that triggers serotonin release. The changes that take place internally and externally influence our behaviour.

These outward behaviours may be taken to reflect your personality, but they could be temporary changes in response to events. For example, you may appear very lively and outgoing when you are under stress, but basically your personality may be more introverted. Others may comment that you are acting out of character.

### Psychometric tests

Psychologists have developed some quite robust tests to measure and analyse personalities. For example, at work you may have been asked to complete a psychometric test, perhaps at an interview. These psychology tests aim to find out as much as they can about your type of personality, your skills and talents, attitudes in general and to work, leadership potential and many other facets of you as a person.

These tests provide an in-depth comprehensive assessment. Most psychometric tests used to be only accessible by trained psychologists, so that a trained administrator was in charge of the testing and also, importantly, the analysis and interpretation of the results. The reason for the early restrictions of access to psychology tests was to keep the interpretation as professional as possible and also to maintain ethical responsibility when giving feedback. These days, you can have access via the Internet to many types of test; it is important not to let the test results dictate who you think you are. The tests aims to measure, not provide, a definitive analysis of you as a person.

For Dummies has a whole book devoted to this topic: *Psychometric Tests For Dummies* by Liam Healy (Wiley). It provides a detailed background and explanation of this world of psychometric testing and the exams used in the work selection and appraisal situations.

## Testing for personality types

You can access many online personality tests, although they're less in-depth than the psychometric tests I discuss in the preceding section.

Finding out about yourself can be interesting and informative; however, bear in mind that how you find out and receive the feedback is a potentially sensitive area. Health professionals often use psychology tests when diagnosing the mental health of people who present themselves for medical advice or are referred by a health or social service. Considerable training and understanding of potential mental illness is essential to be able to help people in the optimum way.

Although you may have some understanding of physical illnesses, you generally go to a doctor for professional advice. The same logic applies with psychological analysis. This book isn't a substitute for seeking professional advice if you or someone you know is seriously struggling with mental health. Sometimes an indication may exist that a personality disorder, in terms of a person's behaviour becoming a serious cause for concern, requires specialist help. Only the medical profession can prescribe medications that can assist in the therapy of people who become ill with mental-health issues.

Having said that, tests are available online that give you a general indication of your own preferences and character.

Nothing is set in stone. Your personality and character may change and develop as you interact in life and different work situations. Finding out that you may tend more towards, say, an introvert personality type doesn't mean that you shouldn't apply for jobs favouring more outgoing personalities. It just means that you may have to work harder to develop more outgoing skills and at times push yourself through your discomfort zones.

This issue is exactly where CBT can help. Discovering the situations and interactions in which you find yourself with uneasy feelings is the first step towards identifying what it is about them that you find unsettling.

Here are some of the personality tests that you can search for online to help work out your personality:

✔ The Myers-Briggs type indicator

✔ The 16 personality types

✔ The Big Five personality test

# Dreading facing the public

Janette worked happily away in her job as admin assistant for the marketing manager and was organised and efficient. When her role changed to include shifts on the customer service desk to deal with enquiries, she became agitated and upset. She dreaded going in to work because she didn't like the public-facing work. She discovered that her preference was to work individually, be accountable to one person and organise her day on her terms. The customer service role meant she had no control over those shifts and what the sessions might bring. She tended more towards the introvert personality and she made herself anxious when she didn't have control.

Using the CBT method, she worked out her thinking: 'I must be in control at all times and if I'm not, I make myself anxious.' With hard work, she was able to change her thinking to:

I'd prefer to be in control, but sometimes the new role means there will be no set pattern to the shifts and although I don't like that way of working, I can cope with it. I may not be brilliant at it but I can work to improve. How is it helping me working myself up into a stew about it? It doesn't. I just have to get on with it and work through the discomfort zones. I'll become less anxious in time.

## Avoiding typecasting people

Everyone makes assumptions about other people. Based on the information you have about them, what they look like and how they behave, you make a judgement about what sort of people they are. The same is true when people meet and work with you.

Human beings need to be efficient information processors and they call on their past experiences to make judgements and form opinions of others. Although helpful, the result can be that sometimes you pre-judge other people and aren't as open to new experiences and possibilities as you can be. This tendency is self-limiting, because you can cut off opportunities to work with people who may have other skills and talents you aren't aware of (I discuss the importance of maximising your opportunities and staying open to experiences in Chapter 8).

Although first impressions are an important source of information, don't close yourself off to the possibility that someone you may consider as an introvert, for example, may be shy and not want to join in social activities.

# Taking a Look at Your Own Personality

Often you can make assumptions about yourself, usually based on reflections of your past behaviours and actions. For example, perhaps you consider that you're a certain type of person, along the following lines:

- ✔ Dislikes studying
- ✔ Enjoys giving presentations
- ✔ Friendly
- ✔ Good at exams
- ✔ Loves going out socially
- ✔ Needs quiet times on your own sometimes
- ✔ Prefers sports activities
- ✔ Shy

I'm willing to bet that you tend to consider your negative characteristics and faults quite readily when thinking about your character, but are less forth-coming in recognising your positive side. As a result, getting feedback from people who know you is a relevant and meaningful approach and can be enlightening.

Here's a simple exercise that often yields surprising results. Ask three people to tell you three positive things about yourself. You may feel uncomfortable doing so, but I guarantee that you'll find it rewarding.

I had one client whose friend reported back to me, as the therapist, that she thought I was mean asking only for three positive words or phrases. She decided to write three amazingly affirming paragraphs about her friend for this exercise. My client said it was one of the most significant and valuable information exercises she'd ever received.

## Reacting to personality feedback and tests

You can get insights into your personality in a number of ways, including: feedback from friends; an appraisal system at work, based on your performance in your job; and via an online test-yourself questionnaire or quiz (though they yield only limited information).

However you obtain the information or opinions, and no matter what type of personality you may think you are, you're not stuck with it. If any aspects of your behaviour or outlook are a source of concern or dislike for you, you can decide to work on changing them.

After all, labels are just labels. The authentic you is how you behave in the world, at work and in your relationships. Therefore, if anything is problematic, you can work to change those aspects by using CBT as a start.

## Finding out how you prefer to work

Don't leave finding out how you work to chance; use research skills to investigate yourself:

- ✔ Look back at jobs you've chosen or had to accept because of circumstances and reflect on how well (or otherwise) you worked in those roles.

- ✔ Make a list of likes and dislikes about various jobs.

- ✔ Start to examine your strengths and preferred ways of working.

Don't concentrate on any weaknesses. Although you may not have shone at or enjoyed a particular job because it didn't fit with your personality and how you prefer to work, learn from those experiences – don't dwell on them as some sort of evidence that you're a 'failure'.

## Identifying your positive attributes

Take some time to consider your own skills, talents and useful characteristics. You may find that looking at yourself under the following four headings is helpful (I also include some example strengths):

- ✔ **Personal:** Resilience, tenacity, stickability.
- ✔ **Social:** Good at talking to people, organisational skills, patient, good listener.
- ✔ **Intellectual:** Enjoys learning, adaptability, has interests and diverse activities, creative.
- ✔ **Emotional:** Empathy, good intuition, integrity, compassion.

If you feel awkward about listing your strengths and skills, it can be because, ironically, your humility characteristic means that you're not used to 'blowing your own trumpet'. If so, note that you can work on this skill. Recognising your talents gives you personal positive feedback and can help you to progress further and increase your confidence.

## Admitting your unhelpful characteristics

Note that I deliberately don't head this section identifying your negative characteristics! That's because in the past you may be very good at putting yourself down and berating yourself for perceived weaknesses and mistakes.

But that was then and this is now! Today you can use CBT to turn around such negative emotions, because you know that engaging in self-deprecation is unhelpful. The best action you can take is to allow yourself to admit that some of your actions and behaviours may, at times, not be in your best interest and use CBT to address them.

## Tweaking the self-defeating parts of your character with CBT

You may think that some aspects of your personality have been present since birth, and provide you with a basic character. But in fact, many things along the way have influenced how you've developed.

Use CBT to work on the bits of yourself that you want to change as follows (I provide an example situation as well):

**1.** Select your perceived unhelpful qualities.

- Look at the list of traits you see as negative.

- Write them down.

- Prioritise which one you want to work on first, for example, control.

**2.** Assess your negative thinking.

- Look out for 'should, ought and must' thinking: for example, 'I must know exactly what I have to do each day at work'.

**3.** Realise your self-defeating actions.

- For example, 'I make myself anxious, start getting irritated with co-workers and get snippy and short-tempered with them'. This is self-defeating, and being dismissive or less than well-mannered with people is unhelpful.

**4.** Look at your unhelpful behaviours.

- What do you find irritating? 'When Erika doesn't get her report ready in time, I feel angry'.

- What are your thoughts about this person? 'I think Erika should get her report ready in time'.

- What do you feel when you're around this person? 'If she doesn't, I just wind myself up because her action is unforgivable'.

**5.** Use CBT to change the 'should' thinking to 'prefer' thinking.

- 'I'd prefer that Erika gets her report ready on time, but look, she hasn't'.

- 'I can wind myself up insisting that this shouldn't happen, or I can change my thinking to preferring that she was ready, and feeling annoyed but accepting that this has happened. I don't like it but I can accept it, because how's winding myself up helping me?'

- 'It's not. Accept it – feel annoyed – move on – learn'.

- 'Next time I'll try to find constructive ways to maximise the chances that Erika gets her report ready on time'.

# Linking Personality Types to Different Jobs

Different people are clearly attracted to different ways of working. You can experience discontent and unhappiness when a mismatch exists between your personality and what your job requires.

When you've gained some insight and understanding into your own personality and characteristics (refer to the preceding section), you can start to be a bit scientific about what jobs are probably better for you. Although finding jobs that suit you or you really prefer to do isn't easy, if you don't take time to analyse your preferred areas and ways of working and make a plan, you reduce your chances of getting what you want.

Here I help you discern what may be right for you and how different personalities gravitate towards certain types of jobs.

# Choosing a job you can enjoy

I was listening to a lecture by psychiatrist Dr Raj Persaud and was struck by how he summed up his views on life coaching: 'If you don't know where you're going, you're unlikely to get there'. This seemed so obvious and true, but had never occurred to me in such simple terms.

He shares the following exercise that helps you to see what things are important to you:

1. Plan your perfect day, with no limits or restrictions on money, resources, activities or on what you do.

2. Write down what you do for the entire 24-hour period, including whom you share the day with, if anyone.

3. Reflect on the day and how you feel when imagining it.

Although most people don't have the luxury of working in a dream job, you can start to look at what things interest you and start checking whether your current job and career path match up. Many people conclude that something's wrong with them when they become unhappy at work. It is not that there is anything wrong with them, but it may be the situation they find themselves in. You may find that you've drifted into work roles that really don't require your best strengths and are at odds with your preferred interests and strengths. Or you may find that you are very successful financially in the role you are in, and everything seems perfect to those around you, but you feel unhappy because there is something missing – it may be hard to admit this to yourself and especially to others, but this is your true feeling. Sometimes people become the victims of their own success, but are not doing what they want. For example, if you really want to be a writer, you may have to find time and make a conscious effort to include it in your life.

Raj Persaud did this exercise with a very successful, wealthy client who shared that his life felt unfulfilled because he really wanted to write a book and be published. The client described his perfect day as flying to Monte Carlo for breakfast, and then taking a group of friends on a luxury private oceangoing liner to a secluded island for swimming and fishing. They returned in the evening to visit a spa, prepared for a wonderful dinner and finally visited the casinos.

Raj Persaud asked him where writing fitted in. The client realised that he'd never planned to write and so he was unlikely to ever have a book published!

### Creative types and depression

Some professions seem to be more closely associated with different types of personality; for example, creative types are thought to have a higher likelihood of greater variance of moods. Some famous painters, for example, Van Gogh, are known to have gone through periods of depression. In his book *Strong Imagination: Madness, Creativity and Human Nature,* Professor Daniel Nettle includes the data for the incidence of mental disorder in different jobs and professions.

People working in the arts – for example, musicians, writers, and artists – are among the highest incidences of conditions such as depression (for more on this issue, check out the later section 'Tying mental health to different professions'). In contrast, people working in other categories, such as explorers, workers in the natural sciences and the military, have lower incidences of mental disorders in general.

### Pessimists and optimists liking certain jobs

In Chapter 8, I discuss the ideas of optimism and pessimism and how some people naturally fall into one category or the other. You need to take these aspects into account when considering what type of work to aim for.

For example, people who tend more towards being pessimistic and introverted are often better suited to jobs that require, patience, diligence and attention to detail; they enjoy the challenge of precision and accuracy. These types of jobs include roles such as accountancy. Some of the other characteristics of pessimistic people have also been found to include some of the above strengths. Not only are people happier working in a job that requires these strengths, but society needs them to do so.

On the other hand, optimists and extroverts, with their penchant for going more for the bigger picture, being outgoing, thinking more divergently and, for some, having a tendency for risk-taking, may not be the most suitable for managing financial affairs.

One psychologist writing about the 2007–8 financial crash in the UK analysed the personality types of the workers involved in money trading and discovered a high percentage of people in the risk-taking extrovert categories. The addictive nature of stock market trading strategies can attract people with a higher predisposition to developing addictive behaviours – and society certainly suffered in this case. On the whole society needs extroverts for their imagination, creativity and innovation; you also need to be aware that vigilance over risk-taking is important, too.

## Imagining the worst at work

Your attitudes and views about your work situation impact on how you feel about your job. You may have the sort of personality that tends to imagine the worst, catastrophise frequently about what's going to happen and feel powerless to have any say. Unsurprisingly, you're then unhappy at work. The more you think like this, the more likely you are to continue to feel negative about work.

But this in itself may not be a problem. I've known quite a few people in different places whose default is to come into work with a negative attitude and whine and complain about most things constantly. When challenged to consider looking for other work, however, they baulk at the very thought and give lots of reasons why they can't possibly do so!

People have to want to change if their current behaviour is making them unhappy. Some people have no problem with complaining about how things are for them. In fact, you can find that having to listen to such people's endless complaints and grumbles becomes a problem for you. But then CBT can help you to find a way to accept them and not upset yourself with their behaviour.

## Tying mental health to different professions

Psychology isn't an exact science in that human nature isn't easily measurable and quantifiable. So as regards researching which professions have the highest risk of precipitating depression in their workers, the results can reflect more about general observations than scientific fact.

Therefore, if you decide to examine the various publications – by employers, insurance companies, organisations and the results of studies – which list high-risk categories of work where the incidence of depression is high, remember how they're compiled and keep the info in perspective. Also, be wary of reading psychology magazines and articles making claims that aren't backed up by scientific study. They may make interesting reading but you can't necessarily apply their findings to yourself.

The important aspect of depression and work is how you feel in a job. CBT can help you identify whether you're having difficulties and encourage you to seek assistance. Finding out what's contributing to your low emotional state helps you to start making changes and move towards recovery. Only you know the following: how you're feeling; whether your job is contributing to your struggles; whether you aren't suited to certain types of work; and whether your feelings are temporary and natural or heading towards more long-term conditions that may include depression.

# Adopting the Role of a Successful, Happy Worker

*Do what you can, with what you have, where you are.*

—Theodore Roosevelt

How you view yourself and manage your roles in life, at work and in your family relationships determines the course of your career and personal life. CBT can help you to see that you have options in all these matters.

You can choose to be passive and let events unfold around you and respond accordingly. Or you can be proactive and take time to reassess what's going on in your life, and maybe take some steps to make changes.

In this section, being proactive takes the form of deciding on how to present yourself to your current or a potential employer.

You can only do your best: try to work hard to be the best you can. You can also work hard at expanding your abilities and attributes by continually being open to experience, learning from others and yourself, and moving forward.

You're responsible for your own life. Other people may add to your happiness or sense of wellbeing, or conversely impact on you in negative ways, but ultimately you're the one who makes the decisions.

I suggest that you use the analogy of being an actor applying for a part in a production; you can consider what you need to interpret and get yourself into the role required for the part you're auditioning in a work situation.

## Auditioning for the part of your job

In the preceding sections in this chapter, you spend some time getting to know yourself better. Here, you get to put this knowledge to good use:

1. Imagine you're writing the advert for your current job. Note what you're looking for and what the job requires in terms of job and personal specifications.

2. Picture the job of your dreams. Again, write down what you'd be looking for and what the job requires for both job and personal specifications.

3. Look at what you've written for the two jobs. How does each one match up to what you've discovered about yourself in terms of what you like doing, your skills, talents, interests, preferences and attributes?

4. Draw your own conclusions about any current mismatches. Where would you like to be and what areas of your life do you want to work on?

Consider going to a professional life and career coach or organisation, and signing up for a complete personality profiling assessment. I think doing so at least once in your life can be a great investment.

I never received career advice at school and had my first such session from a local authority service when I was 40: I found it life changing. It was more of a discussion with no tests, but it really helped me to see myself differently with far more skills and talents than I'd ever imagined I possessed.

## *Acting in your own best interests*

Research by social psychologists in the 1970s shows that the more awareness and self-knowledge you have, the more successful you'll be at directing your life and heading in the directions of your choice. Also, the more willing you are to work out what's needed in different situations and to adapt to fit the bill, the more successful you'll be in the role.

You may question the personal ethics of being willing to change like a chameleon to suit outside requirements. But what you're doing is simply trying to minimise discomforts at work and maximise the positive aspects. When you're happy and successful at work, it benefits you, your employer and society. You're making the best use of your knowledge and insight for your own advantage – not deliberately at the expense of others, but for your enlightened self-interest.

This philosophy in ethics states that people who act to further the interests of others, or the groups to which they belong, ultimately further the interests of themselves. Thinking and acting in this way ultimately benefits society and yourself. You work in the best ways for you, and these benefit your work and also make your life less stressful and better for your physical and emotional wellbeing.

Your authentic core self gives you stability in all you do. You can then make informed, conscious choices about how you want to present yourself to maximise your opportunities and positive experiences.

## *Getting into character*

Deciding to be proactive in your professional life means that you need to be vigilant about how you present yourself in different situations. Having self-awareness and giving thought to how you want to be takes hard work. Like using the CBT toolkit (from Chapter 3), self-presentation management requires conscious effort.

Choose a role model and ask yourself: 'What would my hero do in this situation? How would she behave? What would she think about this?'

You aren't changing yourself into an overly compliant person with no mind of your own, wanting only to please people. Quite the opposite: you're practising what's called conscious compliance. You work out what's best in a situation and decide that your best interest is to present yourself in a certain way, because that's more likely to produce a favourable outcome for you.

# Chapter 10

# Creating Your Own Philosophy for Work

*In This Chapter*

▶ Discovering how you think about work

▶ Spotting and dealing with dissonances

▶ Moving forward with confidence

*L*iving the good life doesn't necessarily mean having a materially wealthy lifestyle (though reducing money worries can certainly help); the phrase can relate to living a meaningful life, influenced by your attitudes, values and beliefs. This idea links to the CBT theory and methods that you can apply to reduce your unsettling emotions.

This chapter encourages you to look at your views and attitudes towards work. In essence that involves discerning your personal philosophy. But don't worry . . . you don't have to retreat to a study to struggle with words such as 'compatibilism' and 'epistemology' or plough through interminably long convoluted arguments! Instead I discuss how your attitudes and actions form your personal philosophy and influence the way you approach work and the world at large. I focus on the fact that CBT is about identifying your personal beliefs and attitudes and then considering how helpful (or unhelpful, when they clash with your actions) they may be.

# Delving into Your Attitudes toward Work

Here's a useful definition of philosophy (the word comes from the Greek, meaning 'lover of wisdom') to bear in mind: 'a theory or attitude that acts as a guiding principle for behaviour'.

Everyone has a philosophy of life, whether he uses that phrase or not. People use statements such as 'that's a guide I use' or 'my general rule is . . .' to help them make decisions or cope with life. Problems arise, however, when you're unaware of how your attitudes influence the way you behave.

Fortunately, CBT is all about solving problems and so read on . . .

## *Identifying how you view work*

As you go about your life, you accumulate knowledge and experiences and formulate your own opinions, which all make up your own philosophy of life. You try to make sense of the world, particularly your world of work, when you come up against policies and practices that don't sit comfortably with you.

For example, you may wonder why other people aren't bothered with some issues about which you feel passionate. Your views on justice and fairness at work may seem quite different from others and this can be a source of disquiet and, at times, anguish.

Take a look at the following sayings that express people's different opinions and reveal their underlying philosophy about life. Although they seem similar, they express differences in how people view life:

- ✔ Always expect the worst and you'll never be disappointed.
- ✔ Expect the best and even better will happen.
- ✔ Expect the best, prepare for the worst and expect to be surprised.
- ✔ Expect the best. Prepare for the worst. Capitalise on what comes.

How many of the sayings resonate with you? Perhaps you even use some of these attitudes as a guide for yourself at work. (Clearly, these attitudes link to being optimistic or pessimistic, as I discuss in Chapter 8.)

CBT can encourage you to look at the worst things that can happen and to prepare yourself mentally for that eventuality. Facing the ultimate challenge (often through the process of therapy, in a safe environment) can help reduce the fear that may be lurking in your subconscious.

So, perhaps of the preceding four sayings, the last one is most useful as a philosophy of life.

Say, for example, that you have a natural tendency towards catastrophising thinking: 'we're all doomed!' Negative automatic thoughts (NATs; see Chapter 8) spiral round in your head and you struggle to get a grip. You can face the fear and use CBT to prepare yourself for what may happen.

Catastrophising thinking raises anxiety levels and so use the CBT toolkit from Chapter 3 to intervene to change this irrational thinking to rational thinking, so reducing your anxiety levels.

As Franklin Roosevelt said: 'The only thing we have to fear is fear itself'. You can capitalise on your knowledge of CBT as a technique to help you rationalise the fearful things in life.

## Appraising what you want from work

The contemporary philosopher Alain de Botton writes about how humans moved from self-sustaining groups in agricultural societies to creating purpose-built places of work and division of labour into employers and employees. He observes that originally the concept of work was meant to be a drudge and something that you were expected to get on with. Early cultures didn't have the concept of enjoying work. Work was a means to an end: you do it, get paid and live off your earnings.

A passage from de Botton's book *The Pleasures and Sorrows of Work* states: 'We should temper our sadness at the end of our holidays by remembering that work is often more bearable when we don't expect it to reliably deliver happiness'.

In today's world, you may find that your expectations aspire beyond basic drudgery and you want to do meaningful and interesting work. Yet circumstances can dictate at times that you do any paid work you can find.

CBT can help here, because how you cope with this non-preferred state of affairs and how miserable or otherwise you feel about work is within your control. It can be useful in difficult times, for example, when you have to do tough jobs that are not well-paid to survive, or helpful in aspirational times, say in the case of an unpaid internship to increase your chances of gaining paid work.

Developing a survival philosophy, where you give some thought to what you're doing and more importantly get a perspective on why you're doing it, can aid you through these times. Your job situation itself doesn't cause your negative feelings of misery and discontent – your views about your situation do.

You may not be able to change the current situation, but you can implement CBT techniques to change how you view it to avoid going into a downward spiral of despair (check out the later section 'Pinpointing Unhelpful Beliefs with CBT').

## Aiming to get what you want from your job

If you've never sat down and written out what you expect from your paid work, doing so is a revealing exercise. Having clear aims and preferences can encourage you to formulate a clear pathway of your desires for the future in your working life. It helps you work towards finding those opportunities that may maximise your chances of getting what you want. Through this type of analysis, your own philosophy emerges.

Consider the following list and see what items are important to you about paid work (of course, add any of your own ideas as well):

- ✔ A fair contract
- ✔ Fair pay for a fair day/night's work
- ✔ Manageable tasks
- ✔ Reasonable working conditions
- ✔ To be treated ethically
- ✔ To be valued

Even if over the years in work you've come to the conclusion that you'd like to run your own business, you can still find it helpful to make an assessment of what you do expect from a job. As well as the practicalities of the job, you also need to look at how a specific job may fit (or not) with your values. After all, a key aspect of getting along with other people and your work is sharing similar values.

Your own conscience is an expression of your internal values, and you won't be content or satisfied if your inner sense of right or wrong is in conflict with the company you work for. For example, if you take a job in a loan company charging extremely high interest rates, that way of working and earning money may well not sit easily with you. For more on this type of clash of values, check out the later section 'Identifying Dissonances between Your Beliefs and Your Actions'.

## Discerning your values about work

The people you work with have been chosen for the skills they bring to the job, not because they necessarily have the same values and goals for living as you do. CBT can help you come to terms with this reality and accept that others have different views. Although at times these differences can be a source of conflict or clashing of personalities, you can reduce your potential for negativity by working towards an acceptance – see it as a management technique.

CBT doesn't aim to make you capitulate to other people's views. It encourages you to see that you're unlikely to change other people and therefore the most healthy approach is to work on accepting them – not necessarily liking them, but reaching a stable, workable set of relationships.

To work out and develop your philosophy, reflect on the way you live your life now, your actions in the past and your goals for the future. Doing so may uncover values and beliefs of which you weren't previously aware.

Ask yourself the following questions:

- ✔ How do I want to live my life?
- ✔ What things are important to me?
- ✔ Do I have a sense of justice?
- ✔ What are some of my beliefs?
- ✔ How do I judge myself?
- ✔ How do I judge others?
- ✔ Who are some of my role models and why do I respect them?

Also, think about your friends: You may discover that the reason you like being with them is because you share many of the same ideas and opinions.

If you have very strong beliefs and attitudes that you'd prefer others shared, don't insist that colleagues agree with you; you're simply likely to experience disruption and upset.

## Learning from people who went before

Philosophy has been around for millennia. As people became knowledgeable about the world and yet still suffered in it, their curiosity widened into questioning the very reason for the existence of life. Ancient Greek philosopher Epictetus was born a slave and yet studied hard and was eventually given his freedom. One of his famous quotes is, 'Men are disturbed not by things but by the view they take of them': that is, other people, events or circumstances don't disturb you; you upset yourself by clinging to your views. Amazingly, this sentiment from almost 2,000 years ago is the basis of today's CBT. In fact, writings from Ancient Greece reveal that they used a form of CBT.

Another important aspect of Epictetus's philosophy is that you can't control everything you want to and you should try to make yourself aware of what is within your control:

> 'Some things are in our control and others not. Things in our control are opinion, pursuit, desire, aversion, and, in a word, whatever are our own actions. Things not in our control are body, property, reputation, command, and, in one word, whatever are not our own actions'.

# *Identifying Dissonances between Your Beliefs and Your Actions*

When you think one way and then act in a way that's opposite to what you think you believe, you're displaying an inconsistency. Of course, no-one's perfect and everyone's fickle and inconsistent at times. But if you find that this inconsistency is resulting in problems, you may want to use CBT to examine what's happening in more detail.

Dissonance is where an inconsistency exists between some of your beliefs or between your actions and beliefs. You believe one set of values and yet your actions are at odds with those stated beliefs.

Imagine that you strongly believe that people should stick to the allotted time for coffee breaks at work, particularly because a rota for breaks is in place. When people go over their allotted time, others can't go on a break until they return. Yet one day you get deep into a conversation with a friend on the same break time and you're ten minutes late returning. You may experience upset when you realise this, because you didn't stick to your own beliefs.

Dissonance creates a sense of unease, maybe even guilt, within you: you're aware that you've crossed one of your own boundaries. More specifically, the term cognitive dissonance describes the psychological tension that arises when a discrepancy exists between your attitudes, beliefs or values and your actions, or when new information becomes available to you.

For example, when I was looking to upgrade my mobile phone, I was encouraged to buy one much smaller than I was used to. I was concerned at the size of the keypad, but was assured by the salesperson that people got used to it. One week later I returned to the shop and a new version of the phone had come out which had a larger keypad; I would have preferred to have the larger model and asked to change, but was told I was locked into my contract. The salesperson told me later when he had left, that he felt bad about selling me the phone as he knew the larger one was coming out a week later. This may have caused cognitive dissonance for him, but it also gave him a commission payment and helped clear the shelves of old phones.

Not only do your own views of work and what it means to you vary as you experience different situations, but also people you work alongside may view their roles at work in a different light. This reality reflects each individual's reasons for working and his philosophy regarding employment.

# *Handling differing views and attitudes toward work*

Being in a work environment requires you to comply with certain expectations and behaviours: committing to certain boundaries and working times, achieving goals, co-operating with colleagues, meeting deadlines and perhaps observing a dress code in service industries. Plus, legislation is often in place to ensure that employees appreciate the importance of implementing social, cultural and gender specific issues of equality and inclusivity. Finally, health and safety rules may require you to stick to procedures and practices set out in company or organisation statements.

These requirements may not necessarily match your preferred way of working or behaving. Perhaps you'd prefer to work more informally, but you know that you need to comply in order to keep your job. Sometimes you need to accept that your personal views are out of sync with your company.

How you deal with the differences between your opinions and choices and your work demands reflects your personal philosophy regarding how you go about in the world. It's also important to your sense of wellbeing and so you need to deal with any dissonance effectively.

Use the CBT techniques to deal with uneasy feelings of dissonance at work and to aid your rationalisation of the situation. Consider the following terms that describe attitudes to work and see whether any apply to you and your work colleagues, in belief and/or action:

- ✔ Committed
- ✔ Compliant
- ✔ Conscientious
- ✔ Co-operative
- ✔ Disinterested
- ✔ Dismissive
- ✔ Enthusiastic
- ✔ Motivated
- ✔ Obstructive
- ✔ Positive
- ✔ Professional
- ✔ Resentful
- ✔ Unrealistic

You may find that you need to accept the current situation but that your future constructive action includes working on trying to change what you see as an unfair or unjust policy. As Confucius wrote: 'Discontent is the first step in progress'.

## *Unearthing conflicts in your professional and personal views*

Unless you own the company you work at, you can't choose the people you work with.

Therefore, to avoid discomfort and conflict at work you need to try to accept the people you work with. If you struggle, use CBT to identify and adjust any feelings of strong emotions that you may experience (see the next section). You don't have to like everyone you work with, but for your own sanity rationalising your negative thinking about each of them is worthwhile, to come to a point of acceptance. Learning to deal with people you can't stand is an ever-useful skill! Flip to Chapter 11 for more on this subject.

Here I'd like you to think about how you view your friends and work colleagues. It could be that you will tolerate less from work colleagues than from friends and that you are more forgiving of faults in friends. A friendship you have chosen works because you both get something out of it. You don't choose your work colleagues, and you may be less accepting of their faults. Look at the following three lists and check out how you view your friends and colleagues. You can see these items as points for checking out potential discrepancy areas – for example, that your expectations of your friends in your personal life differ from your expectations of work and your work colleagues. Add your own attributes too – these suggestions are just to help you get started:

✔ Expectations of friends and the attributes you look for:

  – Amusing

  – Considerate

  – Ethical

  – Fair

  – Honest

  – Kind

  – Punctual

  – Reliable

  – Respectful

- Responsible
- Supportive
- Trustworthy

✔ Expectations of work/employer:

- Be organised
- Efficient
- Ethical
- Regular pay
- Reliable
- Respectful
- Sense of fairness
- Trust

✔ Expectations of work colleagues:

- Acceptance
- Co-operation
- Fairness
- Honesty
- Respect

You're less likely to have as much in common with the people you work with as you do with your friends. At times you're going to have to work with people you really don't like. Don't expect to like everyone you work with.

# Pinpointing Unhelpful Beliefs with CBT

Where you locate mismatches between your personal values and beliefs and those of the workplace, you can find that you experience periods of discomfort as the differences become apparent. Perhaps you pick up an atmosphere of disquiet or even a more obvious clash of personnel and heated verbal exchanges.

But don't worry. This situation is the trigger for you to give some thought to examining your own opinions and beliefs about the differences of these surfacing views. And remember that you can be responsible only for yourself in these situations.

## Picking up on tensions

When you feel uncomfortable or even detect a flash of anger boiling up, bring out the CBT toolkit from Chapter 3 to help bring your emotionally charged feelings down to a manageable level.

Think back to a time when you experienced an uncomfortable atmosphere at work:

1. Identify the situation and picture the scenario.

2. Recollect the issues under discussion.

3. Remember how you felt, including what particularly was uncomfortable for you.

4. Recall what you were thinking at the time, including identifying any 'should, ought or must' thinking.

5. Try to pinpoint the discrepancy between what you believed should happen and what was actually happening.

6. Step back from the situation and see whether you can put it into a different perspective.

7. Consider how you'd do things differently if you could replay that event.

CBT is great for reflecting on situations that still cause uncomfortable feelings, because it allows you to work on reframing them into more rational thinking. If unsettling feelings about this incident persist, see whether you can apply the ABCs of the CBT method (that I outline in Chapter 2) to rationalise your thoughts.

## Devising a holding bay

You may decide to make yourself aware of potential flash points at work. Being prepared with your CBT toolkit at the ready to defuse strong emotions maximises your chances of steering a steadier course in life.

Devise your own strategy for recognising emotional flash points and place them in a holding bay. Doing so gives you time to implement CBT or stay in your holding pattern (refer to Chapter 3) until you have time to work out what's happening and can examine your thinking and the beliefs that caused the flash of emotion.

I like to use the strategy of saying nothing in the immediate moment. An old saying from the north of England goes 'If in doubt, say nowt': meaning if you're unsure what to say, say nothing. I used to be too ready to retaliate verbally and make my views known immediately. But in the long run, expressing my views in a state of heightened emotion wasn't often in my best interests.

Saying nothing rarely makes the situation worse, and if other people mistakenly interpret it as silent defiance or insolence, that's not your problem.

If you're tackled further to explain your reaction, say something like:

✔ I can see you feel strongly about this.

✔ I'm not sure what to say right now.

✔ That's interesting.

This response gives you time in the holding pattern to prevent negative emotions escalating.

For a difference of opinion to be perceived and escalated into a clash, a situation needs at least two differing views to be expressed.

## Agreeing to differ and not losing face

Some people criticise CBT for recommending that you stay calm and not express your views: they think that it encourages people not to care what happens. I think these criticisms are wrong, but sometimes you can find yourself thinking, 'I should say something. This is outrageous and I won't stand for it!'

This reaction is sometimes called a secondary emotional disturbance. If you spotted that it's just another level of 'should' thinking, well done!

When you start thinking that you should intervene and wind yourself up if you don't, the emotional outcome is the same: anger and outrage. Instead, rationalise why you aren't responding in the instance (because making yourself angry isn't the best thing for you). Wait until the adrenalin flash subsides and work out what you can do in the future and what you can't.

The ultimate goal is acceptance – not necessarily liking the outcome, but not upsetting yourself. You aren't 'losing face', but simply thinking and behaving as a rational human being who works on what you can change and accepts the things you can't control.

# Staying Put or Leaving Your Job

CBT shows that you always have choices about work. You may not like any of the options, but you do have the power to work out a cost–benefit analysis of the various options.

Imagine that you're unhappy at work and you see three options:

✔ You can decide to leave a job, but if you're unemployed the consequence may be that you're unable to pay your bills.

✔ You can decide to stay in your job but continue to make yourself unhappy about it and complain and whine and continually upset yourself.

✔ You can use CBT to rationalise your view of your job and decide to accept that, although it isn't the ideal job for you, for now you're going to have to stay there and make the best of it.

Persistence, resilience, motivation and application of CBT form a good combination to help you approach making tough decisions. Check out the links here to the philosophy of Stoicism in the nearby sidebar 'Staring at Stoicism with resignation'.

---

# Staring at Stoicism with resignation!

Recent times have seen a revival of interest in ancient philosophies, particularly Stoicism. It seems to be relevant in today's hectic and uncertain world and can be helpful in providing strategies to cope with tough times. The connection between Stoicism and CBT is strong.

A school of Ancient Greek philosophy, Stoicism emerged at a time of great turmoil. The philosophy was developed to help people find some calm within the turmoil and discover ways of relying on themselves and their inner resources, thoughts and beliefs to benefit their emotional life. Stoicism advises recognising that you can be in control of your thoughts and actions and use them to cope with life.

Generally speaking, having a stoic attitude conjures up a picture of not flinching in the face of adversity, being strong and not complaining when things go wrong. The word resilience has come to mean similar attributes, in having the ability to face up to difficult situations and recover from hard times.

In his book, *Philosophy for Life and other Dangerous Situations,* Jules Evans describes Stoicism in the context of today's world:

> 'The world is beyond our control. It's a rough and unpredictable environment that is constantly changing. The only thing we can really control are our own thoughts and beliefs. If we remind ourselves of that, and focus our energy and attention on our own beliefs and opinions, then we can learn to cope wisely with whatever the world throws at us'.

For more details, check out 'Stoicism Today', a group that regularly publishes articles, blogs and resources. The team includes philosophers, psychologists, CBT therapists and classicists. See the latest discussions at http://blogs.exeter.ac.uk/stoicismtoday.

## *Making tough decisions*

Allowing yourself to acknowledge your unsettling feelings as they arise and making a conscious effort to examine the root of the disturbance helps you to work out how to address the issues behind them.

But only you can make the decision to want to change and address the difficulties you encounter. In CBT terms, you can't create change without at least some discomfort. You need to go through the discomfort zones to change and move on.

### *Knowing yourself builds resilience*

Knowing your strengths and limitations will help you work out if you are just going through a difficult time in your job or if has become intolerable. There may come a point where you realise it is in your best interests to look for another job. This will be a very difficult decision, but it will be helped by the CBT of evaluating the pros and cons of staying in the present situation.

The original use of the word stress was in the context of mechanical engineering (when designing machines and buildings, mathematicians worked out the maximum loads and pressures that could be exerted before objects cracked under the pressure). But in the 1970s, the term entered general usage to describe feelings associated with experiencing overbearing (often work) situations likely to result in negative emotions. Part of dealing with stress is building the necessary resilience to it.

Here's one useful definition of stress: 'when the perceived demands outweigh the ability to meet those demands'.

### *Changing reality of employment*

The changing nature of the world of work and the huge advance in technology impacts many areas of life. Recent decades have seen the following changes:

- A move away from 9–5 jobs, five-day opening hours for shops with a half-day closing, and limited communications by land-line telephones
- An increase in the number of people who extend their education and go to university
- The learning of new specialist skills
- The rapid expansion of jobs in technology markets
- Increased demands on employees to be more available and respond more quickly to changes

### Riding to the rescue

In response to these issues, Professor Martin Seligman used positive psychology to investigate the effects of stress on emotional lives and find ways to combat it. His research on measuring resilience in people and how this factor affects their chances of happiness and emotional wellbeing is extremely helpful. He devised Resilience Training programmes, which are used in the military and have wide applications in industry and for the general public. It is designed to be proactive, rather than waiting to see who has a negative outcome following stress. Many employee assistance programmes offer workshops, and online resources offer exercises in resilience training to help build up responses to stress.

Having some understanding of positive psychology and the links with the ideas and practices of CBT gives you a good overall basis for getting the most out of life, in and out of work.

Seligman identifies happiness as containing three aspects:

- ✔ The Pleasant Life: Appreciating things such as friendship, the natural world and meeting your basic needs, such as food and shelter.

- ✔ The Good Life: Finding out what your unique virtues and strengths are and using them creatively to get the best out of your life.

- ✔ The Meaningful Life: Using your unique strengths to recognise a greater purpose than just yourself.

Being aware of these three categories and taking time to look at how your life includes these aspects or where there are gaps can lead you to be proactive in finding your own balance.

### Gaining a new perspective

Spending some time considering your views on work, relationships and life in general as I describe in this section can help you discover your own philosophy and perspective.

The more you invest your time in obtaining a deeper understanding of yourself, the more you get out of life.

# Chapter 11

# Exploring Your Relationships at Work

*In This Chapter*

▶ Recognising different types of people at work

▶ Considering the impression you convey to others

▶ Developing friendships in the workplace

**Y**ou don't work in total isolation. Even if you're self-employed and work for yourself, you probably interact with and affect other people in one way or another.

I used to think that things would be different at work if I changed professions, in my case, away from education into the business world. I was sure that work-relationship problems – the annoyances, impatience and exasperation I felt at times with some colleagues – were down to the profession I was working in. A friend who'd only ever worked in the business world advised me that 'the problems will be the same, just in a different setting'.

I didn't believe him. But over the years I've worked in business, finance, the leisure industry, retail, public services and other areas, and he's right. The characters you meet at work – the problems, struggles, unfairness and issues – seem universal.

Clearly work relationships cause people a lot of distress. In this chapter, I discuss such relationships from both sides. I provide a number of exercises that help you discover more about yourself and your work colleagues, as well as ways to reduce your stress at work and so become a happy, better co-worker. I also consider the importance of the friendships that you build at work.

# Taking a Hard Look at Your Colleagues

At work, you're thrown together with people you haven't chosen to be with but need to work alongside. Obviously, you may not like or get on well with some of them. Fortunately, CBT strategies and training can help you accept other people and their behaviours without upsetting yourself unduly.

The only constant and reliable resource is yourself. You encounter many different issues and struggles in work, no matter where you work, but by developing a strategy to deal with 'people you can't stand', you give yourself invaluable coping skills.

Consider the truth and the implications for your attitude and behaviour of the following two quotes. The first one is a poignant statement that a psychologist I used to work with in California wrote in a youngster's psychological profile:

> *The most useful skill this person can develop in life will be an ability to suffer fools gladly, as she will meet a lot of them.*

The second comes from Robert Greene's book, *Mastery*:

> *The most effective attitude to adopt is one of supreme acceptance. The world is full of people with different characters and temperaments. We all have a dark side, a tendency to manipulate, and aggressive desires. The most dangerous types are those who repress their desires or deny the existence of them, often acting them out in the most underhanded ways.*

This quote echoes the goal of CBT in that working toward acceptance of yourself and others creates a healthy outlook for you. This is not to say that you have a lie-down-and-take-it attitude, but that you have a realistic understanding that others around you may not always be what they seem.

## Categorising your workmates

Carry out the following exercise. If you're currently in work, use your present job; otherwise, think back to a previous job you held.

Taking some time to actually think about your workmates individually and in some detail can help you get a more realistic view of those around you. For example, manipulative people can seem very pleasant and helpful on the surface but may sometimes let you down in unexpected ways. Look for patterns in others people' work which will help prepare you to anticipate their future behaviour.

Ask yourself these questions:

 ✔ Who was your favourite person to work with?

 ✔ What about the person did you like/admire?

 ✔ What were the person's qualities/strengths?

 ✔ Did the person have any annoying habits?

Now ask yourself the same questions about a person you didn't like:

 ✔ Whom did you really not get on with?

 ✔ What about the person did you really dislike?

 ✔ What were the person's weaknesses/shortcomings?

 ✔ Did the person have any positive qualities?

 ✔ How did you deal with this person?

Looking at your answers, you may see that some of the descriptions of each person refer to professional attributes and some to personal characteristics. Doing so helps you to get a more accurate picture of how she is as a person and how she behaves professionally. What you are looking for is any differences between how she acts as a person and how she is at work.

## Appraising the horrors and the lovelies

You come across many different types of people at work. But bear in mind that many people feel that they need or want to show only some aspects of their personality at work. As a result, sometimes your views of colleagues change when you spend some time with them in a social situation. In particular, the 'office party' has a reputation for people opening up and showing different sides of their personalities, which can be quite revealing!

You can encounter every conceivable sort of person at work, from world-weary, whining saboteurs to self-deprecating leaders and sneaky malcontents. You need many skills to be able to deal with all the different types, because if someone really 'gets under your skin' and you feel discomfort or intense dislike, your work is likely to suffer.

Use CBT to work out what about the person seems to elicit such strong negative feelings from you. Doing so helps you to rationalise your views about the person and work towards reducing them. Every time you get a flash of uncomfortable emotions about a colleague, apply the CBT method to rationalise what you're thinking and reduce the feelings of antagonism or general uneasiness (refer to Chapter 3 for more on using your CBT toolkit). That way, you don't get swept away with negative feelings of anger, guilt, frustration, jealousy and so on.

Work towards accepting this person. I'm not asking you to like such difficult people, but accepting them frees you up to think more constructively as to how you can deal with them.

# Seeing the character types in work

The different characters you meet at work may have very different motives to be there. For example, some people live to work, to feel busy and engaged; others may just do it for the money; still others may just go to work for companionship and to have someone to talk to and to talk about. This exercise helps resolve the true natures of people you work with, and recognise sources of conflict.

1. Choose a person from your work experience, past or present, with irritating, negative characteristics.

2. Create four columns so that you can add entries for her characteristics, work behaviour patterns and social skills, as well as the emotions that this person stirs up in you.

3. Use the CBT toolkit from Chapter 3 to identify the ABCs:

    • A: Actual person or the thought of that person.

    • B: Beliefs or attitudes your hold about the person.

    • C: Consequences, in this case, your feelings about the person.

To show you what this exercise can mean in practice, here's an example from my own life. I use Rosie (name changed, of course!) as an example because I used to find her behaviour at work annoying and unhelpful. Her constant whining was a source of irritation for me and her reluctance to take on new initiatives frustrating:

✔ Non-verbal characteristics:

   – Poor personal appearance

   – Stooped shoulders

   – Always in dark-coloured clothes

   – Negative tone of voice

   – Frequent sighing at her desk

   – Continual comments as she opened emails

✔ Work behaviour patterns:

   – Always moaned about her work

   – Around 75 per cent of what she said was negative

   – Appeared world-weary

- Saw injustice all around

- Sometimes unco-operative about new suggestions

- Obstructive to implementing new working practices

- Arranged frequent meetings with bosses over trivial things

✔ Social skills:

- Kind and thoughtful to others on a personal level

- Keen to champion others' perceived injustices

- Brought in cakes regularly to share

- Liked to talk about her children (though some might find this irritating)

- Ran clubs outside of work to teach skills to youngsters

✔ My emotions:

- Irritated by her lack of co-operation

- Angry at her refusal to take on new ideas

- Exasperated at having to repeat requests for work to be completed on time

- Her making me feel depressed through her negativity

I only saw another side of Rosie while talking to her outside of the work environment, or when the office had a birthday cake to share or the occasional company event.

Work on separating out the professional from the personal. Remain open to the idea that the person you're trying to work with may be quite a different person in a different setting.

I put my CBT training into practice and what I discovered changed my outlook and view of Rosie; actually I really liked her as a person but found her behaviour irritating as a co-worker. By accepting that she was a person with 'whiney ways', I no longer wound myself up about it. She was, I realised, quite happy moaning about work and it wasn't my responsibility to try to change her.

That old saying, 'misery loves company', rang true with Rosie. She sought out others to complain to. But I didn't have to be caught up in the downward spiral of despair if I chose not to. I had no obligation to listen to her, but that didn't mean I was rejecting her as a person, just as a whiney co-worker: it was okay to walk away. She was just a human being with tendencies to moan at work.

Someone's behaviour doesn't make the person that particular personality type all the time.

# *Dealing with people you can't stand*

Once you recognise that there are some people at work you really don't like, and that that is okay because you cannot like everybody, and equally not everyone is going to like you, you can move on. Don't waste time and energy worrying or upsetting yourseslf about particular people at work. Accept that this is the way work is. Finding some strategies to maximise communication with colleagues is a more helpful use of your time. I often used to conclude a conversation at work 'well we will just have to agree to differ about this'.

Interpersonal communication is essential at work and can be the making or breaking of harmonious and productive relationships. The ways in which people communicate in the workplace, across the workplace and in customer interactions are varied and potentially full of opportunities for misunderstanding and/or unhelpful outcomes. If you can read these clues and modify your behaviour accordingly, you can avoid problems when dealing with other people.

Before technological advances in computers, faxes, electronic mail, voice mail, conference calls, video conferencing, Skype and so on, people communicated face-to-face, over the telephone or by sending letters that they composed, considered and checked before sending.

With the advent of emails, however, you lose the nonverbal and auditory signals that people give out when actively interacting with others at work. Some studies seem to show that when people interact with others face-to-face, one third of communication between people is verbal and two-thirds is nonverbal.

Some nonverbal signals are conveyed via:

- ✔ Appearance: Their choice of clothes and personal image
- ✔ Eye contact: Whether they make or avoid it
- ✔ Facial expressions: Such as relaxed, anxious and so on
- ✔ Gestures: How they move to express themselves, for example, hand movements
- ✔ Posture: How they stand or hold themselves
- ✔ Tone of voice: How they sound to others

I expand on these signals in the following section.

Humans are very good at gleaning information from the nonverbal signals as to the authenticity of what's being said. As the old saying goes, 'the eyes are the window to the soul'. Modern research backs up this insight: when video footage of people's faces and in particular their eyes is analysed, people can detect tiny microexpressions by the eye movements. If someone is saying one thing but her body language seems to indicate another view, you may find that you feel a flash of emotion like anger if you interpret her non-verbal signals as being challenging. For example, if someone says: "yeah, right, that's a good idea" in what you interpret as a sarcastic tone. Use your CBT to look at your emotional reaction. People can and will say whatever they want. It is your interpretation that brings about your emotional response.

# Considering the Way You Come across at Work

A working relationship is a two-way process. Therefore, taking into account the impression you give to other people is an integral part of understanding yourself.

When you're sitting alone in your office, working outside on your own or perhaps analysing results in a laboratory, how you appear to others isn't so relevant. But when you're in an environment where you mix with other people, work colleagues, other companies, people you're responsible for or the general public, how you present yourself has an important impact.

## Thinking about self-presentation

Just as you pick up clues about the people you meet at or through work (refer to the earlier section, 'Taking a Hard Look at Your Colleagues'), so different components are involved regarding how you appear to others. Verbal (how you say something as well as what you say) and nonverbal interactions convey a lot of information to others, and so you want to be aware of what you're communicating – one way or another!

Some ways in which you may be saying more than you intend include the following:

✔ Appearance: Your dress sense, hairstyle and so on (see the nearby sidebar 'Dress for success and to impress!'). If you are in a sales or customer-facing position, there is an expectation that you will comply with conventions of dress. Dressing otherwise may show that you don't take the job seriously.

✔ Expressions: Facial expressions are universal across the world, such as smiling, smirking, laughing, frowning, and tight-lipped, although when they're appropriate to use may vary in different cultures. The main emotions conveyed by facial expressions are anger, disgust, sadness, happiness, surprise and fear.

✔ Eye contact: Too little and people may think you aren't listening; too much can come across as threatening.

✔ Head movements: Such as looking away or appearing unfocused. People speaking expect you to maintain eye contact to show you are interested.

✔ Posture: Alert or slouched? Again, it indicates level of interest and engagement.

✔ Proximity: How close you get to others or holding your distance. This is very much a cultural feature: societies vary greatly in what is acceptable.

✔ Voice: A loud, dominating voice can be perceived as threatening; a quiet, hushed voice may indicate reluctance to be involved in communication.

  – Tone: Assertive, compliant, aggressive, dominant, unsure.

  – Pace: Restrained, animated, hesitant, pausing.

✔ What you don't say: Silences can also be very powerful.

## *Picturing yourself at work*

Paying some attention to how you appear at work can be helpful in considering the impression you give. For example, someone who obviously takes more care over how she dresses may be thought of as being able to pay more attention to detail at work.

## Dress for success and to impress!

Understanding the impact of colour analysis is another tool for you to use and include in your CBT toolkit. It can influence other people and help you as well.

My friend Pauline was a 'colour consultant'. She helped people analyse which colours in clothes and accessories suited them best, enhanced their overall look and improved the impression they made to the world.

At the time, I worked in an institution for youngsters with emotional and behavioural issues. Pauline offered to do a lunchtime session for the older teenagers. This kind offer had the potential to be a challenging situation and I was concerned for my friend. In fact the session was well-attended and went swimmingly. The youngsters were interested, which considering that 80 per cent were male, was highly encouraging.

They weren't the only ones to learn something: I discovered a lot about the use of colours and how they impact on other people. I've used this knowledge ever since. If I'm feeling tired or know that I need to present something in the public arena, I'm more likely to wear something bright to create an impact and raise my own spirits.

### Presentation

People don't often take time to consider how they present themselves to others. Going into work can become a habit and people can assume over time that what they look like no longer matters.

1. Close your eyes and picture yourself at work: If you work at a desk, use that image. Otherwise, choose a place you frequently find yourself in.

2. Consider what you look like: Your clothes, your hair, your posture and the expression on your face.

3. Picture a person at work coming up to ask you something: How do you look as you're approached? Are you turned away, do you look up, are you smiling, serious, irritated, distracted or do you have any other expression on your face? As the person talks to you, what do you think you look like in response?

4. Imagine yourself in a wider context: Perhaps in a meeting, at the reception desk or in a customer-services interaction. How do you enter the room or public space? Are you smiling? Serious? Worried? Frowning? Lethargic? Animated? Do you initiate contributions in the meeting? Are you likely to be more of an observer and not interact much? When people come up to you, do you greet them with a smile?

Some customer-service training takes all these presentational aspects into account and helps people to train themselves in new habits. This training helps to increase positive experiences for the customers, but also helps you to feel better about yourself as well.

### Smiling and grimacing

When you smile, scientists have discovered something called emotional contagion, which means that it has an effect on other people and they're highly likely to smile back. Plus, you feel better in yourself when you smile.

Smiling sends out the message that you're relaxed and approachable and it generally increases your attractiveness and likeability. Use it to your advantage.

According to Dr Mark Stibich, smiling:

✔ Boosts the immune system

✔ Increases positive effect

✔ Reduces stress

✔ Lowers blood pressure

✔ Enhances other people's perception of you

Studies suggest that even 'false smiling' can have some of these benefits. As Buddhist monk Thich Nhat Hanh says, 'Sometimes your joy is the source of your smile, but sometimes your smile can be the source of your joy'.

The same 'contagion' applies when you express disgust: the person seeing you is likely to return a similar expression. In evolutionary terms, communicating disgust is an important way of warning others of potential hazards to avoid – although fortunately eating poisonous mushrooms isn't a situation you're likely to encounter in many work environments today!

So don't frown or grimace, unless you want people look at you with disgust!

## Remembering how you were before work

The effects of growing up and entering the work arena can creep up on you over time. Work can make significant, but importantly temporary, changes in your personality, and so matching yourself to your work makes a big difference to how happy you are.

Seeing how you develop as a young adult and progress through your jobs and career can provide you with an interesting insight into yourself. Have a go at the following exercise, which covers thinking about how you were before you entered the world of work and how you are today at work:

1. Reflect on how you were at school. Picture yourself as a young teenager mixing with friends and taking part in hobbies and out-of-school activities. Maybe you see yourself as a happy-go-lucky child, enjoying playing, laughing and racing about on bikes. Describe yourself in six words:

   _____   _____   _____

   _____   _____   _____

2. Consider how you are at work these days. Picture yourself mixing with colleagues, taking part in projects and going about your job daily. Also include going out socially with work. Again, describe yourself in six words:

   _____   _____   _____

   _____   _____   _____

3. Ask yourself whether you notice any changes in yourself, aspects that you wonder how they ever happened. Maybe you see a serious, focused adult who's mostly private and doesn't have much time for laughter.

For a look at my personal experience, check out the nearby sidebar 'Team power'.

---

## Team power

When I reflect back on some jobs I've had, I hardly recognise myself. When I felt under a lot of pressure, with highly emotionally charged roles requiring intense concentration, I see myself as tired, stressed, anxious and certainly not smiling very much. I had sleep disturbances and physical ailments flared up: I wasn't a relaxed or fun person to be around.

In the past, I worked with teenagers with behavioural issues in an inner city area: they had little stability in their lives and much disruption and unpredictability. This tension often spilled over into the work situation and staff members had to use crisis-management techniques to bring some control. Working for long periods in highly stressful and potentially disruptive situations resulted in many exhausted workers.

Yet when I reflect on that job, the team spirit, co-operation and support helped it to be more manageable: working together created a worthwhile project. We had laughter and high spirits after we'd dealt with tricky situations. I discovered that I prefer to work with people with real commitment and shared values.

---

 Choosing the optimum job and environment for you is important. Check out Chapter 9, which encourages you to find out about your personality and preferred ways of working.

## *Seeing yourself in different roles*

As a child, you had few roles. You lived in a family situation and mostly responded to what was required: being taken to nursery and school and later maybe some after-school clubs. You may have had a role as a sibling and perhaps cared for a pet, but generally children don't have too many responsibilities.

Around the age of 11 or so, you probably started stating your preferences and likes and dislikes and tried to make independent choices. Your brain developed into having what Swiss psychologist Piaget called the 'capacity for abstract thinking and reasoning'. I hope that people were around to look out for your safety and guide you towards suitable choices, to allow some independence but also take responsibility for your welfare.

By the time you're about 16, your likes and dislikes, talents and skills, became clearer and you developed an inkling of what type of work you wanted to do in the future.

As you grow older, your roles become more diverse. In the present day, you're likely to have accumulated a few roles in different contexts. Here are just some of the many possibilities:

| *Home* | *Work* | *Socially* |
|---|---|---|
| Cook | Job | Friend |
| Cleaner | Colleague | Team player |
| Gardener | Team leader | Social secretary |
| Partner | Manager | Chauffeur |
| Spouse | Driver | Organiser |
| Sister/brother | Co-ordinator | Club member |
| Aunt/uncle | Mediator | Carer |
| Parent | Nurse | Childminder |

Take some time to do a skills audit along the lines of this table of all the roles that you play in your life. Doing so helps you to create a positive view of yourself and remind yourself of all the brilliant things you can do. We often have a tendency to focus on only the negative.

# Making Friends at Work

Your workplace can be far more than 'just a job'. Research shows that having friends at work increases people's happiness. Some employees report that when they have friends at work, their job is 'more fun, enjoyable, worthwhile and satisfying'.

## I'll be there for you

The bonding that creates friendships at work is an integral part of forming a cohesive work unit and establishing a sense of camaraderie and mutual support. Many companies actively encourage this type of bonding by arranging for workers and their teams to participate in corporate challenges, team-building courses, company social events and perhaps even provide for socialising onsite with gyms and sports teams.

CEO Gary Kelly, who's a firm believer in cultivating a sense of community within his company, says that 'spending time with employees, treating people with respect, having fun, being there for them personally and professionally, and putting people first, with empathy, kindness and compassion', are important aspects of creating a culture at work.

For many people, work can be an important source for providing a sense of security. When your personal life is in turmoil or you're struggling with crises at home, going to work can feel like a refuge.

## Friends! Romans! Co-workers!

A study asked a sample of people, 'If you won 10 million on the lottery would you continue to work or would you stop working?' Two-thirds of the people said they'd continue to work and stick with the same employer.

A lottery winner in Nottingham, UK, won £7 million. He'd joked in the past that he needed to win the lottery to sort out a difficult financial time. When he did win, he said he'd put money in the company, because 'I wanted to use some of the money to look after their jobs. They stood by me through hard times, so I thought I'd stand by them.'

Some people give the following reasons why having friends at work is important:

- ✔ They feel more engaged with the company.
- ✔ They met their best friend at work and they've stayed connected for years.
- ✔ They look forward to going to work more when they have a special connection with a friend there.
- ✔ They even say that they wouldn't want a higher paid job if it meant they wouldn't be working with people they get along with.

Going to work seems to fulfil more than the need for money for some people. Also, office friendships appear to have a direct link with how engaged you feel at work, which can increase productivity.

## Not everyone can be your best buddy

Sometimes friendships can turn sour and provide sources of anxiety and distress.

You're at work because it's your job. You may not necessarily meet people that you can relate to, who share your values (refer to Chapter 10) or who you'd choose as friends outside of work.

You don't have to make friends at work and you may actively prefer not to: that's fine. But if you find that you feel left out of friendship groups and this is a source of concern for you, look more closely at what you'd like from making bonds at work.

## *If you want a friend, get a dog!*

One day I heard someone at an HR meeting say, 'if you need a friend at work, bring your dog'. Harsh, certainly, and an inappropriate reaction to someone in dispute with a co-worker, but you can see the underlying point. Needing friends at work can present difficulties if the friendships don't happen to work out.

Here are some important considerations about having friends at work:

- ✔ **Be accepting:** Acceptance of others and their positive attributes and their idiosyncrasies is all part of the CBT approach to life. Everyone has her own ways of doing things, her own opinions and preferences. Unless it adversely affects her performance at work, accept this and move on; doing so is more productive.

- ✔ **Be respectful:** Always aim to have respect for your co-workers. Even if you don't agree with them or even like them very much, your professional etiquette can include not being disrespectful.

- ✔ **Maintain boundaries:** Ensure that you check out the boundaries of your professional and personal lives. If the boundaries get blurred and friendships falter, it can impact on your work relationships.

- ✔ **Don't judge:** Try not to judge others at work based on your subjective opinion. Making your subjective views known is unhelpful and unprofessional. Holding objective views regarding their work performance is different, however, and often necessary when you're in a supervisory role.

# Part IV
# Using CBT in Your Organisation

Work can bring up a whole treasure trove of feeling and emotions, good and bad both. Using CBT, you can tackle some of the difficult ones, and you can help co-workers tackle theirs, such as

- Anger
- Anxiety
- Confidence issues
- Depression
- Embarrassment

- Envy
- Frustration
- Guilt
- Hurt
- Shame

Visit www.dummies.com/extras/cbtatwork for great Dummies content online.

## *In this part . . .*

- ✔ Understand your actions before you embark on any new project.
- ✔ Use CBT to help employees cope with the disorientating changes that accompany transition management.
- ✔ Identify what areas trouble you, admit that a problem exists and use the various ways in which CBT can help.
- ✔ Learn how CBT can benefit employees, from reducing stress, anxiety and depression to improving staff morale and productivity.

# Chapter 12

# Taking Action! Implementing CBT at Work

## In This Chapter

▶ Knowing yourself better

▶ Putting CBT to the test

▶ Tackling your own problem areas

▶ Creating an action plan

Sometimes, like the reluctant heroes of countless Hollywood westerns, you're left with no option but to act. The time for thinking, reflecting and analysing is past and you need to mount your steed and spring into action. Therefore, in this chapter, I look at using CBT methods to attack your at-work struggles.

In the spirit of taking action, I suggest that you get on your emotional bike (yep, I'm switching analogies, keep up!) and ride your way to more confidence, less fear, more resilience, less anxiety and overall a more balanced emotional life. CBT can provide the stabilisers or training wheels for your bike through instruction, but you have to do the hard work that's essential to riding free and having confidence in your own abilities.

On this chapter's cycle journey, you discover the importance of getting clear why you're taking the trip, practising sufficiently so that you're strong enough for the ride, using CBT to relieve your own fears and anxieties, and building a personal action plan. So saddle up and pedal away (see what I did there?).

## Gaining Insight into Yourself with CBT

In order to use the CBT approach to cope with life in your organisation, you need to get to grips with yourself; to take some time and do a bit of homework to get the hang of yourself.

I know that this statement sounds a bit odd, but a good chance exists that you understand the motivations and behaviour of other people better than you do your own; perhaps you're just too close to yourself.

Therefore, before you take action, you need to gain a fuller understanding of your personal motivations and actions.

## Doing your homework

CBT requires you to do your homework in order to change your natural default position of irrational thinking and your 'I should, ought and must' beliefs to a healthier 'I'd prefer' type of thinking.

Moving from intellectualising to making a genuine change in your thinking takes time, patience, perseverance and commitment. People with a low frustration tolerance and the sort of 'hurry, hurry, rush, rush' personality find it even harder. You may want everything now, with instant changes and rewards of feeling calmer, but you need to put in the work.

You can stand the discomfort of developing a new skill in order to move forward, but you need to do more than just read a book or have some CBT sessions with a therapist. The changes you want are within your control. As Marcus Aurelius, the ancient philosopher, writes in his book, *Meditations:* 'You have power over your mind – not outside events. Realise this, and you will find strength'.

The more you set yourself some homework and decide to get to grips with the CBT ideas and how they relate to you, the more progress you make. A good test of whether you've understood something, and to work actively on tackling a specific problem, is to try and teach it to others. Check out Chapter 14, where I discuss spreading the message about CBT in your workplace.

## Understanding your motivation

Numerous reasons may lie behind your decision to develop CBT skills and techniques, but I guess that most people are motivated by the following two points:

- ✔ You want to solve a problem that's causing you suffering.
- ✔ You discover that you're interested in the CBT method and want to find out more.

The last point is called intrinsic motivation – that is, the drive to learn comes from inside you. As you're reading this book, you've presumably decided that you want to find out more about CBT and how you can apply it in your work situation, and so you're self-motivated.

I decided at 18 that I wanted to go to college, but I wasn't sure what I wanted to study: I enjoyed English and was interested in Biology and Chemistry. I did struggle with some aspects of Chemistry, but really enjoyed the practical experiments. The teacher was lively and enthusiastic and above all encouraging. Most of all, I wanted to live away from home for a few years.

I did the work at college because I had to pass the course. When I was 20, with a year to go before finishing, I had a life change. I suddenly questioned that I would automatically leave college, get married, and settle down to have children. I had grown up in a big family and I realised I wanted to explore things in my life before 'settling down' and taking on extra responsibilities. I didn't think it would be fair to get married with those doubts. I started to think seriously about a career and became genuinely interested in a psychology project I was working on. Suddenly I wanted to learn for my own sake. I didn't need people imposing deadlines: I enjoyed the research. I wanted to study further because I was interested not because someone was telling me to. I guess I was taking responsibility for my own learning. This continued during my career and when I came across CBT when studying on a stress management diploma, I realised that this therapy was advocating doing exactly that – to take responsibility for my own emotional life. Instead of whining like I did as a child and teenager that things were just too hard and giving up easily, CBT points you in the direction of helping yourself through your own efforts.

## *Becoming conscious of your actions*

Understanding your actions is important before you embark on any new project.

Your physical body is always trying to achieve a balance, called homeostasis. Your mind too responds to your body's fluctuations, but it's down to you to try to bring your thinking into balance. Up to a point, this is within your control.

Most of the time you operate on a sort of automatic mode as you go about your daily tasks. But if you ignore the warning signs of becoming unsettled or anxious or unhappy for too long, you can tip over into an acute state of negative emotions.

Train yourself to be open to allowing your consciousness to acknowledge when you start to feel 'wobbly'. You can then decide whether you want to act, or whether it's just a minor irritation that may resolve itself in time.

Keep your self-monitoring and analysis at a healthy level. Constantly monitoring your emotions may not always be in your best interests, because you can tip over into obsessive, self-defeating thinking.

If you stray into a crisis mode of thinking, you have difficulty bringing your mind back into balance. Sometimes prescribed medication can help your body back to equilibrium and your mind to be more receptive to returning to balance. If necessary, your GP can help here.

# Seeing the CBT Methods in Action

I encourage you to harness CBT ideas and put them into action for your benefit. You may want to refer to Chapter 2 where I outline the CBT basics. Here I discuss the role of practising, spotting the right time to act, understanding what happens when you get anxious and emotional, and how to combat it.

## Practising before acting

Practising a new way of thinking takes a concerted effort on your part. You may well need to set aside a specific period of time to make regular progress.

As I state at the start of this chapter, you can view applying CBT as being like learning to ride a bike. When things get 'wobbly' at work, see it as your emotional bicycle flagging up a change and a potential pitfall.

Think back to when you learnt to ride a bike. You had to practise for hours to be able to co-ordinate the balance, steering, braking and speed.

Sure, someone introduces you to the bike and gives you instruction, but then you have to go off on your own to try it out. The more you practise, the more skilful you become. After a while, the sequencing and skills become automatic. But the only way to crack the skill is to practise, practise, practise. You always need to pay attention and watch out for pitfalls, unexpected events and signs of mechanical faults. If you start wobbling, you pay more attention and work to rebalance.

You're bound to come across difficult situations in your life, but by discovering how to examine your thinking so that you can detect the faults, and then apply your CBT toolkit from Chapter 3, you give yourself more chance of doing less damage. So keep your toolkit handy in your emotional bike's saddlebags! At times you may want to use CBT in situ, when a tricky or uncomfortable situation arises. Be aware of your key trigger that you're starting to feel any of the following uncomfortable negative feelings (or any other descriptions of being in a state of anxiety):

- Agitated
- Anxious
- Blue
- Bothered
- Butterflies in the stomach (the problem of moths in the mouth probably just need some 'mothwash'!)
- Depressed
- Distressed
- Disturbed
- Flustered
- Frantic
- Fretful (one for guitarists)
- Frightened
- In a stew (in the sense of being 'in a tizz', not in a cannibal's pot – even CBT has its limits for potential rescue!)
- Malcontent
- Miserable
- Mixed up
- Perturbed
- Rattled
- Shocked
- Shook up (or 'All shook up', as Elvis had it)
- Shot to pieces, feeling 'in bits'
- Startled
- Stunned
- Taken aback
- Thrown
- Tied up in knots (you are into nautical pursuits)
- Trembling
- Troubled
- Uneasy
- Upset
- Worried sick

# *Realising that the time has come to act*

When I was learning CBT, I discovered that the most helpful way to understand it was to look at real-life examples where people had applied CBT in their lives. Over time, I also found from practical experience that understanding and applying CBT techniques actually works. Both these experiences helped me to have the confidence to use it.

### *Hitting the road*

After a while, you need to put away the training manual and try the new skill out. After all, reading about how to ride a bike isn't the same as actually riding one. Any child knows that you need to get on that bike and try to ride it.

When you get home with a cut knee because you wobbled and fell off, you may think about what went wrong. For example, what didn't you pay attention to that would've reduced your chances of tumbling off?

What can you decide to try to do next time to make your bike riding smoother to reduce the chances of repeating falling? When you experience a painful impact, you reflect on your behaviours so as to improve next time.

You may even decide that bike riding isn't for you – that it's too risky and you want to avoid future pain.

You always have a choice. But some of your decisions may in time turn out to be self-limiting. If you decide to give up riding a bike, you then limit your experiences. Think of all the great trips you can have if you persevere through the discomfort zone until you become more skilled at bike riding.

### *Conquering the fear*

Sometimes people engage in self-defeating behaviours in order to avoid risk and discomfort. So, too, with your own thinking. You may decide not to apply for a job for fear of being turned down. Perhaps you don't sign up for a new course for fear of finding it too hard. Maybe you're too lacking in confidence to offer to lead a seminar.

Some of your choices and decisions come from your fear. But CBT can help you work through your fears, rationalise your thinking and prepare you to want to go through the discomfort zones so that you can move forward.

I used to be scared of driving on motorways and avoided routes that included them. As a result I often added many miles to a journey and took much longer than necessary. As part of my CBT training, I chose to try to overcome this fear. CBT training courses aren't all academic and book learning!

My teacher made students do practical assignments to put the theory into action. I studied my notes from class in detail. I read them over and over again, to understand what I needed to do to implement the CBT method.

I had to do a 90-mile journey to attend an important meeting in Bristol. It started at 8:30 a.m. and no public transport would get me there in time. I couldn't go the night before due to an important family event.

My two options were to:

✔ Not attend the meeting and as a consequence put my job at risk.

✔ Drive in my car.

Taking country roads would've added hours and so I decided to prepare myself to use CBT to do the drive. I was anxious and very uncomfortable, but I'd applied all the reasoning and rationalising techniques, which prepared me to expect levels of anxiety and discomfort.

On the day, the weather was atrocious: rain, wind and dark skies. I started thinking up other excuses not to use the motorway. But I reread the CBT notes and steeled myself to go.

Spoiler alert! I did it! I was pretty sweaty at first, but as the miles rolled by I became less anxious and settled into the drive.

## *Speaking louder than words – with actions!*

I learnt from practical experience that understanding and applying CBT techniques actually worked.

When you're thinking of doing something that you find stressful, don't just read about doing it: do it! However great you are at reading all about CBT, and whatever a good idea you agree it seems, at some point you have to move from intellectualising to acting. By doing so, you come to know when you've truly changed your thinking – when you genuinely feel different.

You can't fool yourself. Your body gives you tell-tale signs when you haven't truly changed your thinking and beliefs. While you're still anxious, all sweaty palms and tense neck, it means that you're still working hard to change your thinking. But when the new thinking and rational preferences truly become part of your new thinking, and you honestly accept your new outlook, you don't have the symptoms of anxiety.

Expect to spend time learning the CBT method. The principles seem simple but you do need to work at them. Reading and agreeing with something doesn't mean that you've really understood it. You need to invest the time, decide to pay attention and then try it out.

This chapter includes examples for you to model your own experiences on or to use for attacking future struggles.

### Observing the thinking–feeling link in operation

Every day you experience many different feelings. They come and go and mostly you don't pay too close attention to them.

Sometimes, however, you're suddenly aware of a particularly strong feeling, such as one of great euphoria if you've just won the lottery (I can dream!). Equally, your attention can be drawn to the fact that you're experiencing a flash of negative feelings, which can stop you in your tracks. For example, if you're in danger of stepping out in front of a speeding car, or you hear the sound of branches breaking overhead, your attention focuses on the imminent danger and you experience a huge wave of fearful emotion.

In a sense your body is physically taking action, often unhelpfully, which in turn impels you to act. If your action is to implement a helpful CBT-based response, you can quell the body's excessive reaction. In Chapter 2 when I set out the CBT steps, I mention a 'holding pattern' strategy you can use to help. Here is an action I took when making my way home from Docklands on the tube train in London. The train stopped in the tunnel underneath the River. I started to feel sweaty, panicky and light-headed; I had always had some symptoms of claustrophobia in enclosed spaces. I began to realise I was trapped in a tunnel, the doors were locked shut, there was no way out onto the electrified tracks and a huge weight of water was bearing down above. Once I recognised that my thinking was triggering this stress response and these physical symptoms, I decided to use a holding technique of deep breathing, slowly in and out, and then use a distraction technique in the moment to help calm myself down. I got out the newspaper and started reading it. As my anxiety levels levelled out, I looked at my irrational thoughts which had set off this response. The ultimate fear came from thinking 'Oh no I am trapped, I won't be able to breathe. I will die, I must not die'. The rational thinking changes I needed to work on were, I would prefer not to die, but I can stand being stuck in this train, it is uncomfortable, but unlikely that the air will run out . . . and how is my current thinking helping me? The more anxious I make myself, the more likely I am to start shallow breathing and make myself feel light-headed.

### Viewing the body's reaction

Your body reacts in the following way to perceived threats:

- ✔ I feel, therefore I think.
- ✔ I feel, therefore I perceive.
- ✔ I feel, therefore I make conclusions.

The result is fear and anxiety. When you feel such sensations (emotions), they're as a result of changes in your body chemistry. Check out the nearby sidebar 'A look inside your body'.

# A look inside your body

Some of the chemical changes in your body include changes in levels of: adrenalin, endorphins, serotonin, dopamine and oxytocin.

These chemicals and hormones are associated with certain emotions, such as anger, fear, stress, pleasure, happiness, love and pain.

The ever-changing states of your emotions seem to indicate that they're in a constant state of process. You may feel a 'gut reaction' to something that happens and maybe start to feel 'butterflies' in your stomach or have a general sense of anxiety or fear.

Many ideas and theories have been put forward in science with regard to the origin of these reactions and feelings. With sophisticated medical analysis and machines that can scan the human brain to see which parts 'light up' when people experience different emotions, science is discovering exactly what's happening when you 'feel something'. The neurotransmitters responsible for communicating messages from your brain to various parts of your body send out warning signals when a threat is near.

You constantly encounter potential threats in your environment. Your thinking and interpretation of those events can cause your brain to see them as repetitive threats to your wellbeing. Your body therefore releases the chemicals and affects the feelings you experience:

- Your bus is late: 'Oh no, I'm going to be late and miss that meeting'.

- You're stuck in a traffic jam: 'I'm running late for that appointment'.

- You miss breakfast: 'I'm going to have low blood sugar and not be able to concentrate; I'll feel edgy and grumpy at work'.

- Your computer system is down: 'I can't pick up emails; I'll miss the deadline for the submission'.

- Your company's quarterly figures are down: 'This may mean redundancies'.

## Feeling the effects

As your thoughts spiral into imagining worse and worse scenarios and possible consequences (check out the next section for a fuller description of this process), the anxiety levels in your body rise and an outpouring of adrenalin takes place due to the mind–body link. Your body thinks that you're under increasing threats. You start feeling the effects of the hormones.

Your body can't maintain this level of chemical fallout forever. You can have a panic attack, which is an expression of extreme anxiety with the result of partial immobilisation of your body and mind. In other words, you 'freeze'.

The body has pumped loads of adrenalin to prime your major muscles to fight, flee or freeze. It's a natural, if unhelpful, response. On average, it lasts between 5 and 10 minutes. The body is unable to keep pouring adrenalin into the blood stream and so the levels start to go down.

As your thoughts start to spiral into the catastrophising stage of 'what ifs', 'that would be terrible' and 'I couldn't stand it if that happened', you start to get symptoms: racing heart, feeling light-headed, sweating. This biofeedback can then feed your fears even more with thoughts: 'I'm going to faint', 'I'm having a heart attack', 'I'm going crazy' or 'I'm going to die'. This thinking route increases your fear and feeds the anxiety and even more adrenalin is pumped into your body, exacerbating the symptoms and even more extremely unhelpful thinking:

- ✔ 'I'm going to have a total panic attack; people will think I'm really weird'.
- ✔ 'I'll faint and fall in the road or in front of the train'.
- ✔ 'I'll make a complete idiot of myself'.
- ✔ 'No-one will help me if I freak out and I'll die right here'.

But things don't have to go this way, because it's all down to your perception of events. Your thinking and interpretation of events are what give rise to the unsettling feelings, not the events themselves.

Consider this scenario. You and your cat are standing at the bus stop. Well, you're standing up – shuffling anxiously from foot to foot, because the bus is running late. Your cat, on the other hand, is sitting calmly – unperturbed, disinterested yet strangely knowing! Why is this?

- ✔ You interpret the event as a threat to you, because you can think about being late and the consequences of others judging you harshly. Colleagues may complain about you and generally work will be a nightmare all day.
- ✔ Your cat has no perception of being late for work and so doesn't perceive any threat. (Being a cat, he doesn't even know what 'work' is.)

If you change your thinking about the bus being late to, 'Oh well, it's unfortunate, and although I don't like being late for work, it's just one of those annoying things', you don't make yourself overly anxious but just experience a healthy concern. You can calm yourself before emotions build to the position when your body feels the need to react with a flood of chemicals.

## *Spiralling out of control: Negative thoughts running wild*

Generalised anxiety can lurk beneath the surface and give you a feeling of foreboding and general unease. Your thinking can sometimes seem to spiral off seemingly out of your control; it can appear to have a mind of its own, separate from you! You can feel as though you can't stop thinking about negative consequences that may happen and how awful it would be and 'what if' this happened and 'what if' that happened. You build yourself up into a state of massive anxiety and make yourself very distressed.

## *Spiralling negative thoughts*

Unfortunately, if you're like many people, you're probably quite adept at this process, setting off a chain of thoughts in which you think about different possible future scenarios and how each one leads to something even worse with terrible consequences. When your mind acts in this way, you need to counteract it with CBT. Sometimes you discern a specific cause for the anxiety spiral, such as an event in the world around you, perhaps at work; other times you can suddenly find that you're focusing on something 'in your head'. Whether you know the cause or not, the effect is the same: unease or panic as your thinking progresses through various stages of 'Oh no, what if?'

But if you allow yourself some time to reflect on what you're worrying about, you can help relieve the tension; you can deconstruct your thinking and attitudes by bringing them into the present.

Here's the sort of thinking I mean: 'Well, if I'm honest, I'm actually a bit worried about this . . . and this . . . and this too . . .'.

I say, bring it up and bring it on! Use the CBT toolkit (refer to Chapter 3) to weigh up the possibilities, hypothetically, as a written exercise. You can take yourself through the worst scenarios and rationalise your irrational thinking to a point of acceptance and a logical calmer state. Anticipating what may happen and working through it when you're in a calm non-threatening environment can help you prepare.

Allow yourself to bring into your conscious mind the things that are bubbling underneath and worrying you: analyse them, rationalise them, accept them and move on.

Remember a time when you were sitting still, maybe at home or on a bus or driving along, when suddenly a thought pops into your head that starts to send you into a spin:

1. Remember the trigger.

2. Recall your first thought and then the next thought.

3. Consider how your thinking progressed.

4. Think about the worst outcome you thought of.

5. Remember how you felt.

This progression of chaining your negative thoughts can lead to a full-blown panic attack in some people (I describe the chemical realities behind this reaction in the preceding section). Therefore, discovering how to recognise the start of the spiral is vital in stopping the potential progression in its tracks. Otherwise, this way of thinking gets worse and worse, feeding and fueling your anxiety levels to a point where you can't think straight at all.

## Halting the unhelpful thoughts

Whoa there tiger! As I state in the preceding section, finding a way to halt spiralling negative thoughts as they start to rise is much healthier for you.

Using CBT methods, you can employ a technique to hold or stop the negative thinking, which helps the body to cease pouring in the adrenalin so that you don't reach a panic state.

You need to be on the lookout for when you start this type of negative thinking. Only you can do it, because only you know what you're feeling.

When other people, such as work colleagues, seem to be coping perfectly well, you can even add to your own negativity by comparing yourself to them. But they aren't you, so these comparisons are unhelpful.

## Applying the ABC model

Only you know when you start feeling 'wobbly'; and only you can launch CBT to the rescue!

Here's a reality check that's at the centre of CBT thinking: no certainties exist in your work life. Nothing says that just because you want opportunities, promotions, sufficient resources, and fair and honest people to work with, you're going to get them.

Hanging on to your internal beliefs that life should be this way or that way, when clearly it isn't, just means that you upset yourself and make yourself unhappy.

Take action: ask yourself how worrying and making yourself anxious is going to help you, others at work or your family.

You may know the answer already: it isn't. It's fruitless and damaging to your emotional health and happiness. Therefore, implement your CBT knowledge:

1. Change your thinking.

2. Adopt healthy preferences.

3. Keep your anxiety levels lower.

4. Rationalise your thinking.

5. Release yourself to behave in new, constructive ways, which are in your own and other people's best interests.

6. Act upon what's within your control and don't dwell on things outside of your control.

7. Be the best you can, within reason.

Using the fear of driving on the motorway as an example (check out the earlier section, 'Conquering the fear'), here's how I applied the CBT ABC method from Chapter 2. Of course, the steps are generally applicable to your own struggle as well:

1. Name the feeling: Anxiety! Boy, was I aware that I was feeling anxious!

2. Identify the event that triggered the feeling: The thought of driving on the motorway – terrifying!

3. Work out the thinking and beliefs that give rise to the anxiety: I mustn't die in a crash on the motorway. In my case, I needed to identify my beliefs and attitudes to driving on the motorway. I became my own detective for unhelpful beliefs, looking for the 'should, ought or must' thinking, or 'should not, ought not or mustn't' thinking.

The fast connections in your mind process the situation or thought you're focusing on and becoming anxious about. They seem to log into an irrational thinking mode and take you to the worst scenario. As a result, you can be surprised at the huge leap you make from feeling anxious to thinking something as extreme as 'I mustn't die in a crash'. I certainly was when my CBT teacher identified my belief.

Therefore, I'd like to look in more detail at Step 3 of the list, which involves identifying and disputing the unhelpful belief:

✔ Identifying the belief: In my case, this was 'I mustn't drive on the motorway, because I may crash and be hurt or even lose my life . . . that would be terrible; I must live a long life'.

✔ Disputing the belief: To combat your particular belief, I suggest that you tell yourself a relevant version of what my CBT teacher said to me:

*Who said you must lead a long life [or never have work upsets, tough times, unexpected changes and so on]? There are no certainties in life that say this will automatically be true. If you insist on your complete safety at all times, then it is likely you'll avoid anything that you think might prevent you from living to an old age. This will result in you limiting your life experiences. Instead change your absolute belief that you must not crash or die on the motorway [or whatever your personal fear or anxiety is] to a healthy preference, thinking along the lines of, 'I would*

> *prefer not to have a crash or even die, but I have choices: I can either spend my life avoiding motorway driving and limit where I go or add lengthy journey times and mileage, or I can face my fear, go through the discomfort zone and accept that there are no certainties – but making myself over-anxious will not help. I will practise rationalising my thinking, bringing down the anxiety levels and fear by actually doing the driving.*

You can need a lot of preparation and practice of going through the ABC stages in your head before getting to the point where you act. But this exercise showed me that the CBT method can work – and I hope it convinces you too.

# Reflecting on and Tackling Your Tricky Areas

No, this heading doesn't imply that the section is about using a mirror to dry yourself thoroughly after a shower! Instead, it's about learning to focus on your own problems at work. Allowing yourself to remember difficult times and acknowledge that now, looking back, you can see how things got so out of control is a useful thing to do.

Although people may advise you 'not to go looking for trouble', preparing for possible future adversity can be a great way to anticipate potentially upsetting situations and mentally get yourself ready to deal with them.

In therapy sessions, I often encourage clients to identify an event that's worrying them – something that hasn't happened, but about which they're making themselves anxious because they're envisaging negative things.

Here I discuss looking at past problems, rather than hiding from or repressing them, and then using that experience to combat present ones.

 Try this, what I call, my 'if I knew then, what I know now', exercise. Thinking back over your past behaviour when you encountered a tough time can be helpful when learning CBT. You could have a go at reviewing what happened, how upset you were, and how you would have dealt with it differently if you had some knowledge of CBT methods.

In an interview for a job I once went to, I made myself highly anxious thinking about what sort of person I thought the employers wanted for this post. I tried to second guess the answers they wanted all the way through. I wasn't really being me. Also when I am anxious I look pretty serious and don't smile much. Someone else was offered the job. I came second on qualifications and experience. The original person turned down the job and then they offered it to me. After I had been in post a few months, the manager called me in. She said if they had realised how friendly, and warm and flexible I was I would have got that job hands down in the first round. When I think about that in CBT terms, I was being who I thought I 'should' be and in fact this didn't help. Since I trained in CBT, I have viewed job interviews very differently. They are a two-way process, be yourself and they will be choosing the real, self-accepting you, not a version you think they are looking for. CBT helps you to be more confident because you work on accepting yourself.

1. Choose a past tricky situation when you felt negative emotions.

2. Insert the type of thinking that results from: 'I could've dealt with that situation in a better way if I'd had some understanding of CBT'.

3. Consider how you'd have preferred things to be.

4. Accept that 'that was then', and you accept it today as an unfortunate experience.

5. Remind yourself that dwelling on the past and feeling bad about it today doesn't help you.

## Handling problem situations

As crystal balls for seeing the future and time machines haven't yet been invented, any feelings of unease that you experience about things that only may happen are based on your hunches. You look at what's happened before and base these foreboding images on that, or perhaps you use your imagination (and you can very successfully) to wind yourself up into a state of anxiety/fear/panic/depression about what may be.

Even so, these feelings are real and exist in the here and now. The more you imagine these terrible things, the more worried, upset and possibly fearful you make yourself.

Quite simply, give yourself a break. Stop such spiralling negative thoughts that take you up into the stratosphere of disaster and doom. Instead, put CBT to work to rationalise how likely it is that these things will happen. Plus, if the worst scenario occurs and they do happen, work out a plan for how you'll deal with them.

Get out your CBT toolkit from Chapter 3, apply it generously in the safety of your own home or the therapist's clinic room, reapply whenever the thoughts reoccur and wait for the uncomfortable feelings to subside.

Your thoughts are within your control; the future isn't.

### Identifying any patterns in behaviour

As you do the various CBT exercises and practice that I describe through-out this book, you may find that you start to spot repeated patterns in your responses to events at work – and in your overall behaviour. This is where you bring in your detective skills.

You've read it before, but it bears repeating: if you always do what you always did, you always get what you always got.

For example, if you're always the first to volunteer to take on work-experience students, but then you find that you get behind with your own work because you're continually looking after the students, perhaps you want to consider your natural compulsion to offer to help others. Volunteering can bring you enormous satisfaction, but this sort of compassionate and generous act may not always be in your best interests if you continue to jeopardise your other work.

You don't have to volunteer every time just because you're good at something: occasionally saying no is okay. You may feel uncomfortable at first, but in the long run you're more likely to achieve your own goals.

Only you can take responsibility for your own actions.

### *Changing your repeated responses*

After you identify aspects of your behaviour that aren't in your own best interests, you can spend some time examining the following:

- ✔ Being aware of your actions
- ✔ Whether those repeated patterns of behaviour are helpful to you
- ✔ Whether you want to discontinue or moderate them
- ✔ What your thinking behind these behaviours is (by using the CBT ABC model of enquiry in Chapter 2)
- ✔ What to change your thinking/beliefs to

You can then start practising your new approach in earnest.

When you start making a concerted effort to keep an eye on your emotional life at work, and applying some CBT techniques to help you reduce destabilising feelings, you can't assume that all will be well. You need to maintain this level of awareness for whenever something difficult comes up or is coming up in the future.

Your default thinking mode of making yourself worried, depressed, guilty, angry, ashamed and other negative emotions may want you to revert back to thinking unhelpful things. You need to keep up the training and practice to continue to improve at unsettling those unsettling feelings and moving into rational thinking and new constructive behaviours.

Ensure that you devote time to allowing yourself to think about future events and situations when you find that you're starting to worry about them.

Merely deciding that 'I don't want to think about it' is more likely to make 'it' pop up in your thoughts more often.

### *Deploying your CBT toolkit*

When you're armed with the CBT toolkit from Chapter 3, you always have an awareness of it and can employ it at work whenever your view of a situation requires a bit of tweaking to get you through the day. The great thing about CBT is that you can use it for past, present and future emotional ups and downs. I like it because it's:

- ✔ Adaptable
- ✔ Consistent
- ✔ Free to use
- ✔ Light enough to carry with you at all times
- ✔ Logical
- ✔ Practical
- ✔ Science-based (with the ideas of rational and irrational thinking)
- ✔ Universal

Face the fear and CBT it anyway! Armed with your CBT toolkit, you can imagine the future scenario and work out the possible feelings that you have around it before using the ABC framework (from Chapter 2).

Colin is the manager of a healthcare service. The Managing Director tells him that as a result of a review of the company's performance, the firm has to make cutbacks. Colin is tasked with gathering the employees together and making the announcement. He feels himself starting to get into a terrible state of nerves and anxiety. But he knows that using the CBT toolkit can help him to plan how to deal with this situation and reduce his anxiety levels.

Here's how Colin goes about using the ABC approach:

- ✔ A (the activating event): Announcing the cutbacks in the budget to the team.
- ✔ B (his beliefs and thinking): 'I shouldn't have to be the one doing this'. More fully:

    *I shouldn't have to give the employees this difficult news. It's awful, I can't stand it. They'll hate me and think I'm responsible for it all. They'll think it's my fault for not organising the business better. People may lose their jobs. Families will be affected. They'll think I'm a rotten person who doesn't care. I hate myself. I'm weak.*

- ✔ C (the emotional consequence): Anxiety.

Colin starts by recognising C (the emotional consequence) – profound anxiety. Every time he thinks about having to stand up and tell the workforce, he feels sick, anxious, headachy, sweaty and fearful. He wakes up early in the morning and can't get back to sleep. He's edgy, almost as if he's going to burst into tears. He dreads going in to work.

The A (activating event) is having to stand up in front of everyone. At first glance, Colin thinks that A is causing C. But on reflection with CBT-inspired rationalisation, he realises that A isn't causing C. The impeding announcement isn't making him anxious; he's making himself anxious because of the B – his beliefs about the announcement.

Therefore, he sees that he needs to look for the 'should, ought or must' thinking. B – I should not have to give them this difficult news. It's awful, I can't stand it. They will hate me and think I am responsible for all of this. They will think it is my fault for not organising the business better. People may lose their jobs. Families will be affected. They will think I am a rotten person who doesn't care. I hate myself. I am weak.

He recognises that his beliefs about the situation and attitudes towards himself are giving rise to the anxious feelings and his physical symptoms. His tendency to judge himself harshly lies behind his anxiety. He jumped irrationally from learning that he has to make an announcement to deciding that he's a rotten, weak and pretty worthless person. He ends up deciding that everyone will hate him.

Colin deconstructs his beliefs. Here's the new Colin self-speak:

> *Although breaking the bad news is a tough call, someone needs to do it. Nowhere does it say that I absolutely will never have to be the bearer of bad news. Insisting to myself that it 'shouldn't' be is irrational thinking. Just because I think it shouldn't happen in no way guarantees that it won't. Instead of trying to hang on to my irrational belief, I'm going to apply the CBT attitude-changing toolkit and work to change this unhelpful attitude to a rational attitude.*

> *I'd prefer not to have to do this. It's unfortunate and I don't like it but it's not the end of the world. I can, in fact, stand it. It's tough but how is winding myself up into a state of high anxiety helping? I need to accept it, get on with it and move on.*

> *In terms of my thinking spiralling into generalising that everyone will think it's my fault and think badly of me, there's no way I can be responsible for how others think. If I condemn myself as incompetent and worthless then I'm in fact agreeing with them. I'm a fallible human being who may make mistakes and if I have, it's unintentional. I accept myself as a worthwhile human being who has a tough job to do. Some may not like it but I can't have everyone's approval. If some people do view me negatively then it's not the end of the world. I can accept it. I won't like it, but I can survive this.*

I see clients often treating themselves more harshly than they would a good friend. They'd show far more compassion for a friend or work colleague than they give to themselves.

Imagine for a moment that Colin looks at the situation as if his workmate had to make the announcement. He may say something like:

> *I don't think I'd condemn another workmate as being responsible for the difficulties at work and consider him as a weak person. I'd see that it's just a job and someone has to make tough choices and that railing against him and the world won't help. I certainly wouldn't want to see him making himself ill with worry over it.*

You really can have no idea what other people will think. You can conjecture and try to anticipate until the cows come home, but you can't possibly know. Worrying yourself in anticipation of an event or reaction that may or may not happen can't possibly be any good to you. Instead, when you use CBT to rationalise your fear and worries about events, you can face the future with confidence.

# *Drawing up a CBT Plan of Action*

You may find that making a plan of action to be calm is helpful to you (especially if you intend to use CBT at work, which is the subject of Chapters 13, 14, and 15). If you can prepare yourself before you get into work, it will help you to avoid becoming upset. A colleague of mine decided her pre work mantra was 'I do not want to upset myself over work'. She would think ahead to what she would be doing that day, anticipate the potentially difficult meetings or list of 'to do' things piling up and mentally calm herself before the day started. She knew that if she had slept badly or was feeling a bit under the weather, her tolerance levels would be lowered, and she might be more likely to 'snap' at people or show her irritation with colleagues either verbally of nonverbally. She decided to be extra alert to keeping herself as calm as she could through repeating her mantra in her head and deep breathing. She would also try to smile more during the day, knowing that you cannot frown and smile at the same time and that even forced smiling helps raise your happy hormones. She would focus, apply her techniques and finish with 'and rest'.

Try it; you may find it works for you.

Your action plan may include the following entries:

✔ When I'm feeling okay, this is how I am: _____

_____

✔ Be on the alert for these triggers: _____ (Note how you intend to be alerted to impeding upset.)

✔ How I'll know if I'm anxious/worried/upset/fearful or other negative feeling: _____ (This covers how you'll recognise when you're feeling unsettled.)

✔ Strategies I can use to help me to focus: _____ _____ (Note down what strategies you want to implement, such as a holding pattern strategy.)

✔ Any other considerations, or previous patterns of behaviour I need to take into account in my campaign against upsetting myself at work:

_____

_____ (For example, now or later decisions to use the CBT.)

---

# Deciding to be an active learner

If you've come across other types of counselling, CBT can seem quite different. For example, counselling doesn't ask you to write things down, plan goals, do homework and have practical strategies and conscious coping skills at the ready.

Perhaps it helps to look at changing your psychological state as follows: People have the resources within them to find their own way in life, and as they process what they experience they get insights into what's happening for them and how they prefer to be. You may find that

you'd prefer a 'less teaching' type of therapy to help you when you're struggling, or at different times in your life you may find that some types feel more appropriate for you. There's no right or wrong. You're unique and you're encouraged to go with what feels best for you.

CBT is an open and transparent therapy. You're involved in your own therapy and development along the way. Personal and professional responsibility is simply another choice you can make.

# Chapter 13

# Seeing CBT as a Positive Force in the Workplace

## In This Chapter

▶ Using CBT to help employees through work changes

▶ Looking at how a company can improve performance with CBT

▶ Considering relationships, betrayal and survival

*D*iscovering CBT and how its methods and ideas can help you to reduce uncomfortable feelings that arise at work is clearly very useful: it's the foundation of this whole book! But you rarely work in isolation, and so if you can spread the knowledge and understanding of CBT principles to work colleagues and bosses, you can find that it improves the general working conditions across your team and even at management levels.

In this chapter, I discuss doing just that. I describe how companies can use CBT to help employees cope with the disorientating changes that accompany transition management: that is, takeovers, mergers, restructures and the like.

In the modern business world, such events happen more and more frequently. Although they're always stressful and disrupting for employees, the ways in which firms go about handling such changes directly affects the level of impact on staff members' wellbeing, motivation, morale, and so on. In short, companies can handle changes well or poorly. But what is sure is that CBT can be an immensely useful tool for helping the process to run as smoothly as possible.

I also describe how CBT can help firms to improve their public image and their employees' loyalty and performance, and the role it can play in dealing with relationship issues. I am not suggesting that you all become fully fledged CBT professionals and have a complete career change – only if CBT has really grabbed you by reading this book! What I am saying is that knowledge of some helpful techniques based on CBT might add to your skills base when interacting with teams and projects

I base the content of this chapter on requests from participants in my CBT seminars and workshops about how they can reach a greater audience. I support the text with examples from participants' real-life experiences and evaluations of the courses. I'm constantly surprised by the way courses develop at the request of employees and are then taken up by other departments and teams, including when parallel courses for management are rolled out across an organisation.

# Using CBT in Transition Management

Fast-moving, fast-paced business environments, with their economic uncertainties, takeovers, outsourcing, redundancies, 'rationalisations' and transitions, are always part of people's work experience.

Everyone can be affected by these transitions or changes, from employees at all levels through to managers, bosses and MDs. There are always plenty of unsettling feelings around changes at work and anything that can help manage the changes more smoothly is usually welcomed. The changes, by their very nature will create new situations, uncertainties and turbulence. There is not really a blueprint for how to implement changes in organisations. Every situation will be new and different. Everyone will be feeling her way around. One thing that can be a constant is using the same approach to dealing with the emotional impacts of the changes. CBT can be tool for individuals and teams.

In this section, I discuss the importance of keeping employees, managers and even the MD informed and onside, as well as the need for managers to communicate effectively and handle objections sensitively.

Here's the basis of the scenario that I present in this section, which shows you how using CBT as part of a workshop was found to help the employees with the emotional upheavals taking place during the restructuring at work.

I was invited along to a meeting at my employer, which had requested consultation regarding its concern for employees. The firm was about to announce a significant outsourcing of work and reorganisation.

My brief was to provide practical help for transition management for the staff. The company's base was in the United States and it already had pre-written courses and workshops on the subject. I had a copy to review and took it along with a view to proposing it as appropriate for the company's current UK needs.

# Moving from the individual to the team: Engaging employees

You may be becoming a covert to CBT and think it would be great to share amongst colleagues, if it is helping you: I have always had something I call a 'compulsive helping gene'. Since being a child, I have always wanted to join in and help when I can see someone would like some help. I guess I was so grateful that CBT had helped me, I became a bit enthusiastic about sharing what I had learned. I have often found that when clients have found the CBT sessions and the books they have read helpful, they too want to share their new knowledge. After all, if we didn't share discoveries and inventions, we would still each be trying to work out how to light a fire. Below I outline how I found an opportunity to incorporate my CBT knowledge more widely in a work situation than just working with individuals in therapy sessions.

I'd worked in California and had experienced its culture differences and modes of business practices. Although the firm's transition management package was well-written and structured, I felt there was scope to include a practical therapeutic helping strategy – you got it! CBT.

During the meeting with the HR department, I mentioned that I thought introducing some CBT principles and practices to employees would be help-ful for managing the workplace changes. Luckily, the head of HR was well-acquainted with CBT and she was interested to discover more about how we could apply it in the current situation. Initially, the workshops were to be just for the employees to help them cope with the changes.

Tailoring the training to a company's situation is important. The company reviewed the workshop and requested a pilot programme. I presented the workshop to three different groups of employees from different departments and evaluated the responses, which were positive.

Here is a summary of comments taken from reading the participants' evalu-ation forms: You may want to bear them in mind if you ever consider doing something similar as an endorsement of how the workshops actually helped the employees.

- ✔ A very practical and useful tool to help with the current insecurities.
- ✔ It made understanding what I can do in these transition times to help myself and my colleagues to make the best of this situation.
- ✔ I'll be able to use these CBT principles in my personal life as well as my professional life.
- ✔ I feel much less anxious about all the changes now.

✔ I've learnt that there are some things within my control and some things outside my control. Worrying about what I can't control won't help me.

✔ The workshop helped me to rationalise my thinking around how I feel I should be treated in work and reduce my anger at having these changes imposed. I understand it's appropriate to feel annoyed and disappointed at the potential changes, but winding myself up into a state of anxiety and anger won't help me or the situation.

The company set up a programme of workshops on two sites and over 40 groups received the transition management training course. The evaluations continued to be positive and sometimes comments were included, along the following lines:

✔ I'd like our management to receive this training too, so that we can all 'sing from the same sheet'.

✔ This course really opened up communications between colleagues. We need to have the same communication with our managers.

The positive feedback meant that the requests for the scheme to be rolled out to senior staff and managers were acted upon and realised.

## Devising a manager's special

One of the concerns that team leaders and managers frequently voice is that they don't always know how to go about announcing changes to staff members and how to deal with the fallout from angry employees. Of course, managers are usually well aware of their responsibilities for employees' emotional as well as physical wellbeing, as stated in Employment Law legislation, and they're often genuinely concerned at the effects of the changes on their colleagues.

Teaching basic CBT and counselling skills can be a great help in this situation. Managers appreciate having confidence in proven techniques and skills that they can use when talking with their teams. Knowing how to communicate with employees in ways that are unlikely to make the situation worse is highly beneficial. Managers can help people feel that they're being heard and that they have an opportunity to express their feelings in a non-threatening and supportive environment.

I continue the anecdote from the preceding section in order to show you how useful it can be to widen the circle of understanding. When people share the same workshops and material, it means they have common ground. Very often there is suspicion and mistrust around what different sections of a company are hearing and the spiral of rumours can start to spin out of control. I found that many managers were themselves uncomfortable around what they were able to disclose to their teams and what they were required to keep confidential. Their experiences around these changes included an extra layer of anxiety because of their feelings of responsibility to their colleagues. A separate CBT course that covered the basics and also tried to address their extra concerns around how they could communicate information to their teams with the least possible extra disruption was offered.

A review meeting was held to update the current progress of the CBT courses and discuss future programmes. The company already had another management consultancy onboard for the training of the managers, but repeated requests for management to receive the 3-hour CBT-based transition courses (from the preceding section) led to the company enquiring whether I'd formulate a manager's version, expanding it to a 5-hour workshop, and present it for consultation.

I did as asked, including in my proposal training in basic counselling skills, management and leadership theory and practice, as well as more detailed analysis of the process of change within organisations.

The 5-hour 'manager's special' was piloted, reviewed, evaluated and accepted. When the contracts had been signed, the Manager's Transition Management Programme was rolled out nationwide to the various departments within the UK.

## Handling senior staff members' reluctance or opposition

I see quite a few clients in my practice who come for some help in coping with being promoted to a higher position or have started a new job in a managerial post. Sometimes it may feel quite unnerving when you are promoted within an organisation and the colleagues you were once on a level with, you now have to give them directions, organize the projects and make them accountable to you. New manager's posts rarely arrive with built-in training on how to manage this transition. Equally, if you have been appointed to a new company or organisation in a promoted post role, so you have no current knowledge of the setup or people you will be managing, you might feel apprehensive and quite scared! Managers and senior staff are not perfect and have all the answers. They may be struggling just as much as you with the changes and new proposals. They are only human. Sometimes this lack of confidence may present as a reluctance to engage with the team, or in fact blanket opposition to communicate the changes in case they lose their credibility or have to face angry staff. You might find with your understanding of CBT that you can help put forward the case to get some outside trainers to come in and run some CBT-based sessions to help them with their own self-doubts and in turn help their teams to cope with the changes.

This CBT-based training initiative that I continue here from the two preceding sections was delivered from the bottom upwards, from ground-level staff to the senior staff. The different departments held open-forum meetings, where departments that had received the training gave feedback to other departments that were considering providing the training.

This type of spirit of openness frees up communication channels and dispels suspicions and insecurity within and across departments.

I was particularly impressed by the integrity of the participant employees in the 3-hour workshop I describe in the earlier section. Although some of them knew that the changes coming on board might adversely affect their own futures, they were still prepared to give their best to the company and were open and willing to learn about any new ways of how to weather the storm. These compulsory workshops were originally met by some hostility, because not everyone saw taking three hours away from the trading floors to take part in a psychology-based course as a priority. I used to explain that the aim was that the participants would find at least something helpful for the sessions to take away with them. I can honestly say that looking at the evaluation forms they filled in after the sessions, participants reported positively about the usefulness of them.

Here is an introduction I wrote to open a session of CBT-based change management. You may want to consider this approach if ever you find yourself responsible for introducing an outside trainer to a group of people assembled for a compulsory workshop. Some may think this a risky opener as perhaps all the group might walk out during the workshop! I can report I never had anyone walk out. Placing responsibility on your colleagues for their own learning can help them engage more and decide what new learning is relevant to them.

> *I appreciate that you're being asked to take three hours away from your very busy schedules today. I can assure you that I won't be lecturing at you for the whole time, but will include discussions, exercises and group work. If you feel at any time that this is really not helpful for you and not a worthwhile use of your time, then please feel free to sign out and return to your work.*

I then introduce myself and my background. If you find that talking about the course being psychological is met with rolling eyes and preconceptions of it being more 'hippy, dippy' than businesslike, you can add: *This workshop will give opportunities for some interactive practical exercises. Nothing is compulsory; if you feel you don't want to take part in all the dancing and chanting, then please feel free to opt out.*

## Moving from sceptic to advocate

In the dozens of workshops I've delivered, only one participant seemed determined not to pay attention or participate – until we discussed the cycle of loss and the notion of acceptance toward which CBT works. A light seemed to go on and he commented that this idea could apply to people's personal lives, too.

From that moment he was engaged and made some great contributions during the session. He requested extra resources and became almost evangelical in promoting the workshops to other departments. He was one of the people who gave feedback that senior managers should receive these workshops and encouraged others to request the same.

This was a significant learning point for me, too, as a trainer. I did feel quite anxious at the start of the session as this person sat there in the group eating his takeaway lunch as he said he didn't have time to eat before the session. I had flashbacks to working with challenging behaviour from adolescents I had worked with in educational settings. I used my best CBT on myself, considered the options, to ignore him or challenge his behaviour (probably make him worse), to acknowledge his irritation at having to be in the workshop, or call for security to frogmarch him out (only joking). I went for option three: I said he sounded annoyed, with which he agreed. I explained I would prefer that he didn't continue eating in the room, but that was his choice. This was the first time I used the paragraph above with the disclaimer that if at any time anyone felt the workshop was not a worthwhile use of her time, then to sign out and return to work. Some days people may be distracted by their own worries at work, they may not be feeling up to par or they may have had some unsettling news in their life. Interpreting their presenting negative behaviour as a personal slight on you and possibly becoming defensive or dismissive of them will result in you upsetting yourself. Take some time to empathise with the person and acknowledge her behaviour; it may help to calm you down and be in a positive frame of mind to deliver the workshop.

When they realise that I'm not serious about the dancing and chanting – and that I won't be asking them to survive naked in the forest for a month in order to commune with their spirit guide! – people seem to relax. In the spirit of openness and authenticity, which mirrors the CBT ideas, this type of introduction helps participants to engage and take responsibility for their own learning.

## *Including HR in feedback and evaluation of CBT courses*

Anyone running a CBT course or workshop should always provide evaluation forms to participants, and ensure that the feedback is automatically sent to HR and other interested parties within the company. I often find that as well as ticking the option boxes, many participants also write comments.

Record these so that others can see how useful, or otherwise, the session has been.

It can be helpful to give all participants on a CBT course a handbook, which has been specially customised for the course, to allow them to keep a record of it. The appendices can include booklists and lists of resources to encourage people to discover more about CBT. I even offer email addresses to account for any further enquiries and information the participants may require.

## Offering to enlighten the MD on CBT

Large and small companies often send employees on courses, encourage team-building exercises, arrange away-days and generally seek to enhance the communication and share skill sets within the firm. Many successful start-up companies, which go on to become large and thriving organisations, appreciate the need to engage employees and maintain the motivation and enthusiasm for their work by varying their experiences and hoping to help employees feel valued.

Although these experiences are mostly rolled out to mainstream employees, finding managing directors (MDs) participating is more unusual.

But I can't stress enough the importance of keeping MDs in the loop so that they're aware of the activities and outcomes of such, often quite expensive, ventures.

If you can, why not follow what I often do and recommend that the firm incorporates executive CBT coaching. Doing so gives MDs the opportunity to receive feedback on the mood of the employees as well as gain information about the workshops.

## Communicating a Consistent Message throughout Your Company

You can help your organisation and work colleagues to tackle changes and problems when the whole company has similar attitudes to how the issues are viewed and dealt with. This goal is easier to achieve in smaller firms, but when a company offers similar training courses across the company, so that employees and managers hear similar messages, it can help identify and address some of the problems.

Time and time again, I hear the same complaint from employees that the communication within the company is a problem. Different sections of a company may hear different messages from their line managers, or team leaders or whomever they are directly responsible to. Rumours abound and can create havoc. Anything that can help create consistency within the company will help in the long term.

When you intend to spread the CBT word to your employer, whether informally or formally with courses and workshops, you can play an important role in achieving this aim. In this section, I discuss ensuring that your firm is pulling in the same direction, and attending to its culture, public face and how it treats its staff.

## Helping a community to cope with change

A manufacturing company in the UK was facing tough times financially. The firm had been a household name for decades, going from strength to strength over the years.

But things change. In the early 21st century, the company was sold and working practices in some of its UK factories were changed radically. The affected workers experienced much anxiety and distress, because they had to change their shift patterns to accommodate a 24-hour working day. Also, the factories were an integral part of the local community and many families were affected by these changes. As a result, social and community cohesion was undergoing a change. The managing directors of a local branch contacted an employee consulting organisation to see whether it could help with the transition management for its employees. It offered transition management courses, incorporating CBT principles, to the workforce. The working patterns didn't allow them to receive the training during their working hours and so employees signed up to come in on their own time. Over three days, all the employees attended a workshop of their own volition. Such was their concern; they saw it as a potential investment for their own and their families' futures.

The courses were well received and the feedback was positive. The courses had the added value of giving employees the opportunities to air their concerns together and receive practical guidance on how to minimise their anxiety and insecurities. The sense of community was apparent as they discussed their concerns for fellow workers and how they'd all manage this new shift pattern and still look out for each other and their families. The natural rhythm of the community was changing and they were determined to try to reorganise their social lives to ensure continuity of communication and mutual support.

Teaching some of the basics of CBT can be just one of the practical strategies that could help workers during distressing times. A combination of effective communication and a little bit of CBT can go a long way to mitigating discontent.

## *Standardising your company's strategic aims*

*Of all the forces that make for a better world, none is as powerful as hope. Without hope people are only half alive. With hope they dream and think and work.*

— Anonymous

Another aspect of planning and achieving goals can be seen when your company considers its aims and objectives and shares them publicly. Having a consistent policy toward aims and goals can help create cohesion and a hopeful vision.

These can be grouped together and then described as the strategies your company will endeavour to adopt for the company as a whole and also be broken down into smaller aims and goals:

- ✔ Strategic aims: The overall large goals that a company wants to achieve by implementing its identified objectives.
- ✔ Strategic objectives: The smaller steps needed to be able to work towards achieving the overall aims.

The strategic objectives are a detailed analysis of the business plans. In order to facilitate the smooth running and operation of the company, the workforce needs to be onboard.

Clarity in the company's perspectives will create a practical framework for all to work toward.

## *Appraising the work culture*

When applying CBT principles and practices to your workplace, make sure that you include consideration of any issues in the context of the company's culture, such as its views on business ethics and its philosophy as a whole.

Many businesses develop Mission Statements that set out the purpose of the company or organisation. If you have the opportunity, read this document, and in any workshops you take part in, include how you view and plan to implement these goals. Also, if your place of work has explicit guidelines for business ethics and company values, work these aspects into any CBT presentation too: ask participants to consider how they fit in at work, comparing their personal values with their employer's. Check out Chapter 10 for more details on doing this exercise for yourself, which can in turn guide you in leading colleagues to do the same.

Many companies like to support and sponsor good causes in the communities; in fact, sometimes businesses compete to be seen to be supporting ethically sound ventures, locally and globally. Apart from the philanthropic message it gives out, endorsing worthwhile projects also makes good commercial sense. While this may not seem at first to directly link with workshops you might attend, the value of helping others as a company encourages bonding, team spirit and a 'feel good' factor within the company, which is a strong motivator.

## Thinking about your company's reputation

How your company is viewed in the local surroundings and the impact it has globally are increasingly important.

High-speed media opportunities mean that a company can be highly visible in its attitudes towards work practices and how it treats its employees. In addition, customers and pressure groups readily notice environmental issues, such as how ethically your firm sources, markets and sells-on its products. If its workforce is seen to support the company and it demonstrates good working practices and ethical business plans, the result is a healthy working environment and the reputation as a good employer.

Each year, *The Times* newspaper publishes a Top 100 list of small businesses. Here I list the attributes that count towards achieving a place in the much-coveted list. (***Note:*** the 25 Best Big Companies and 100 Best Companies share the same criteria.)

Flip through the following list and notice how many of the categories concern employees' subjective experiences: called the affective components of their jobs. Clearly, employers need to look after employees if they're to attract the most skilled workers. Scoring well on these issues makes good commercial sense too, because high endorsements reflect success and attract investors. A successful company sends out a strong message that it's being managed effectively.

The criteria for the Top 100 small businesses include:

- ✔ Leadership: How employees feel about the head of the company and its senior managers.
- ✔ Wellbeing: How staff members feel about the stress, pressure and balance between their work and home duties.

✔ Giving something back: How much they think that their employers put back into society generally and in the local community.

✔ Personal growth: To what extent staff members feel that they're stretched and challenged by their job.

✔ My manager: How staff members feel towards their immediate boss and day-to-day managers.

✔ My team: How staff feel about their immediate colleagues.

✔ My company: Feelings about the company itself, as opposed to the people they work with.

✔ Fair deal: How happy the workforce is with its pay and benefits.

## Sustaining your firm's human resources

Human resources – the employees and staff of a firm – are a significant and necessary component of the workplace. CBT can help your company to hear a consistent message of a practical way to help yourself and others pull together at work.

Surveys show clearly that how employees feel about where their work – how they're treated, managed and valued – is paramount. Spotting a company that has high staff turnover can be the first indication that all isn't well and that it may not be a place you want to work. The reality is that employees who are satisfied with their jobs are less likely to give them up.

As I discuss in Chapter 10, your job means far more than just the financial rewards. Consider, for example, the lottery winner who still continued to go to work.

Companionship, self-worth and a sense of being valued are significant aspects of having a job. On the flip side, absenteeism can also be an indication that people aren't happy in their job.

Communicating CBT through your company can help make people aware of brewing discontent and also help tackle it, for the benefit of all involved. Here are some of the reasons to watch out for that may lie behind high staff turnover and absenteeism:

✔ Not feeling appreciated

✔ Poor working environment, such as too cold or hot room temperature, inadequate working spaces, problems with equipment, lack of investment in facilities, and health and safety issues

✔ No career prospects

✔ Staff appraisals low on the list of priorities

✔ Inadequate training and supervision

✔ Lack of respect

✔ Poor wage structure

✔ Culture of coercive management

# Facing up to Relationship Issues at Work

Relationships are just as essential at work as they are in your personal life. Unfortunately, for something so important, relationships of all sorts are about as complicated and fraught with problems as anything you can imagine!

How a company treats its employees and how they treat each other can cause a ripple effect out into the community at large, which is why most successful companies prioritise their customer-relations interactions.

When you combine CBT techniques with some knowledge of counseling skills, you can set yourself up to promote healthy customer relations in your workplace.

I used to have many students on the introductory counseling skills courses who reported that doing the course had helped them to deal with the general public in an empathic way without upsetting themselves if there were disputes or confrontations.

It wasn't that all these students were intending to be counsellors, but that they found having knowledge of some counseling skills helpful in their work.

Many companies in service industries run counselling skills training for employees. These skills can be useful and helpful not only in promoting good customer relationships, but also in helping employees protect themselves from too much stress and anxiety when dealing with difficult situations. Check out Chapter 15 for more on counselling skills.

The key aspects for improving your own and your work colleagues' relationship skills involve respect, efficiency and authenticity. Counselling skills help people to:

✔ Detect when others are 'walking the walk and talking the talk', but not being genuine.

✔ Spot insincerity in the tone of voice in a phone call.

✔ Pick up on the body language of others when they aren't really paying attention.

## *Winning customer respect*

High-quality training and respectful attitudes within and outside the workplace create good customer relations. When a firm puts into practice customer-relations training consistently across the company, the result is to win customer respect.

A positive customer experience encourages people to:

✔ Form positive attitudes towards that company

✔ Use the company again

✔ Tell others about the company

Some of the indicators of achieving respect include regular customers returning, fast responses and accurate records being kept and regularly analysed.

Social media means instant feedback and messaging, which can reach many people very quickly. News about poor customer relationships travels fast!

## *Maintaining trust in relationships*

Trust is immensely important in work relationships. A good relationship requires the maintenance of a high level of integrity.

### *Seeing the elements of trust*

In essence, trust implies a consistency of your expectations being met. As a result, when your trust is broken, you experience a whole gamut of negative feelings, some of them quite strong and distressing. You may then find that regaining trust is very hard.

When you think of trust, what words and phrases come to mind? Check out my own list: strength, integrity, confidence, honesty. Also, when you have trust in someone, you:

✔ Believe in that person

✔ Have confidence and hope in that person

✔ Entrust yourself to that person

✔ Don't fear that person

## *Reacting to broken trust*

Sometimes you build up certain relationships in which your positive experiences and interactions lead you to form an attitude of trust and respect. As a result, one act of betrayal can shatter your illusions about, say, a co-worker, manager or even the company as a whole.

Understanding CBT has certainly helped me to reduce emotional disturbances in work situations where betrayal of trust occurs. I wish that I'd had some CBT skills up my sleeve in the past, because I think it would've helped me in the following situation.

This event occurred in my first job as a primary school teacher. It had a strong impact and formed a huge lesson for me: you can't always trust the people you work with.

I went into the staffroom one morning. A disgruntled group of teachers were complaining that the principal wasn't going to be at school that day due to a funeral he had to attend. He'd been away from school frequently that term and the extra burden of responsibilities was beginning to take its toll on other staff. I volunteered that if they felt so strongly about it, they should call a meeting to discuss how best to manage the situation.

I then went off for the day with a party of children on a school trip.

The next day, the principal summoned all staff to the staffroom. He announced that he didn't want any discussion around what he was about to say, but that he was appalled that a member of staff would create a petition complaining about his frequent absences with a view to sending it to the Board of Governors. He said that he couldn't understand why he hadn't been approached personally and he'd never trust that member of staff again. One teacher asked who'd done that. He replied that those who'd signed the petition knew who'd created it. The teacher persisted in knowing because she hadn't seen it.

The principal announced that it was me!

I was shocked.

I tried to protest my innocence but the principal swept from the room and repeatedly refused to discuss the issue. Whoever told him about the petition obviously knew it wasn't true, as did the four teachers who'd been approached to sign it.

This was a huge lesson for me that you cannot always trust the people you work with.

I did ultimately discover who'd told the principal about 'my petition'. She was an older member of staff who apparently held a grudge that I'd been promoted quickly after my probationary year.

I tried to talk to her about it once, but she stayed silent except to say, 'Wasn't I the first to congratulate you after your promotion?' I also went to the principal and assured him that I hadn't created the petition and that I was disappointed he'd believed the lie.

Overall, I was distressed and shocked that people behaved in that way.

I became very upset and dwelled on the event, making myself ill with worry and anxiety.

Today, with my CBT training, I'd view the situation differently. I wouldn't waste so much time dwelling on the event. Instead I'd think along the following lines: People have their own agendas. They can and will say whatever they want. The only control I have is to move towards accepting that this is so. I don't like it, but upsetting myself to the point of depression isn't going to help. I have my own truth and integrity and no-one can take that away from me.

Some of the other staff, who played a part in this 'conspiracy', gave me little gifts over the next few weeks. My conclusion is that some people behave in unfathomable ways. I learnt to be more wary of people's behaviour, but understand that people can behave in manipulative, deceitful ways, out of step with my own code of ethics.

Incidentally, the principal was seen on the TV news the evening of his 'Auntie's funeral' singing in a male voice choir competition, recorded that same day in another part of the country. Ho hum!

The one certainty you have is yourself. If you can anchor yourself with a strong sense of your own ethics, standards and self-belief, that becomes your constant in the changing situations of your working life.

# Chapter 14

# Communicating the Benefits of CBT to Other People

### In This Chapter

▶ Leading the way by how you live

▶ Spreading CBT ideas at work

▶ Knowing when to recommend professional help

. . . . . . . . . . . . . . . . . . . . . . . . . . . . . . . . . . . . . . . . . . . . . . . . . . . . . . .

*W*hen you've experienced the benefits of CBT for yourself, you may feel the urge to spread the good news to people at work. Doing so is a win-win situation, because as I describe in Chapter 13, using CBT more widely in the workplace is useful for you, for your colleagues, for your general working conditions and for creating a consistent, positive culture within a company.

You may be thinking, 'that's all well and good in theory, but how about a few concrete suggestions for going about widening CBT's applications?' Well, since you ask (!), in this chapter I discuss the ways in which you're the best example for CBT's benefits, how to spread the word effectively and sensitively, and how to know when to steer other people towards consulting a medical professional. You can carry out my suggestions in this chapter with confidence, because they're based on my experiences of taking CBT into work situations and case studies of how CBT has helped people across companies and industries. I also provide outlines for giving formal presentations in Chapter 15. If you decide your company might be interested in sharing some CBT ideas around, it is important that whoever delivers the courses is a trained, experienced HR professional who is qualified in CBT. As with any professional development course, you need to have professionals at the helm. These sorts of workshops, seminars and courses can bring up many emotional concerns, and training in how to manage these feelings in a safe, secure and confidential environment is paramount. A fully qualified CBT therapist would have trained on an accredited training course and be on the national register in the UK or hold a recognised license in the United States, for example.

This book is intended as an introduction to the ideas of CBT and an outline of some of the emotional struggles you can find yourself experiencing. It is very important you seek medical advice if you feel you need to. This book is no substitute for sound medical advice backed up by a team of mental health professionals. Mildly disturbing emotional struggles are outlined; serious mental health issues are not covered in this book. You can only be there as a concerned friend for your colleagues, not an expert on mental health treatments.

# Testifying to CBT by Your Example

When you've developed some CBT skills and found them useful, you can discover that other people are interested in knowing how you manage to stay so cool at work! Demonstrably reducing your anxiety and stress is unlikely to go unnoticed. Past clients report back to me that their friends and colleagues notice changes in them at work and are curious to find out why: nothing's more powerful than a personal recommendation.

The beauty of CBT techniques is that they aren't just for work but for your whole life. The courses incorporating CBT techniques that I outline in Chapter 15 are popular because they help people with their professional and personal lives. Work–life balance issues (which I mention in Chapter 16) become clearer as participants make their own assessments of how they want to live their lives and how they can rationalise, for example, their guilty feelings about not repeatedly staying late at work.

Here I discuss how you can act as a CBT role model, by encouraging rational thinking in difficult moments, admitting your errors and presenting a great example to your co-workers.

## Acting as an ambassador for acceptable behaviour

People are required to work with all kinds of colleagues during their working lives. As you've no doubt found, you encounter some people you admire and can work alongside happily, whereas others you're less keen on. When you discover which working styles you prefer for yourself (refer to Chapter 9), you can then act as a role model for other people.

When you know what sort of person you want to be at work, you can function more effectively as a role model for others. Here's an exercise to help you discern your ideal work colleagues, which in turn helps you to become an ambassador at work for other people. Picture one or two people at your current or a past job whom you admire:

✔ How do they look?

✔ What clothes do they usually wear?

✔ How would you describe their personality?

✔ How reliable are they?

✔ How trustworthy are they?

✔ How would you describe their emotional outlook?

✔ Why do you admire them?

This exercise can help you to focus on working styles of people and think about how you would like to be at work. From the information you get from this exercise, you can find some pointers about how you want to be. When you show the world that you can cope at work, and that you aren't likely to get into a rage or display other irrational behaviour, you attract others by demonstrating a sense of security and composure. Others want to learn from you as you become an ambassador for acceptable work practices.

## *Demonstrating rational thinking*

When people ask you about CBT, having an example to hand of someone demonstrating CBT-influenced rational thinking and behaviour is helpful.

In the following, I show an example of an employee who was passed over for promotion, but instead of jumping up and down, complaining to all and sundry and railing at the world generally about how unfairly he had been treated, he worked out that it would not serve any purpose to do so. He quietly worked out his future plan of action to maximize future opportunities. Note how he did not go into 'knee jerk' reaction. He helped bring down his immediate 'hot headed' emotions by thinking through what the consequences might be if he displayed his anger. He showed that he could keep his cool.

A leisure company was reorganising its staffing structure within a hotel. Simon had been working for the company for a couple of years. The head of guest services took him to one side and said that he'd recommend that Simon be made head of housekeeping services. He explained that he wanted to put Simon in the department at grassroots level to start with so that he got experience of all the roles and responsibilities that employees fulfilled in that department. Simon spent six months in this role and worked hard alongside the others. One lunchtime, another member of the team announced that he'd been told that he was to be made head of housekeeping services, to start the next month. Simon was devastated. He felt a flash of anger and then, in the moment, knew that he had to decide whether or not to challenge this other employee, and show his anger, or hold on to it until it subsided and then think about what to do. In other words, Simon was choosing to go into a hold-ing mode (as CBT recommends), to stop his anger from escalating, until he was able to think rationally about what had happened.

Putting this incident into the CBT ABC framework (from Chapter 2):

- ✔ A: His workmate's announcement
- ✔ B: Simon's beliefs about what should be happening
- ✔ C: Simon's emotional consequence, that is, his anger

Simon decided not to respond while he was feeling angry. He knew that he'd probably say something he'd regret later. He held on to his feelings until they subsided and then made an appointment to see the head of guest services to discuss the situation. He rationalised that he could do nothing if the other person had indeed been appointed. But he could express his surprise and disappointment and request that he be considered for future appointments. Simon asked for a debrief to give him feedback on what experience or quali-ties he'd failed to demonstrate as being suitable for the post, and what ele-ments he should work on to enhance his CV to make him eligible for future promotion roles. He also discovered that you can't always trust what people tell you and that changes will happen that are out of your control. Then again, acting and behaving in unhelpful, obstructive, mean ways does have a habit of catching up with people: the Head of Guest Services post was later made redundant and smaller self-governing sections were created. Simon was appointed to head of customer relations in the new organisation.

His ability to stay cool and focused, and his wide experience within the organisation, paid off. He reflected that if he'd become angry and made com-plaints at the time of his disappointment, it probably wouldn't have helped his future career.

One of the teachers I trained with used to say: 'Life isn't fair. Who said it would be fair? Accept the things you can't control with grace and act upon the things you can have some control over.'

Simon believed in himself, knew he'd done a good job and didn't upset him-self in a self-defeating way, which may have affected his future opportunities within the company. Moreover, perhaps the Head of Guest Services' inconsis-tent actions hadn't gone unnoticed.

# Reap what you sow

If you have belief in yourself and act with integrity and with the best intentions, in general good things happen to you – and vice versa. If you go through your life behaving with integrity and genuine purpose, you're more likely to engage in positive situations – that much is fairly logical and rational. You attract people who respect and admire you for how you behave. Of course, you may also infuriate others, but that's their problem, not yours.

## *Being the first to admit your mistakes*

When you act as an ambassador for CBT, or indeed any aspect of your life, you're going to make occasional mistakes. How you deal with them affects not only others' opinion of you, but also your perception of yourself.

Your aim is to show the world that you accept yourself, even though you sometimes make mistakes, but that you don't judge yourself harshly. This strategy in the workplace helps you and presents a great CBT example to your colleagues.

## *Dealing with your errors*

Here's the healthy response for when you make a mistake, especially when you're trying to persuade work colleagues of CBT's effectiveness:

1. Admit to yourself promptly that you messed up this time.

2. Don't go into denial and try to ignore the uncomfortable feelings, but accept that your behaviour wasn't as good as it could've been.

3. Use CBT to remind yourself that making yourself feel guilty isn't going to help you or rectify the mistake.

4. Shift to acceptance, as follows:

   *Okay, it wasn't a great thing I just did there, but I'm not going to beat myself up and make myself feel really bad. I can accept that sometimes I make mistakes. Just because I made a mistake it doesn't make me a bad person. Careless perhaps, or at this moment in time somewhat incompetent, but I'm not going to rate the whole of myself as essentially useless. I'll do what I can to make amends but if that's not possible, I'll accept this and move on.*

   In other words, have healthy regret that you made a mistake but not an overriding sense of guilt and repetitive negative thoughts.

Get used to voicing your concerns in 'CBT speak' to others; for example, 'I made a mistake back there. It's not great but hey, I'm not perfect. I'm a fallible human being. I accept that wasn't the best decision but I'll learn from it and move forward'.

Studies show that leaders who admit they make mistakes and show their human vulnerability can endear themselves to their audience more. As co-founder of Apple Steve Jobs said:

> *Sometimes when you innovate you make mistakes. It's best to admit them and get on with improving your other innovations.*

Check out Chapter 5 for more about looking after yourself at work, one of the aspects of which is accepting yourself.

### Realising that sorry isn't always the right word

Sorry may be the hardest word to say, but it's not always the best one.

Instead of saying sorry when things go wrong or you make a mistake, try changing that to 'acceptance'.

Some definitions of 'sorry' include words such as unfortunate, deplorable, tragic, regrettable, or even distressed, grieved and full of sorrow: the latter terms come close to suggesting a disturbing state of mind. Yet the purpose of CBT is to help reduce disturbing emotions, not bolster them.

Instead, follow an alternative way of viewing situations that don't go as you hoped. Choose to follow the CBT route of: 'I regret my behaviour, but I accept it and will try to make different choices in the future'.

You may find that you say 'sorry' quite frequently, in differing contexts: for example, when you bump into people or misunderstand what they say. This response is an automatic polite statement to acknowledge transgressing ways of behaving and is fine. It's quite a different use of the word and isn't necessarily expressing feelings of being upset.

Incidentally, the Head of Guest Services role was made redundant in the previous example in a later re-organisation. Acting and behaving in unhelpful, obstructive and just generally mean ways does have a habit of catching up with people.

# Advocating the Use of CBT at Work

When you provide a positive example of CBT by how you behave at work (as I describe in the preceding section), workmates and even managers may want to know more. They can ask you simply to chat about it or perhaps request a more formal approach.

In this section, I cover spreading the CBT word, informally and formally, handling any criticism and tailoring the level of information to your audience and their requirements.

## *Sharing CBT with interested colleagues*

A good way to discover whether you understand CBT techniques and theories is to share them with other people. Without being too evangelical, if someone at work is having a hard time and asks for your opinion, go ahead and share some of the CBT ideas and practice with him. Similarly, when people ask for your opinion around work matters, it's an opportunity to start sharing CBT.

Obviously you have to be careful when sharing CBT with other people, in case they misconstrue your gesture as implying that they 'should' or 'need to' get some help. But you can support a genuine concern for others with your knowledge and understanding.

Share any helpful resources: for example, if you find this book useful, tell others. Spreading the word helps you to find out more about how other people cope at work, and also gather strength in numbers. After I held some CBT workshops at one company, a few departments set up a voluntary monthly lunchtime session for people interested to see how the course was being implemented and give each other tips. The mere action of holding a group meeting is supportive and helpful in itself.

---

## Know a Gouda book to read?

An innovative idea that's taking off globally is to hold not just book clubs and discussion groups for popular fiction books but 'bibliotherapy' groups, where the reading is self-help and therapy books. I remember a short book called *Who Moved My Cheese?* taking off in a big way in early 2000, as word of mouth and company endorsements caused the publishers to work 24/7 to fulfil orders. The author, Spencer Johnson, wrote the book to illustrate the importance of being able to deal with unexpected change. He also wanted it to be a motivational book for anyone looking for less stress and more success. He wrote it in the form of a parable about four mice and how they go about looking for their 'cheese': their goals, their purposes in work, are represented by the availability of the cheese.

## Offering to present your CBT understanding to a group

You can extend your informal sharing of CBT knowledge into a more formal approach if you like. In Chapter 15, I include the outlines of a few workshops, for you to use as a guideline to create your own presentation.

The best test of whether or not you really understand a concept is trying to explain it to someone else.

Here are some ideas:

- ✓ **Finding a way in:** Often, some of the most relevant and helpful information is driven 'bottom to top'. The people at the grassroots level are the most knowledgeable about a business's mood: the difficulties, anxieties and problems that they and their colleagues may be experiencing. A good leader and manager wants to know this info. A less secure manager may feel anxious about asking for feedback on problems – but if you don't ask, you don't get an opportunity.

- ✓ **Approaching your team:** A good starting point is often to get word of mouth from your team about what they think of spending some time considering CBT training to help them deal with work. The hardest part is being heard initially and getting CBT seen.

- ✓ **Proposing some CBT in a meeting:** You can make a point of asking for this proposal to be on the agenda of a team meeting. Being proactive in professional development can be a real bonus. Time is always short and people are very busy, but just having your suggestion as an item on the agenda can raise awareness.

- ✓ **Creating a short presentation:** If you manage to have the subject raised at a meeting, be prepared to offer to do a short presentation on the ideas behind CBT. A presentation of 10 to 15 minutes is a start, with a follow-up of a longer workshop being a possibility.

- ✓ **Expanding the presentation to 45 minutes:** Chapter 15 provides you with the basics for a 45-minute presentation.

The emphasis in CBT is to show people the basics and how to apply them so that they can become their own 'therapist'. The same is true of explaining CBT in the workplace. Using the basic framework, some theory, practice, case studies and examples, along with material to take away, you can make a good inroad into whetting people's appetites to want to discover more. Obviously suggesting that everyone buy a copy of this book, or better still, asking your company to fund the bulk-buy book purchases, would be even better!

# Handling challenges

When spreading the word about CBT, you're bound to meet sceptics and challenges from some colleagues. People have their own opinions about psychology and professional development and may not be as open to learning some new ideas as others.

But criticism doesn't throw you off-track, because you know that CBT is all about dealing with unhelpful thinking – whether it's from yourself or colleagues. Therefore you can welcome the challenges in the spirit of CBT.

### Being prepared for criticism and suspicion

Some people always find reasons not to embrace new ideas, seeing change, new ideas and new ways of working as potentially threatening and causing them to feel insecure. So if you're proposing introducing some CBT methods into your workplace, prepare yourself for criticism or at least suspicion. You may get negative feedback, people who want to block and obstruct your efforts, and even those who try to sabotage your initiatives and try to make life difficult for you.

Don't worry: use your CBT on yourself to remember that these objections reflect their issues, not yours.

They may have a problem, but it's not down to you – you cannot be responsible for other peoples' upsets. You don't upset them; they do that all by themselves by the way they view the situation.

You probably really have enough to do working out your own problems without taking on everyone else's too.

### Converting criticism to constructive feedback

Explaining the difference between negative feedback and constructive feedback can be an eye-opener:

- ✔ **Negative feedback:** When you're simply criticised and judged negatively, which is unhelpful. An example is 'Your report is rubbish'.

- ✔ **Constructive feedback:** Objective commenting that's helpful, in that it gives you information that you can do something about. Constructive feedback is issue-focused and specifically intended to give objective information – for example, 'Your report didn't contain all the data required to reach a clear conclusion'. Constructive feedback is specifically focused on giving objective information, and is issue focused.

### Adopting a stoical attitude

Having the attitude that you've decided to share CBT because you believe it can help people is useful to help you keep going when introducing new ideas. Accept that not all people are open to these new ideas, but that in the great scheme of things you're unlikely ever to get everyone's approval.

Don't be put off. You can only do your best to offer to share these ideas with others; even if just one person is interested, that may be very helpful for them.

## Recognising the different levels and depths of CBT

When you're asked to give a more formal presentation about CBT, you need to adapt the amount of information that you share according to the level of interest shown, how much time you're allowed and the background of the potential audience. Some groups may already have ideas about psychology and different forms of therapy; others may have no knowledge at all. You need to adjust the information to suit the groups you're addressing.

But you can explain the basic framework of CBT very simply (see Chapter 15 for some suggestions). In my experience, people from all walks of life and employment situations can pick up the basics of CBT readily.

A good idea is to demonstrate how to apply CBT to particular contexts and emotional upsets by providing specific information. Make the examples and case studies relevant to the target audience for an engaging process.

Some of the most frequent emotional difficulties I've observed, on which you may want to focus in the work situation, include the following:

- Aggrieved
- Anger
- Anxiety
- Confidence issues
- Depression
- Embarrassment
- Envy
- Frustration
- Guilt

✔ Hurt

✔ Shame

Going through the CBT basics, applying the framework to problems from any of these categories, can help people to easily understand and apply CBT. Asking people to volunteer situations where any of these issues have arisen and applying the CBT to those situations makes your session more relevant.

If you decide to ask for examples of troubling situations and feelings, I strongly suggest that you ask for these before the workshop, until you get really experienced in working through the CBT ABC model. Asking for people to volunteer their troubling feelings can open the way for a workshop to be potentially hijacked by one person wanting instant therapy in the session, unless you are prepared. Also it could be that someone has a very serious issue which they just decide to share, which you would not have time or be in the most appropriate place to give help. If you ask in advance, you can select which troubling situations can be managed in this environment. If you ask people to write them on previously prepared slips of paper, then anonymity of the ones selected will be maintained, as you will be in charge of the selection.

Running training sessions where personal problems and emotional reactions are shared takes an experienced facilitator. Don't underestimate the skills and training required to 'hold' a group safely and ensure they get appropriate professional help, that participants aren't left feeling more troubled without anywhere to go afterward to get appropriate professional help.

You don't need to limit your resources for helping others to CBT. It's only one method out of dozens that you can use for helping employees manage difficulties at work. Many other types of counselling, coaching and psychological theories and practice are available to read about, train in and apply.

# Using Your CBT Experience to Help Other People's Struggles

CBT is proven to be effective for working with people who have persistent and chronic emotional problems. But this book is intended as an introduction to the ideas, methods and practises of CBT in the workplace, and not a replacement for seeking a full medical assessment and treatment for continuing debilitating problems. You may wonder how you'd know if someone, or even yourself, has a more serious psychological struggle.

One baseline for indicating that a consultation with a health professional may be helpful is how far the difficulty is impacting on a person's everyday life.

In this section, I discuss how best to help other people who come to you for advice, including some of the psychological conditions that people experience in their lives.

Having an awareness of what happens when you break a leg, for example, is absolutely no substitute for going to a medical centre for a full assessment and individual plan of action for the best ways to help you to heal and be restored to full strength. If you carry on walking on a broken leg, your health will deteriorate further. Having an awareness of CBT is no substitute for a full assessment of your mental health if you are struggling.

The issue of boundaries and confidentiality were always included in the training programmes for Transition Management. Learning about when and how you can handle distressed colleagues, so as not to make things worse but be as professional and supportive as you can, was reported to be one of the most helpful aspects of the training.

## Recommending that people seek professional help

Knowing when you can help others in distress and when to step back and call in professionally trained healthcare professionals is highly important.

The general indication is that when people have been struggling for longer than you'd expect for feeling a 'bit down', they need to visit their GP and relate how they've been feeling as a first port of call. Doctors are trained to assess mental health as well as physical health.

If someone feels embarrassed or a little unsure of what to say when visiting their doctor about feelings of anxiety, stress or generally feeling disorientated, ask them to write a list of what they've been experiencing. Also, taking along a friend or family member who can read the list if they have difficulty talking or start feeling 'wobbly', means that the information is still passed on.

You may well know from your personal experience that people can feel alienated from themselves when dealing with stress or depression, so much so that they can't always recognise themselves. Understanding that these feelings are natural, don't last forever and that time and perhaps assistance to get better are required, is an important step to dealing with the emotional turbulence.

## Feel free to bring a friend

Psychotherapists are human beings and get depressed and struggle at times, like anyone else.

When I was having a particularly tough time in a job and then suffered a physical attack at work, I went on a downward slide emotionally. It was a temporary job and I knew it would come to an end, but I was determined to see the contract through. I wasn't sleeping much; I felt highly anxious and ultimately became distressed.

A natural break in work arose, and when I was away I went into a state of depression. Friends were concerned and persuaded me to see a doctor, one volunteering to go with me. I wrote down how I'd been feeling, but in the consultation felt unable to speak. Having the list to give to my friend to read out was very helpful. The doctor reassured me that these feelings were natural and to rest and relax and come back in a week.

 Remind people that admitting that they feel out of kilter and accepting that they aren't themselves is the start to moving forward. Make sure that they don't beat themselves up.

### *Watching for warning signs*

 If someone confides in you at work that they're experiencing some of the following warning symptoms and they are troubled by them, they might decide to see a doctor or other trained health professional:

- ✔ Feeling very alone and isolated
- ✔ Feeling anxious, 'jumpy', tense and nervous
- ✔ Not being able to cope
- ✔ Not liking themselves; feeling inadequate
- ✔ No energy or enthusiasm
- ✔ Not feeling well frequently: headaches, colds, infections, pains and muscular aches
- ✔ Feeling emotional and having outbursts of crying publicly and alone
- ✔ Sleep problems: difficulty getting to sleep and/or early waking
- ✔ Thinking that they have no friends
- ✔ Feeling ashamed about things they've done
- ✔ Blaming themselves for the state they're in

- ✔ Feeling overwhelmed by their problems

- ✔ Feeling numb; unable to have feelings for others

- ✔ Constantly worrying about things; repetitive thoughts going round in their head

- ✔ Having unwanted pictures flashing into their mind; disturbing thoughts and feelings

- ✔ Thoughts of hurting themselves

- ✔ Feeling hopeless, as if 'there's no point to life'

- ✔ Hurting themselves or taking risks with their life

- ✔ Believing they have no future and no way out of their difficulties

- ✔ Getting angry with other people, snapping at others or feeling irritable

- ✔ Making plans to end their life

When a person feels alone and isolated and struggling with life, being able to share with someone (such as a GP) how they're feeling can be a first step to getting help and moving towards reducing some of these symptoms.

Be on the lookout for colleagues at work and friends who may be struggling. Changes in their patterns of behaviour can be a warning sign. The sooner they can explain to someone how they're feeling, the sooner they can get help and prevent a slide into worse feelings.

### *Noticing damaging levels of self-medication*

When people are struggling, they sometimes find that eating or drinking certain things give them a temporary 'lift' and helps them cope:

- ✔ Alcohol

- ✔ Coffee and tea

- ✔ Energy drinks and energy-boosting substances

- ✔ High carbohydrate foods – cakes, biscuits, sweets, chocolate, crisps and snacks

- ✔ Pain-relieving drugs

- ✔ Smoking

In moderation, these ways of helping to get through the day aren't a problem. But if you spot longer-term changes in a person's eating and drinking patterns, it may be a sign that they're struggling.

When people go through an intense period at work, perhaps a project that creates many demands and deadlines, they may turn to some of the preceding items to help them cope in the short term to get through the stressful time. A problem can arise if they then find that they're increasingly dependent on outside stimulation and self-medication.

In the long term, such coping strategies can increase a person's problems. Here are some of the possible risks:

- ✔ Addiction
- ✔ Weight increase to unhealthy levels
- ✔ Taking illegal substances
- ✔ Increasing ill-health

### Asking for help at work

In the work situation, your company may have an Occupational Health department that can help to organise some support for a colleague. Your employer may even have a contract with an Employee Assistance Programme, which provides a confidential helpline telephone number.

Or it may have a Human Resources department, which can possibly advise your colleague.

## Spotting when colleagues may have a specific emotional problem

If you notice that a colleague is struggling, or you wonder if they are showing signs of mental health problems, you may be concerned what you can do to help. You are not an expert on different types of mental illnesses, nor can you decide how serious the problems may be. Your first port of call could be to ask the person how they are in an open and non-judgmental way. If your show of concern is rebuffed and you have serious worries about this person, it important to let someone else know. This could be their manager. It is not for you to decide what to do. An employer has a duty of care not just for physical wellbeing but also for emotional wellbeing. This plan of action also takes the burden of responsibility off you. You will have done your best to offer support or to alert the relevant people to your concerns.

✔ **Social anxiety:** A fear of interaction with other people that brings on self-consciousness and feelings of being negatively judged and evaluated, and as a result leads to people avoiding interpersonal contact.

Different degrees of social anxiety exist. In severe cases it prevents people from mixing with others in all situations, though you're unlikely to come across these sufferers at work, because they probably can't cope with work.

Less-serious levels and situation-specific forms also exist, however, including avoidance of social situations. You may be able to recommend some CBT practice for people suffering from the following:

- Fear of standing up in front of others – for example, giving a report or presentation to a group
- Anxiety about meeting new people
- Worries about having the attention focused on them
- Fear of being asked to 'introduce yourself' in a group
- Worries about being watched while carrying out tasks
- Anxiety about encounters with people in authority
- Worries about being made fun of or criticised
- Difficulty making friends at work or in their personal life

✔ **Obsessive Compulsive Disorder (OCD):** At times people can have the same thoughts going round and round in their heads.

Check out Chapter 3 for more about repetitive thinking. When people are worried or anxious, this type of thinking can be a natural occurrence.

Sometimes, however, merely irritating symptoms tip over into a more deep-seated problem and become an OCD. The symptoms to watch for in yourself and others include:

- Experiencing an obsessive, repeated, unpleasant and unwanted thought, image or urge
- Feeling anxious, uneasy, scared or disgusted
- Needing to carry out some special behaviour repeatedly, to relieve the unpleasant feelings brought on by the obsessive thoughts

OCD symptoms range in their severity. For mild OCD, applying the CBT methods from this book may help people to rationalise their unhelpful thinking to a point where they don't need to engage in those behaviours to reduce their anxiety.

For medium to severe repetitive thinking and behaviours, consultation with health professionals is important to help set people up with appropriate treatment.

✔ **Post Traumatic Stress Disorder (PTSD):** A psychological condition that can occur after people experience a trauma that leaves them with ongoing symptoms of distress. The difference between PTSD and a normal response to a shocking event or trauma is the severity and length of the symptoms.

Here are some examples of events with the potential to traumatise those involved:

- Death of a relative or friend
- Disasters
- Physical injury
- Pregnancy and birth
- Relationship breakups
- Surgery
- Violence, to the person or those around them

After a shock, experiencing symptoms of distress such as the following is normal:

- Anxiety
- Bad dreams
- Detachment from normal life
- Disorientation
- Fear
- Images from the event flashing into the person's mind
- Keeps thinking about the event
- Lack of trust in others
- Numbness
- Out of control behaviour

Any of these symptoms can last for a few days or weeks, but they usually ease off and become less intense.

PTSD is recognised when the symptoms don't go away and keep coming back and disrupting life. The three main indicators of PTSD are as follows:

- Re-experiencing the traumatic event

- Avoiding any reminders of the event

- Feelings of anger, anxiety, fear, disrupted sleep patterns, lack of concentration and feeling on 'the lookout' all the time

PTSD is extremely distressing and can hugely impact people's everyday living. They may not even realise what they're experiencing, but work colleagues or family and friends do see worrying changes. A visit to a health professional can help establish whether a person is suffering from PTSD.

Sometimes sufferers develop skillful strategies to keep work and their personal life separate, but they can't expect to repress all their emotions indefinitely. When events impact on a person's emotional state, they need to allow themselves to acknowledge them at some point.

The impact of any event is always personal to the person. No-one else can feel what an individual's feeling; only they can know how they're affected.

Urge people to take such feelings seriously and seek professional help if they persist.

**Suicidal thinking:** An area where many companies would benefit from having more information available for the individual, employees, bosses and the firm.

The isolation of experiencing extreme distress and disorientation can leave people feeling very lonely and hopeless; they can decide that only one way is left to stop the interminable suffering. Fearing reactions of family and friends and unable to share their darkest thoughts, suicide may seem the only option left.

Employers and bosses may be afraid to enquire after employees' states of mind, but they do have a duty of responsibility for emotional wellbeing as well as physical safety. Having some information about what warning signs to look out for in employees whose behaviour changes or who exhibit signs of stress can be helpful in deciding what people can do to help.

Discovering more about when and how you can help distressed colleagues, so as not to make things worse but be as professional and supportive as you can, is very helpful. You cannot diagnose disorders in colleagues, like depression, but you can express your concern if you suspect they are struggling.

# Chapter 15

# Introducing CBT Methods to Your Organisation

## In This Chapter

▶ Considering CBT use for your own company

▶ Benefitting your organisation financially

▶ Delivering CBT training sessions at work

▶ Checking out basic counselling skills

*A*fter practising CBT for a period of time, you begin to feel more confident in using it and in the benefits it can bring. You may even see yourself as a walking witness to the improvements that CBT can have on a person's emotional life. Even so, making the move from discovering CBT and offering to share the ideas in your workplace (refer to Chapter 14), to putting together material to present to a group more formally, can seem quite a leap.

But don't worry; this chapter has it all sorted. Here I outline some suggestions for your company to make some provision for more people to learn about some of the ideas of CBT and its benefits. Of course, I am not suggesting that armed with this book you could venture into delivering CBT courses yourself, but there are national registers of qualified CBT therapists like www. babcp.com that could provide you with contacts to approach who could come in and do some CBT coaching introductory sessions and seminars. I also discuss how you can persuade the people who matter at your firm that CBT is worth investing in, and I provide suggestions for CBT training materials that I've tried, tested and used successfully in workplace settings. Showing the initiative and motivation to want to lead professional development helps not only your company and other people, but also assists you in consolidating your own CBT practice.

# Including CBT in Your Workplace

If you're self-employed as a sole trader, reading this book educates you in CBT in a work and home setting at the same time. But if you work for a small business or a larger company, you're just part of an organisational culture created by the people who work there. The decisions, policies and practices have evolved over time as the organisation was created and expanded.

Any business wants to know how including professional development, in company time, is going to benefit that organisation.

Here are some of the potential benefits to help persuade people that training employees in CBT can help the company:

- ✔ Reduced stress, anxiety and depression
- ✔ Reduced staff absenteeism
- ✔ Increased employee engagement
- ✔ Improved customer relations
- ✔ Reduction of stress-related illnesses
- ✔ Raised staff morale
- ✔ Improved motivation and productivity
- ✔ Enhanced colleague and management communications

# Seeing How CBT Benefits Your Company's Bottom Line

Companies want clear reasons as to why they should use CBT in their training programme, and the most powerful, persuasive ones are probably the economic benefits.

To read some background and detailed evidence that you can put before those in charge of your company, check out the nearby sidebar 'Considering the evidence for CBT's benefits'.

# Considering the evidence for CBT's benefits

You have probably heard of different types of 'talk therapies' that have been around over the years. It can be hard to have an idea of how they differ and why anyone might prefer to have one treatment over another. It is very confusing; like the evolution of mobile phones from the big bricklike ones with huge battery packs to the keypad ones that just did calls and texts to the amazingly slimline touch screens with access to the Internet, there will always be debate over which is best. So, too, with these therapies and types of counseling. There is no definitive evidence that 'one size fits all', but CBT based therapy does seem to be increasing in popularity, due to a number of reasons.

Research into evidence-based methods of psychological therapy, most comprehensively on CBT, show that it can help people to reorder their thoughts and manage their feelings and behaviour in an effective and healthy manner. For anxiety disorders, for example, the typical recovery rates were over 50 per cent and on a level with recovery rates when just using medication. Depression recovery rates were similar after four months using either CBT or antidepressants, but, crucially, patients who used CBT were much less likely to relapse.

The importance for mental and emotional wellbeing in the workplace was noted in a test case in the UK in 1984. A social worker for Northumberland County Council went off sick with a nervous breakdown due to the stress of his work; he returned later to find conditions hadn't changed and became ill again. A judge ruled that the employer had a responsibility for workers' mental health and safety as well as their physical safety. The judge decided that although the authority chose to continue to employ him, it provided no effective help: 'In so doing it was in my judgement acting unreasonably and therefore in breach of its duty of care'.

In 2006, a report published by The Centre for Economic performance Mental Health's group, headed up by a Professor of Economics called Richard Layard. He was looking into the incidence of depression in the UK society and its impact on the economy of the UK World Health Organization; statistics predict that depression will become the most debilitating illness in developed and developing countries, even though effective treatments exist:

- Globally, more than 350 million people of all ages suffer from depression.

- Depression is the leading cause of disability worldwide and a major contributor to the global burden of disease.

A 2006 report by The Centre for Economic Performance's Mental Health Policy Group called for thousands of CBT therapists to be trained to help alleviate people's distress and in turn benefit the economy. A programme called 'Improving Access to Psychological Therapies' (IAPT) was drawn up and implemented in 2008 in the English National Health Service. By 2011, a report for implementing NICE (National Institute for Health and Clinical Guidance) guidelines for psychological treatment for depression and anxiety disorders was published. This showed a commitment to training particularly focused on CBT.

## *Balancing the costs and benefits*

In 2007, a paper entitled 'Cost-benefit analysis of psychological therapy', in the journal The National Institute of Economic Review, outlined the economic benefits of providing more access to CBT psychological therapy by implementing a training programme to provide more CBT therapists:

✔ The cost to the UK government in time lost from incapacity due to the estimated 6 million people suffering from clinical depression or anxiety to work is enormous.

✔ The cost of training extra CBT therapists could be recovered within 2–5 years by the savings in incapacity benefits and extra taxes that result from people being able to work.

The case was put forward that the cost of training the extra therapists to help people with depression and anxiety would be cost effective in saving the economy money by helping people stay or get back to work and not increasing bills due to lost productivity and sickness pay benefits.

The economic arguments for the benefits of looking after the mental health of employees, as well as the legal responsibility for care in the workplace, may well have influenced the rise of organisations making such provision.

One example is the Employee Assistance Programmes (EAPs) delivered by specialist companies. EAPs have been around for longer in the United States than in the UK, but increasingly companies are arranging for access to physical and psychological care services by buying contracts so that their workforce can access this provision in complete confidence and anonymity.

Smaller companies and self-employed individuals may well not have the budgets to buy this sort of EAP provision, but they still have a responsibility to their employees. Professional development training sessions are a start to educating their teams in the CBT form of emotional support. Check out the nearby sidebar ''Earing all about EAPs' for more on EAPs'.

> *Investing in the future of the company, you can never be overdressed or overeducated.*
>
> — Oscar Wilde

The more you understand about yourself, your life and the world in general, the more you get out of everything. In addition, you bring yourself, your knowledge, your skills and your attributes to work, which all benefit the company in some way.

## 'Earing all about EAPs

When I worked in California, I was covered by the employer's health programme, which included access to the Employee Assistance Programmes (EAPs). We had detailed health checks, with evaluations, support and suggestions for addressing any self-concerns we identified in the assessments. I was impressed with this service, never having had this facility in the UK.

I told my husband how generous and considerate I thought the employer was. Being more cynical, he pointed out that keeping the workforce healthy was in its interests, in order to get the most out of staff. Nonetheless, the service was very motivating and encouraging.

EAP programmes can vary considerably in terms of the types of support they offer, but most include clinical and non-clinical elements designed to support employees on a broad range of personal and work-related issues. Typical clinical elements can include telephone counselling, often delivered by counsellors directly employed by the EAP provider, and face-to-face counselling, usually delivered through a network of contracted affiliate counsellors. Increasingly providers also offer online access to counselling, through live chat, secure portal communication systems or self-directed computer platforms.

When you feel valued by your employer, not only for the job you do but also in terms of your overall welfare, you're more likely to be a loyal and motivated employee. Dissatisfaction and unhappiness at work often happen when a lack of communication and apparent disregard for staff is present. But when you're actively engaged in your work and feel a part of a whole, which includes regular feedback in both directions, you feel valued and have a positive sense of wellbeing.

Including professional development in your job description, during work hours, is an investment not just for you but for the company as a whole.

A company's success depends on a happy, educated and motivated workforce. It needs to invest in human resources as well as physical ones.

# *Leading CBT Workshops and Seminars*

A small amount of learning about CBT principles and practice can be helpful in many different work settings. I've given CBT presentations to varied groups, from UK government departments to agricultural workers, including psychology students, business networking meetings, small and large international companies, conferences, village halls and cruise-ship lecture programmes. With the information I provide here, you can do so too!

In this section, I let you into the secret (not really!) details of some material that I use when introducing CBT to groups. The short presentations and longer workshops are of various lengths and depth.

You may find it useful to see how the seminars and workshops integrate the CBT ideas. This material is not intended for you to run off and volunteer to present workshops yourself, but just to give you an insight into the sort of layout of the sessions. It took me many years of training and weeks of typing away into the night to put all this together for the companies I delivered to. Participants in the sessions seemed to find it helpful and told me that it made sense and often asked for a copy of the presentations afterwards. I was more than happy to send the presentations over to their departments, so they could spend looking back at the content. Some of them even told me they were signing up at their local colleges for introductory courses in counselling and CBT courses.

The basis for these presentations is a simple lecture that I used to introduce CBT to a human-resources team in a medium-sized company, which was considering finding practical help to guide its workforce though changes. The firm had heard that CBT was a practical-based psychology tool adaptable for use in transition management. The original presentation briefly covered so-called talking therapies, how CBT developed, what it is and the simple ABC model (from Chapter 2) in context.

To share your enthusiasms and knowledge of CBT at your own level, I will use this analogy to warn against taking on too much too soon, in your enthusiasm to share your new-found CBT knowledge.

You may have had a great piece of cake and ask the cook for the recipe. You have a go at making it and are pretty impressed with your results, and so are your friends you give pieces to. They want the recipe too. You print it out and share it. Feeling flushed with success you are keen to tell more people about it. This doesn't mean, however, that you can now go off and set up a cookery school! The same with the CBT knowledge; by all means, share your interest in it with others, but remember you will need to bring in skilled and experienced trainers in CBT-based courses for anything at a higher level than just presenting the recipe.

This is how I presented a 45-minute CBT introduction. In the following, I outline the sort of topics I presented to a new group.

The first four numbered points in the following list are headings for you to consider to your own work situation. You may want to use a recent instance of changes in your company.

1. **The changes that are happening in your work:** I ask the group to tell me what's been happening for them in their workplace and how they are being affected.

2. **Talk about concerns:** I hand out slips of paper and ask participants to write down three concerns they're currently experiencing. I collect the slips of paper so that I can keep the whole process anonymous.

I tell the group I may be reading these out to the group later, so not to put their name on the paper; otherwise, indicate if they don't want their concern read out.

3. **Reasons for run this workshop:** I describe to the group what my role is that day for being asked to come along and run the workshop. I explain I am a psychologist (groan from audience) and a psychothera-pist (double groan), and how the workshop would be interactive. I always expect questions such as did their company think there was something wrong with them, and some worries that they might have to bare their soul, or even take part in chanting and dancing, in the session. But I soon dispell these concerns by saying how it is all confidential and their participation, apart from initially having to show up, was voluntary. I explain how I would share with them some practical ideas on how to manage change at work.

4. **Check what's covered in this session:**

    • Psychology theories.

    • What is CBT?

    • How can an understanding of CBT help employees at work?

5. **Read the concerns from the slips of paper collect in Step 2:** And I show how many concerns are common to the group. I explain that the session demonstrates how a particular 'toolkit', based on psychology research and practices, can be helpful for reducing the intensity of some of these concerns.

6. **See psychology in action:** I include a section to briefly describe what the group may already have heard about psychology and throw in a couple of names which might be familiar. There was no expectation for people to go off and research psychology, just to outline the background of how there are different types of psychology knowledge.

These headings are just the tip of the iceberg in studying psychology. There is no way I can comprehensively cover all these topics in a 45-minute workshop, but if you are interested in finding out more about psychology, there is a great book called *Psychology For Dummies* by Adam Walsh. Studying psychology is a huge area, but I found many people have an interest in it and some knowledge, and I want to set the background for them, so I just introduce the following brief definitions.

    • Different types of psychology (studying the human mind)

    • Different types of counselling and therapy (using different methods from psychology to help when there are mind difficulties)

7. **Freud:** Psychoanalytic psychology and therapy. This is just one theory and practice in psychology of a mind-helping therapy. I ask who has heard of Freud and what they knew about him.

8. **Humanistic psychology:** I explain another type of counselling, which is not a directive type of therapy but allows people time to find themselves. A leading light of this type of counselling was Carl Rogers, who believed that people know themselves best: the counsellor listens and is alongside the person as she finds insights and ways forward.

9. **Behaviourist psychology:** I briefly tell the group that this type of psychology looks at changing people's behaviour through rewards and incentives.

10. **Thinking psychology:** Sometimes called cognitive psychology. I explain that although behaviour can be changed it doesn't necessarily involve any thinking but more just changing a reaction to a stimulus. Some people wanted to study more about what people are thinking and how changing their thinking brings about changes in their behaviour. Cognitive means 'thinking'.

11. **Cognitive Behavioural Therapy:** A combination of Behaviourist and Cognitve psychology:

    • Cognitive – Thinking

    • Behaviour – People can see

    • Therapy – Leads to change

12. **Cognitive Behavioural Therapy 2:** 1950s interest in treating stress:

    • Practical and teachable

    • Become your own therapist

    • 1970s depression report in UK

13. **Economic cost to countries of mental ill-health:**

    • World Health Organization statistics

    • Depression and mental ill-health worldwide

    • CBT evidence-based therapy

    • NHS chooses CBT for the health services

    Check out the earlier section, 'Seeing How CBT Benefits Your Company's Bottom Line' for more on these.

14. **What does CBT actually do:** I show how to use CBT to reduce:

    • Stress

    • Anxiety

- Mild depression

- Anger

- Frustration

- Guilt

- Relationship problems

- Damaging effects from change management – personal, professional and company wide

- Interview anxiety and nerves

- Unsettling feelings at work

- Show that thoughts give rise to your feelings

- Negative thinking leading to negative feelings

15. **Example of negative thinking (from Chapter 2):** Describe how two people, Jeff and Ben, react differently to the same situation when a car pulls out in front of them on the way to work – one makes himself very angry; the other is just annoyed.

- Jeff and Ben and the drive to work

- Same route, same situation, both react differently

- Why? Because of how they view the situation

16. **The ABC model** (from Chapter 2):

- A is the Activating event.

- B is the Belief or the view you hold about what happened.

- C is the Consequence – how you feel.

17. **Unhealthy negative emotions:**

- They're unhealthy because people upset themselves.

- If people don't want to experience negative feelings, they can change the way they view these events.

  How to stop upsetting yourself:

  - Work on changing your thinking.

  - You then still feel healthy negative emotions, and you still may not like what happened, but you don't wind yourself up into a state of anxiety, anger, guilt, or embarrassment or any other of the upsetting emotions.

Check out Chapter 2 for how you can work on changing your negative thinking.

18. **Using the ABC model:**

    - Identify the unsettling emotions first – the C.

    - Pinpoint the actual situation that happened – the A.

    - Work out your views, thinking and beliefs about the situation – the B.

19. **Using an example – Jeff and Ben:**

    - A – the car pulling out

    - B – the beliefs about how people should drive

    - C – the emotions: Ben is angry; Jeff is annoyed

20. **Considering 'should, ought and must' thinking:**

    - Your strong beliefs

    - The consequences of hanging on to your strong beliefs

    - You wind yourself up

    - You can make yourself ill

    Find out more about avoiding should, ought and must thinking in Chapter 2.

21. **You can change your beliefs:**

    - Develop CBT methods and change the way you think.

    - You've had years of thinking the way you do now – old habits die hard, but it's possible.

    - It takes lots of practice!

22. **You can change unhealthy negative emotions to healthy negative emotions – for example:**

    | *From* | *To* |
    | --- | --- |
    | Anxiety | Healthy concern |
    | Anger | Annoyance |
    | Depression | Appropriate sadness |
    | Low confidence | Acceptance of self |
    | Guilt | Healthy regret |

23. **'I will not 'should' on myself':** I explain to the group that when you hear yourself saying 'I should not' or 'I must not', or 'I ought not to' do something, then these are the types of phrases that are followed by feeling tense and upset. If you can stop yourself from thinking like this and putting yourself under pressure to make these unbendable demands, you give yourself a break.

**24. Change your 'should' thinking to:**

- 'I'd prefer not to have messed up, but it has happened. I don't like it but I accept that winding myself up about it doesn't help. I'm annoyed but not inappropriately upset'.

- 'I'll learn from this instance and use the knowledge to try to avoid it in the future'.

**25. Healthy preference thinking gives rise to healthy negative feelings, neutral or even positive feelings:**

- 'I'll change my natural default irrational thinking to rational and helpful thinking'.

- 'It'll take much practice and be an ongoing project'.

- 'I'll look out for those upsetting or 'wobbly' moments and be alert so I can use the ABC model to help me rationalise my thinking'.

CBT is for your whole life, not just for crisis moments.

I explain to the companies employing me that if they want me to extend this 45-minutes presentation into a 2-hour workshop, I could do that. This would mean that I'd include some time for small-group work, practical exercises and discussion time.

## Holding a 3-hour interactive workshop

One of my most popular training workshops is called 'Transition management: Moving ahead with organisational change'. Based on the presentation in the preceding section, this workshop covers broader topics and puts the CBT model into context for each specific team and organisation.

The general session objectives are as follows – adapt them as appropriate to your work's situation:

✔ As a result of this session, employees will be able to:

- Identify the process of change as it affects them

- Acknowledge their reactions to these circumstances

- Recognise and explore the change model

- Attain some strategies for dealing with the degrees of discomfort

- Have an awareness that all the choices people make will have different consequences

- Be aware of professional and personal responsibility issues regarding uncertainty

- Move forward towards a healthy and balanced outlook

✔ The different parts of the workshop covered are (in this order):

- How individuals handle change.

- The change model.

- Managing during times of change.

- Degrees of discomfort: unsettling emotions during periods of change, including physiological, psychological and behavioural signs.

- The ABC model of disturbance (refer to Chapter 2): 'People are disturbed not so much by events as by the views they take of them'.

- Cognitive consequences and how they precipitate unsettling feelings: stress, anxiety, anger, shame, self-doubt, harassment, rejection, worry, sleep problems, illness and depression.

- Normal reactions to change – 'change curve', which looks at the stages people go through when changes take place. Some of these stages include denial (you don't want to admit something is happening) and resistance (you don't want to change and you fight it through to the stage when you do take on board the changes you adapt and integrate the changes into your work).

- Problems during transitions.

- The cycle of loss: Swiss psychologist Elizabeth Kubler-Ross worked with terminally ill patients, and noted that people who were close to the patients went through similar stages of reactions to their loss - denial, anger, bargaining. She went on later to describe these changes as being similar when other forms of loss are experienced, like loss of job, redundancy, divorce, depression and acceptance. I liked this model as I had seen people go through these stages and it seemed to link to the ultimate goal of the CBT in that it was acceptance.

- Coaching during transition: cognitive behavioural therapies. The idea of coaching is to work with people to help them achieve their personal or professional goals, to manage life changes and provide guidance along the way.

- Using CBT techniques at work to reduce emotional disturbances.

- Examples in your current situation.

- The way forward: your preferences.

- Managing future choices.

✔ Feedback from employees who participated in the workshops and filled in evaluation forms (from over 50 workshops in different locations to different teams and departments):

- Employees reported discovering that although they can't change the current situation, they can change their view of it and they do have choices – these insights came through strongly.

- The choices may be tough ones, but individuals can take charge of how they view the options and are responsible for how they make themselves feel.

- The opportunity to voice experiences and concerns in a small group was helpful.

- Employees welcomed the chance to see tools for recognising when/where they're emotional and how they can move forward.

- Employees appreciated the respect and commitment of the organisation in providing workshops and acknowledging and providing support for the potentially difficult times.

- Requests from many groups to want to share this knowledge with managers was apparent.

- A key factor was the motivation for two-way communication with managers and wanting to move forward together.

This outline of this proposal for a 3-hour workshop is intended as a suggestion for a suitable qualified external provider to get started running CBT-based change workshops. I trained other colleagues to deliver this type of workshop so we, as a team, could reach more companies.

## Creating a 5-hour manager-training day in CBT

This managers' training day includes the same material as for the 3-hour session in the preceding section, plus an introduction to place the transitions of their company in context.

Again, these suggestions for expanding the workshop into a 5-hour day course are intended for ideally the same qualified presenters who delivered the shorter workshops to the 'employees' to deliver to the managers. Having outside providers is important so the confidentiality of the sessions is observed and the participants are on an equal footing. This mirrors the confidentiality needed when providing counselling for employees. You need to use outside providers as you would be hesitant to bring up your true feelings in an environment where the person giving the counselling was another employee in your work. You have to know that confidentiality won't be breached.

Follow the guidelines in this section and your training day is sure to go a whole lot smoother than detective Ethan Hawke's in the film *Training Day!*

The course objectives can include:

- ✔ Placing the transition management workshop in the context of the organisational and structural changes in the company
- ✔ Experiencing and understanding the workshop presented to the other employees (such as the one in the preceding section)
- ✔ Placing employees' reactions into the context of manager relationships
- ✔ Considering visioning, strategic plans and culture change
- ✔ Providing tools to enable communication to take place
- ✔ Integrating and moving forward with the vision and mission

Here's a suggested course overview:

- ✔ Introduction and background
- ✔ Employee presentation
- ✔ Department/team reaction
- ✔ Organisational context
- ✔ Manager's perspective
- ✔ Employee/manager communication
- ✔ Tools for assisting the transition process
- ✔ Coaching employees and managers
- ✔ Problems during transitions
- ✔ Communicating during change – skills, techniques
- ✔ Managing stress
- ✔ Way forward

The managers receive the same 3-hour session as the other employees the in the second half of the day; they also receive the manager-specific 2-hour additional course.

I suggest delivering the 3-hour session in the morning and then have at least an hour lunch break before the 2-hour session in the afternoon.

The afternoon session concentrates more on teaching the managers the basic counselling skills they can use to help create the right environment for effective coaching to take place. Basic counselling skills lie behind all CBT interactions (flip to the later section 'Looking at Basic Communication Skills'). You need training in counselling skills and then specialist training in CBT to offer an effective combination.

After the section teaching the counselling skills, it then broadens out to encourage a wider discussion around how the managers tell their teams about the proposed changes and the concerns they have around this.

### Communication during change

The message that managers send to their staff prepares them for changes. They want assurances of what's going to happen and support to deal with the changes. This goal can be a pretty tall order when managers themselves probably don't quite know what's going to happen, and most importantly, don't know how they're going to be affected.

A team depends on the managers and looks to them for answers. Without communication, the rumour machine runs rampant. An important point is to deal with change as it happens, both collectively and on a one-to-one basis.

Here's what to communicate:

- ✔ Reasons for change
- ✔ Facts about the marketplace and the group's competitive position
- ✔ An understanding about what's coming and what's expected of staff moving forward
- ✔ The part staff will play in the strategy
- ✔ How the change will affect staff
- ✔ How managers are dealing with change (and their personal emotions about the change, too – they're only human, after all)

Here's what staff members want/expect:

- ✔ Facts
- ✔ What's in it for them
- ✔ Truth, candour
- ✔ Honesty regarding what the manager doesn't know
- ✔ An understanding of how they'll be affected personally
- ✔ When the decision was made, and who made it

Check out these guidelines for effective communication:

- ✔ Encourage two-way communication.
- ✔ Listen to what employees are telling the manager – use the counselling listening skills in the next section to help employees feel heard and reduce any hostile feelings.

- ✔ Ask for employees' opinions and reactions – use the counselling skills to handle these in ways that don't inflame the situation or are seen to be taking any particular 'side', and which help reduce potential conflict.

- ✔ Encourage ideas – let people be heard in a safe and respectful environment.

- ✔ Act on employees' suggestions where possible.

- ✔ Encourage an atmosphere of respect, honesty and trust.

- ✔ Tell people what you know/don't know.

- ✔ Use counselling skills to listen, maintain professional boundaries and don't promise things outside of your control.

- ✔ Demonstrate commitment to other employees.

- ✔ Give personal bad news in private – use counselling skills to handle the emotional reactions in a respectful and safe way.

- ✔ Be honest and build trust.

- ✔ Clear up rumours and misinformation.

- ✔ Keep employees updated on a regular basis.

- ✔ Give information again, again and again.

- ✔ Be accessible and available.

- ✔ Create a climate of mutual respect and trust.

# Looking at Basic Communication Skills

In order to help create the best climate for communication, you can guide people, such as group managers and team leaders, in some of the basic communication skills that I learnt from my counsellor training days described in this section.

The skill straining is not aimed at giving the managers individual psychological support but teaching some of the ways in which they can convey information to others in a way which will not 'make things worse' when talking to the individuals in their teams.

Over the years, I've received feedback indicating that developing these skills gives managers confidence in working with their teams, helping them to know how to approach people in a one-to-one situation in an effective way that doesn't make the situation worse.

Here are some main points of communication skills which I learnt from the counselling skills training I undertook.

Research suggests that in mass communication to groups, only about 70 per cent of the audience take onboard what's presented. The communication is much more effective when it's conveyed on a personal basis and at an individual level. Although more time-consuming, you can see it as an investment for the company in helping people to go forward, saving time and expense in the long run by reducing stress, sickness and absenteeism. Using communication skills, sometimes referred to as coaching individuals, can be very helpful in getting to the root of problems and people's true perceptions and interpretations of events, as well as helping to allay fears and misconceptions. Insecurities often go hand in hand with negative and disruptive emotions.

To create a facilitative environment for the coaching, three criteria are essential for communication and understanding.

- ✔ Respect
- ✔ Empathy
- ✔ Non-judgmental interactions

Using any of these skills is no substitute for professional counselling.

If you as a manager have any serious concerns about how an individual is coping with the changes, you must be aware and arrange individual professional help.

## *Creating a trusting environment*

In order to create a safe and trusting place where people feel they can open up and tell another person their worries, demonstrating the preceding three conditions will help to provide this. There is no way you are expected to act as a counsellor in the professional sense, but helping to build up trust may facilitate a more open relationship at work.

These three essential elements are the core conditions necessary to create a climate of trust and openness and facilitate the communication to take place.

Professional counselling isn't someone listening while people pour out their hearts. The counsellor is actively using skills to help people share their deepest concerns, without fear of being judged, rejected or worry that the counsellor will tell others of their struggles.

Being a professional counsellor is clearly not what is expected of you as a manager. In fact being aware of the boundaries and knowing when to refer on for professional help is an important part of your role.

However, anyone can use the same considerations and skills if they want to listen and help another person to open up. These skills can be useful in any situations where communication is taking place.

## Talking in a respectful and professional manner

Be objective; reflect back what the person is saying: for example, 'It must be a very difficult place for you right now'. Also, be aware of other people's insecurities – you may find them on the defensive or on the attack.

Whatever another person's responses, a golden rule is never to take it personally – the trigger is the situation, not you personally. In the context of CBT and the ABC model (from Chapter 2), people have responsibility for their own reactions to events and changes. You can't be held personally responsible for what's happening to them.

As a manger talking to a person on your team, resist any feelings that you need to 'rescue' people and make things better. You aren't responsible for others' feelings. You can help by introducing them to skills to deal with difficult emotions, but you can't do that for them.

Some of these tools to help in the one-to-one sessions can be taken from using basic counselling techniques of 'active listening'.

## Hearing about active listening

Some of the tips in the preceding section to help in one-to-one sessions connect to the basic counselling technique of active listening.

These active listening skills are useful in many work situations, in your personal life and when dealing with relationships and interactions generally. If you have an awareness of how you're interacting with others, you take more control over how you communicate and how you're received.

### Framework for listening

This framework helps you understand what people are saying, feeling and thinking, and how they're behaving:

> ✔ Experiences: What people experience as happening to them.
>
> ✔ Behaviour: How people act – what they say and do.
>
> ✔ Feelings: What they feel about a situation.
>
> ✔ Thoughts: What sense they make of the situation – of their own behaviour and other people's – and what beliefs they have about themselves, other people and recent events.

### Listening to silences

A conclusion I reached having worked with many clients over many years is that:

> *Whenever there is silence, there is never nothing going on.*

This double negative points out that silences in the one-to-one situation can be a powerful tool.

It is important to allow silences to allow the person you are talking with to reflect and reach their own conclusions. As a manager, you may need to practise being comfortable with silences. In the busy work environment, a silence may seem like an eternity and a luxury but the benefits for the person are worth it. Giving them permission to have some space to think will help them feel really listened to.

Silence can be a way of 'speaking volumes', and listening to people's silences is as important as listening to their words. You gain clues about what they may be thinking or feeling when they're silent. Body language communicates a multitude of messages. For example, you may discern that a person's body language seems to indicate she's feeling hostile or upset, or that she's just reflecting on the situation. You can invite the person to say what's happening for her at the present time, thus giving her the opportunity to talk and making the atmosphere more congenial for opening up.

# Reflecting for better communication

The term reflective skills applies to certain ways of communicating that have the intention of trying to better understand what other people are thinking and feeling. You can use reflective skills consciously to help you communicate your understanding of a person's perspective or frame of reference.

The reflective skills of restating, paraphrasing and summarising are important for communicating an understanding of people's concerns from their perspectives. Reflective skills when used consciously can enable you to communicate your understanding of the employee's perspective or frame of reference.

### Restating

Restating involves repeating back to the person single words or short phrases that she used. It's an efficient way of prompting further discussion.

Restating can feel strange, but it helps the other person to feel that you're trying to understand her point of view and that you're listening to her. The technique encourages further elaboration and enables the counsellor to get some insight into the person's frame of reference.

When restating, the counsellor repeats a word, which is emphasised and emotionally loaded, as follows:

> Person: 'I feel so embarrassed'.
>
> Counsellor: 'Embarrassed?'
>
> Person: 'Yes, I thought I was doing well. I had no idea I was underperforming. I feel such a fool'.

As you can see, restating provides minimal direction to the person and isn't as intrusive as the question, 'What do you mean by embarrassed?' or 'Why were you embarrassed?'

Restating is a useful skill for maintaining the focus in a session, but overuse sounds stilted and contrived. Use appropriately and not like a robot repeating everything back . . . click . . . repeating everything back . . . click . . . repeating everything back. Reboot!

### Paraphrasing

Paraphrasing is the skill of rephrasing what you understand to be the core message of the person's communication. For example:

> Person: 'It's alright for you. What do you know about failure? I bet you've never been rejected. All my life I've been successful and now I'm being told I'm underperforming. I'm the one who's affected by this'.
>
> Counsellor: 'You're angry that I'm not able to share what you're going through?'

Paraphrasing can be an excellent skill for helping people to clarify for themselves what they mean. In order to move on, they need to understand themselves and where they are. For example:

> Person: 'I feel really disappointed with this appraisal and don't know what to do next. I thought I was getting along well – and now this bombshell'.

Counsellor: 'This must have come as a surprise to you because you thought you were on the right tracks and now you're confused as to what you can do next.' Person: 'Yes, I'm not sure what this means'.

Counsellor: 'Would it be helpful to look at the options and start to address some of the issues?'

Here are some useful guidelines for paraphrasing:

✔ Be tentative and offer your perception of what the person has said.

✔ Be respectful.

✔ Use your own words: repeating verbatim isn't paraphrasing.

✔ Don't add to what the person says; evaluate or offer interpretations.

✔ Be genuine and don't pretend to understand, if you don't. Instead, say something like, 'I want to understand . . . let me just check with you'.

✔ Be brief and direct.

✔ Keep your voice tone level: paraphrasing in a disbelieving or surprised tone of voice is unlikely to communicate acceptance.

### Summarising

Summaries are essentially longer paraphrases. Using them enables you to bring together salient aspects in an organised way.

They're a useful way to accomplish the following:

✔ Clarify content and feelings.

✔ Review the session.

✔ End a session.

✔ Begin a further session.

✔ Prioritise and focus.

✔ Move a session forward.

# Probing with questions

Probing skills primarily include asking questions; they're useful for gaining information and changing the focus.

Probes declare the counsellor's perception of what's important to address. When using probes, the control over content is shifted away from the person to the counsellor and the latter is relatively more directive than when reflecting (see the preceding section).

A counsellor has to gain information from people and encourage them to be specific, perhaps in order to direct them to areas that need further exploration.

### Asking questions effectively

Anyone who wants to encourage other people to explore their true thoughts and feelings needs to be aware of the effect and impact of different ways of asking questions; done effectively, it can be a great tool to add to your communication and counselling skills.

Generally, well-timed, clear and open questions have several positive effects:

- ✔ Help people to focus and to be specific
- ✔ Assist information-gathering
- ✔ Open up an area with a person

How you phrase and pose questions affects how successful you are in eliciting a helpful response. Here I take a look at various ways to ask questions.

### Open questions

Open questions are useful forms of questions for eliciting information and encouraging people's involvement. They demand a fuller response than yes/no answers. They generally begin with 'what', 'where', 'how', 'who', 'describe' and 'tell me about'. For example, to someone talking about difficulties she encountered in a work transition, you can ask:

- ✔ 'What specific aspects of the transition have you had difficulty with?'
- ✔ 'How would you describe the difficulties you've encountered?'
- ✔ 'When did you first notice you were experiencing difficulties in carrying out this function?'

### Hypothetical questions

Hypothetical questions are open ones that you can use to focus on what might occur in the future. They're useful for helping people to articulate their fears and explore in the relative safety of a one-to-one feedback session. When they put some words to their fears and beliefs, they're available for modification by challenging.

Hypothetical questions are also valuable for helping people to visualise positive outcomes and imagine working in a different way.

To a person expressing anxiety about the future, you can ask:

- ✔ 'What do you imagine this will be like?'
- ✔ 'What's the worst thing that can happen?'

These types of challenging and thought-provoking questions are in line with the practice of CBT methods. By imagining the worst, facing the fear and rationalising the thinking, this can help reduce anxiety.

Of course, a manager's concern can that by giving this space for the person to open up and voice their innermost concerns, they might reveal that they are feeling hopeless and they can't see the point of going on. Any hint that the person has serious thoughts about hurting themselves or others must be referred for medical help without any doubt.

I have been in a position on a few occasions when I explain the confidentiality clause to clients that everything we discuss is confidential unless they reveal they have thoughts of hurting themselves or others that confidentiality will have to be broken, if they have in fact admitted having these thoughts. We have strict guidelines and procedures how to deal with this. A manager would not be expected to do any more than make an onward referral.

### Unhelpful questions

When I was first learning counselling skills, I found the section on different types of questions quite a revelation. In particular, discovering that unhelpful questions tend to close people down as opposed to helping them communicate was very useful in the work situation.

These unhelpful types of questions are the 'why', 'closed' and 'leading' kind:

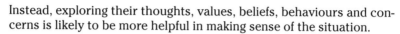

- ✔ **Why questions:** To ask people in an appraisal why they're having difficulty accepting the outcome, doesn't help them: generally, people don't often want to understand why they behave as they do. They know they feel upset.

  Instead, exploring their thoughts, values, beliefs, behaviours and concerns is likely to be more helpful in making sense of the situation.

- ✔ **Closed questions:** The 'yes' or 'no' ones, such as 'Do you feel this appraisal is unfair?' or 'are you having difficulty accepting this appraisal report?'

  These questions just invite people to say 'yes' or 'no'. They don't encourage any exploration of how they're feeling and can often simply silence people.

✔ **Leading questions:** These communicate that the questioner expects a certain answer, or that the listener should hold specific beliefs, values and feelings.

Nonverbal communication can have a strong influence in these cases. You don't encourage people to open up if you 'put ideas in their head', give signs that they 'should' be able to accept their appraisal without question or imply that they aren't living up to the expectation of the company's policy.

# Part V
# Next Steps and the Future

> *Only you can control your future.* – Dr. Seuss
>
> *Avoiding a lapse into old ways of thinking. If you always do what you've always done, you'll always get what you've always got.* – Henry Ford
>
> *Taking responsibility for your whole life and wellbeing. We make a living by what we get, but we make a life by what we give.* – Winston Churchill
>
> *And once the storm is over, you won't remember how you made it through, how you managed to survive. You won't even be sure whether the storm is over. But one thing is certain. When you come out of the storm, you won't be the same person who walked in. That's what the storm's all about.* – Haruki Marukami
>
> *Change is inevitable – except from a vending machine.* – Robert C Gallagher

 Visit http://www.dummies.com/extras/cbtatwork for great Dummies content online.

## In this part . . .

✔ See where you can easily apply what you've learned about CBT outside of work and into your personal life.

✔ Understand the importance of being flexible and adapting yourself to the changing situations that life throws at you.

✔ Learn to handle responsibility, consider a change of career direction, and even entertain the idea if self-employment is the path for you.

✔ Understand that how you deal with changes is greatly influenced by your attitude and your openness to new experiences.

# Chapter 16

# Transferring Your CBT Practice to New Situations

. . . . . . . . . . . . . . . . . . . . . . . . . . . . . . . . . . . . . . . . . .

*In This Chapter*

▶ Casting your CBT net wider

▶ Using CBT in your personal life

▶ Looking after your whole self

. . . . . . . . . . . . . . . . . . . . . . . . . . . . . . . . . . . . . . . . . .

*A* study conducted by the Carnegie Institute of Technology and published in 1936 found that even in technical areas of work, such as engineering, only about 15 per cent of the financial success of the company is down to technical knowledge. In contrast, a massive proportion of 85 per cent is down to skills in so-called human engineering, which includes the ability to get along with people, leadership skills and personality.

Of course, this book covers how you can use CBT techniques to reduce the emotional roller coasters in your life at work, such as anxiety and other unsettling feelings. But you don't completely isolate work from your personal life, and so in this chapter I look at how what's happening in your work and personal lives is part of your whole being. Therefore, I discuss using your new-found CBT knowledge and skills in other areas of your life, which nonetheless impact on your work as well. These include your personal relationship, with family, partners, friends and acquaintances. You are just as likely to experience emotional ups and downs in your life and relationships outside of work, when you have challenges and decisions to make as you have in work. Some people can keep their work and home lives separate; however, sometimes you can't help but bring your personal problems to work with you.

# Widening the Application of Your CBT Skills

One of the most frequently occurring comments I receive from people who complete my work-focused CBT-based transition management course is that they can easily apply what they've learnt in the sessions outside of work.

One participant said that the course had changed her life: she'd rationalised her working hours, firmed up the boundaries between work and home, finally set the date for her wedding and built in time to work on a project with her partner. Previously, she'd made work her constant priority, which adversely affected her personal and social life. She had felt guilty and unhappy, but CBT helped her to rationalise her views about work and make a number of positive changes.

Your working life is often intricately interlinked with the rest of your life. In this section, I discuss your need to display adaptability and confidence.

## Being flexible in your CBT approach

Holding rigid views can sometimes mean that you experience negative emotional consequences (refer to Chapter 3 for more on this). Holding on to such beliefs for the sake of it, or because you've always thought that way, just isn't in your best interest.

You can, however, train yourself to be more open and flexible in your views and actions, including in the situations in which you choose to use CBT, even if your default mode is to be rigidly in control and hang on to certain ways of thinking and behaving.

You can find that changing your views is difficult, however, because you experience discomfort when you actively work to change your 'I should', 'I ought' and 'I must' thinking to more 'I'd prefer' views. Holding on to rigid beliefs for the sake of it, because you have always thought a certain way, may not be in your best interest. Using the CBT techniques in this book to help you practise being more open and flexible is going to benefit you over time. For more on this aspect of CBT in particular, check out Chapter 17 about how adjusting to transitions at work can equally apply to adjusting to changes in your personal life.

## Spotting the contextual clues for CBT use

When are you likely to choose to be more flexible in how and when you use CBT? Only you can know the answer to this question.

When you feel emotionally unsettled at work, socially or home, you have two overall options:

✔ You can decide to feel upset and let these feeling spiral out of control: tipping over into your life generally, keeping you awake at night, making you feel irritable and anxious. Doesn't sound much fun, does it?

✔ You can stop and pay attention to these feelings, choosing to focus on what's occurring and use the CBT techniques to work out what's happening.

Be on the alert for feelings of unease in your home and social life. For example, if the phone rings and your heart sinks when you recognise the caller ID, that could be the trigger for deciding to set some time aside to work out what it is about that person that sets off these feelings. A bit like installing an app on your phone to alert you to incoming potential trouble ahead:

✔ The clue is in how you feel.

✔ The context is that you can feel upset in certain situations.

✔ The CBT techniques can be used in any context where you experience emotional discomfort.

## *Taking confidence into new environments*

Armed with your CBT toolkit from Chapter 3 (which is with you at all times if you choose to pay attention to it), you can deploy it in any situation. Your new CBT skills and methods help you deal with potentially difficult situations or interactions forever more.

No-one can take away your new-found skills. You take that emotional strength with you wherever you go. Some days you feel less strong than others – perhaps you feel tired or are coming down with a cold – and you may find it harder to cope. But you know that you have that strength available to use if you need it.

You may not always perform as well as you'd like to, but the key is to not wind yourself up and mentally punish yourself. Accept that today isn't a great day or that your particular response or decision wasn't the greatest, but also that dwelling on it and creating more negative feelings doesn't help.

You're a fallible human being. Sometimes you make a mistake: it's tough but not the end of the world. Accept – be appropriately annoyed, but not angry – and move on.

As one of my guests on the cruise ship lectures said: 'Build a bridge and get over it'. That bridge can be your mental efforts to rationalise your thinking and your views of yourself and move on.

## Believing in using your skills and experience

When you go through a tough time and are on the receiving end of challenges, don't lose sight of the fact that you have many skills and talents that no-one can take away from you. If you find self-doubt creeping in and nibbling away at your confidence, remember your beliefs in yourself:

'I'm an okay person'.

Make a list of all the things you can do or enjoy. Include anything from riding a bike, baking a cake, playing a computer game, reading a story to children, making people laugh, helping others out of a fix, being part of a sports team, enjoying yoga, singing, playing an instrument, researching, listening to others – anything you can think of.

Whenever I get clients to ask three people to tell them three skills or positive attributes they see in them, the clients often are amazed at what they hear about themselves. You may be very good at finding your own faults but not so great at seeing your own positive characteristics. If you haven't done so already, flip to Chapter 9 and do that exercise now. Then come back here and do the next one; don't worry, I'll be waiting for you.

Take the two lists: the one of the skills that you consider you have and the other one your three friends or family gave you. Keep these lists safe.

Whenever you have a 'wobble' and moments of self-doubt, and you feel yourself dwelling on your actions and behaviours in a negative way, get the lists out and reread them. Tell yourself that this is the person you really are.

# Making Use of CBT Outside of Work

Take some time to think about what happens to you in your life outside of work. For the purposes of this section, treat 'working time' as the time you spend in paid and unpaid work, including:

✔ Time spent in your paid job

✔ Looking after the family

✔ Domestic responsibilities and chores

My focus in this section is your life at times other than these working periods. I help you calculate the time you spend working (in one sense or another) and how dominant work is in your life. Armed with this info, you can then use CBT to enhance your life in all its aspects.

# *Identifying your own working pattern*

No doubt, you have your own unique working pattern.

If you're in paid work, your contract may well specify, say, 40 hours as your basic working week, even if in reality you choose, or need, to work longer hours.

You may have chosen to work part time, out of necessity to fit in caring for others, or because of availability of work. You may have more than one part-time job and work shift patterns.

Make a list of all the hours you work in a typical week. Include not only the time you spend in paid work, but also time spent in unpaid work activity, such as domestic responsibilities, caring for others and any other activities that may not be your first choice of how to spend your time, but you feel are necessary, or you're obliged, to carry out. Go through the list and rewrite it as a 'wish list', of how you'd like your work schedule to be if you could wave a giant magic wand.

The problem is that you can find yourself swept along with feeling that you 'have to' dedicate your time to all these activities, without stopping to look at whether driving yourself towards anxiety, guilt and depression really is in your best interests.

You always have options. They may be hard choices to make, but you can allow yourself to take the following steps:

1. Be honest and take time to list all the options.

2. Work out the consequences for each different choice.

3. Look at your 'should, ought or must' thinking regarding each option.

4. Use the CBT technique to rationalise each of the 'should, ought and must' thoughts that you have.

5. Use that magic wand to decide what you'd really prefer to do, what consequences each choice would bring, and finally make a conscious decision to do certain things and accept them.

You don't have to like your choices and decisions. But by working through them and making a conscious decision to get on with them – because you rationalise that at this moment doing so is in your long-term best interests – you accept them and feel calmer.

## Your work and life is in the balance

During the 1970s in the UK, the term work–life balance was created to recognise a difference between a person's work and personal life. This term was used more frequently in the United States and the whole topic of trying to achieve a healthy work–life balance was widely discussed in companies, HR departments, by employees and in articles in the media.

A sea change in attitudes occurred towards working. The 1960s and 1970s saw an increase in wealth for many countries, greater accessibility to higher education and altered expectations of people in work. The idea of work as an unquestionable necessity and acceptance of working conditions was challenged, as working hours and job descriptions changed.

The boundaries at work have only become even more blurred with the 24/7 access afforded by new technologies. But now undoubtedly people are working longer hours because of their ability to take work home, on holiday, or in fact anywhere, with them.

## *Working to live or living to work*

The concept of a 'work–life' conflict dates back farther than you may think. In the 1800s, anthropologists considered a definition of happiness as occurring when very little separation exists between 'your work and your play', so even back then work and home life seemed to merge into one. For more background, see the nearby sidebar 'Your work and life is in the balance'.

The importance of finding your own work–life balance is not only important for your personal sense of wellbeing. Companies also report that good life–work balances for employees are part of successful and thriving organisations. Research in the UK shows that a good work–life balance can contribute to an outstandingly successful organisation. Factors such as strategy, technology and organisational structure were less important than previously thought.

People are what really matters to companies' success.

If your work–life balance is weighted disproportionately to the work side, when you'd prefer it wasn't, applying some CBT techniques is helpful to work out how you'd prefer the situation to be. Only you can be alert to emotional imbalances and the negative effects they may have on you. Drawing up your own analysis charts and writing down the advantages and disadvantages of how you organise your life currently, or more likely how your life has become as you respond to all the demands and challenges work presents you with, and being proactive in how you lead your life helps you along the road to a happier life.

## Catching up with CBT

Not many people are taught coping strategies for emotional disturbances in school. Granted, the introduction of Personal and Social Education type courses do address some issues connected to emotional development. But not many schools teach students how to recognise and cope with emotional upsets and concerns in a practical and methodological way.

I certainly wish I'd been taught CBT when I was in my teens, because I think I'd have spent a lot less time making myself anxious, angry, guilty and at times depressed. All these feelings are natural parts of life, of course, but having some understanding of why I was making myself upset and some practical information to help

me do something about it would have been welcome. I learnt about CBT in my 30s and I can certainly confirm that my professional life benefitted: I made more rational choices, increased my confidence, was more open to new experiences and less likely to whine and interpret events negatively. I was far more likely to rationalise events and other peoples' actions and far less likely to jump up and down when things didn't go the way I wanted them to. I didn't personalise issues as much, was more accepting and tried to work on moving forward with things that were within my power to control.

# Using CBT in your personal life

CBT is a universal tool. You can use it anywhere, anytime and whenever you want to reduce unpleasant feelings. Don't restrict its use just to work: that would be like working as a mechanic in a garage but not servicing your own car. What a waste of skill!

Education is a progressive process and you build on previous knowledge and skills. The same applies to CBT.

You didn't learn math at school so that you can doodle algebraic functions to while away the hours! No, it's a practical skill that you use throughout your personal and professional lives. Otherwise, you couldn't work out your personal finances, your salary, measurements and so on.

# Combining your emotional and physical health

Although this book focuses on using CBT at work, it wouldn't make sense to not have a look at what you're doing in your personal life to try to keep or create a balance in your body and mind. Often making time to include some 'down time' and some fun and enjoyable pursuits takes low priority. When work takes up so much time, and you have domestic responsibilities and perhaps family commitments, just getting enough sleep could be a luxury. Arriving at work feeling sleep deprived due to outside pressures as well as perhaps having taken work home with you can set you up for putting your body and mind under a great strain. Whilst there is no magic wand to remove some of these pressures, making yourself aware and taking some time to look at how you might make some changes to reduce these pressures will be time well spent. I see many clients who have self-referred themselves for counselling or perhaps been referred from work who somehow make time to come for their hour session each week. The relief of taking an hour out to try to make some sense of how their life is and the insights and changes they make once they jump off the high speed train they find themselves on to take stock has benefits not only to themselves but to those around them, too.

You're a whole person, made up of your physical body and your mind, and so splitting yourself into separate parts risks ignoring this reality. In Chapter 2, I discuss how what your senses perceive physically has a direct effect on your body chemistry. If you see a potentially threatening situation in any area of your life, your body reacts by pouring adrenalin into your bloodstream to prime your muscles to stay and fight or run away.

### Spotting stress symptoms

No doubt you're aware of work-based stress: it's probably the most high-profile type. But plenty of events outside of work can cause you stress as well.

As you go about your daily, non-work life, you're constantly processing information around you. Many 'threats' exist in the environment and your body reacts automatically without you really being aware or conscious of the chemical changes taking place. It doesn't take much to get that adrenalin pumping and for you to suffer stress.

Here are just some examples of everyday 'threats' you can encounter. Each event has an impact on you:

- Waking up late
- Running for the bus
- A long queue for your morning coffee
- Getting a call from school that your child is ill
- Opening a bill to find that it's higher than you expected

These are just some of the 'threats' you might encounter. Each event has an impact on you.

Your mind processes this information and you interpret each event according to your own personal viewpoint: some you pay particular attention to and others just come and go subconsciously.

Constantly experiencing daily hassles can have an accumulative effect on your emotional and physical wellbeing. Sometimes you can start to be aware that you're feeling generally a bit 'stressed'; at other times, your attention can be focused on one event and you're aware only of feeling one of the following emotions, or indeed any other negative feeling:

- ✔ Angry
- ✔ Anxious
- ✔ Guilty
- ✔ Hurt
- ✔ Scared

For more details on other alternative ideas that you may find useful, check out *Meditation For Dummies* by Stephan Bodian and *Mindfulness For Dummies* by Shamash Alidina (both Wiley).

## Adopting a holistic approach

You may want to consider introducing other methods into your life to help you deal with negative feelings and enhance your overall wellbeing. I'm a great believer in using alternative theories as part of a holistic approach in life to enhance wellbeing, such as integrating stress management, mindfulness courses, meditation and yoga, as well as educational seminars on nutrition, exercise, mental-health awareness and a variety of programmes.

If it helps you, go for it, as long as it's ethical, doesn't extort huge amounts of money from you or insist on a long-term financial commitment, and it's practised by well-qualified professionals. After all, only you know what's good for yourself. All knowledge is power for you to make educated choices for your own wellbeing. In addition, modern research using blood-hormone analysis and MRI scanning techniques is proving changes in body chemistries as a result of some of the alternative approaches that have therapeutic effects on people's bodies. For centuries, people intuitively felt that these approaches were beneficial, and now science is catching up.

These days, companies and organisations include many alternative therapies as resources for their workforces. The feedback is very encouraging, not only for the individual but also for the health of the company in financial terms. The European Research Council in 2013 reported that holistic workplace practices are now becoming more common and that incorporating holistic approaches is bringing about positive results.

Offering alternative practices is seen as an investment in employees' overall health, which can help reduce stress, increase awareness of creating a healthy lifestyle, reduce absenteeism and create a support system for emotional as well as physical wellbeing.

## *Seeking balance through exercise*

Making an effort to achieve a balance for yourself outside of work maximises your chances of increasing your wellbeing inside work as well. This reality concerns your physical and emotional lives.

Of course, CBT is useful for looking at your mental wellbeing balance. But just as you become more mindful of recognising when your emotions are getting out of kilter, and use CBT techniques to bring them back into equilibrium, so too you need to be aware of when your body is sending you messages that it's becoming physically unbalanced.

Seeking medical advice for physical symptoms of potential ill-health can help you to restore a state of equilibrium for your body and mind. Some of the symptoms that can indicate physical imbalances to watch out for include:

- ✔ Colds and other infections
- ✔ Increase in aches and pains
- ✔ Gastrointestinal discomfort
- ✔ Headaches
- ✔ Lack of energy
- ✔ Sleep disturbances
- ✔ Loss of interest in sex
- ✔ Chest pain and rapid heartbeats
- ✔ Sweating
- ✔ Grinding teeth at night
- ✔ Clenched jaw
- ✔ Vocal changes

You don't have to opt for apparently wacky alternative practices, go on long courses, wear 'alternativey' clothes or spend loads of cash to help balance your life! Simply being mindful that you want to include some physical activity as much as you can is a great start. Going outside, away from enclosed buildings and having some fresh air and exercise, such as walking regularly, is conducive to physical and mental wellbeing.

# Creating an Overall Consistent Way of Being

Structure, discipline and routine can help your body and mind create stability for your life. Your body is a clever machine with 'autopilots' to make regular changes to adjust to differing conditions. The body tends to seek and maintain a balance or equilibrium internally when the external world changes. For example, the usual internal temperature of a body is 37 degrees centigrade. When the body experiences changes in outside temperatures, it starts to adjust automatically to maintain that 37 degrees.

CBT views the discomfort and imbalances in your psychological states as being derived from your irrational thoughts. You can identify these thoughts and consciously work on them to reduce the tensions, as I explain in Chapter 2.

This section is about the need for stability and consistency across your entire life. Monitoring your emotional states can't be put in a box and just looked at when things really start to get out of control. You will come across new situations continuously and your mind will be taking them all in and you will be making decisions and taking actions. You may find it useful to regularly 'check in' with yourself to be aware of how things are going for you. You may be quite familiar with the idea of making an appointment to see a medical doctor if you get signs of physical discomfort to check out if there is anything you need to do to alleviate the discomfort but the idea of checking in with a professional to see how your mental health is when you have discomfort is perhaps not as usual. Remember – you don't have to wait until things start going wrong to conduct an emotional MOT on yourself. You can start to build it into your life yourself.

## Maintaining an awareness of your overall emotional situation

You can decide how often you may want to 'check in' with your own emotional state. You won't have time, nor would you want to be constantly monitoring your emotional fluctuations but maybe schedule in a time when you reflect over the last week and take a look at how things have been for you. Very often, you may have a 'catch up' with a friend, and possibly this is a time you share what has been happening for you and how you are feeling. Ironically, you may not have time to meet up with a close friend or indeed have time to include regular friends into your life, which in itself is a good reason to build in your own 'catch up' time.

Doing this sort of exercise and using the CBT method to weed out the imbalances that are creeping into your life and plan for future actions to make your life less stressed and giving yourself a better chance for a more enjoyable future will happen if you start to plan and anticipate how you want to be in future situations. Some of these future situations you may be able to be in charge of by making your own choices and some will just present themselves and not be in your control. Either way, the same CBT methods apply.

As Dr.Seuss said:

> *Only you can control your future.*

When something is awry physically, you become aware of discomfort: perhaps a headache or stomach ache, a fever or an increase in aches and pains. You then choose to try to remedy that physiological discomfort.

Well, you need to be just as vigilant for changes in your emotions that give you discomfort. Only you can read your emotional barometer.

The facts show an increasing rise in the incidents of reported mental-health issues. Only you can choose to do something about your emotional discomfort. No-one else can do this for you, unless you become extremely distressed and ill emotionally.

Keep an eye on yourself and be aware of when you start feeling unhappy in different areas. The mind is like any other part of you in that if it starts to weaken, the sooner you attend to the signs and do something to redress the balance, the sooner it recovers and, most importantly, the less likely you are to drop into a chronic state of mental ill-health.

> *Avoiding a lapse into old ways of thinking. If you always do what you've always done, you'll always get what you've always got.*
>
> — Henry Ford

Using CBT methods when you come across situations and events that have flagged up the presence of uneasiness for you in the past will stand you in good stead for preparing you to be on the ball in applying the same methods in new situations. Using CBT in the moment is a skill you can develop and so prepare yourself for any bumpy roads ahead.

Implementing CBT practical strategies to monitor and assume control of your own mental health takes hard work. If you decide that you like the ideas and practices, it's something you can use for the future. CBT isn't a quick fix diet that you get excited about and use for the duration of reading this book; it's something that may well become part of your way of being for the rest of your life.

Like any new ideas you come across, the novelty can keep you focused and engaged for a while, but then you find that you fall back into older established ways of habitual thinking. Like most people, you have a natural tendency to want to return to your comfort zones and familiar patterns of thinking and behaving. If you don't pay attention, you can forget what you learned, misinform yourself about aspects or even choose to ignore it. Constant revision and application helps you to be mindful of the techniques to help yourself.

Many clients I've seen, who report feeling much better after learning CBT and starting to use it regularly in their lives, start to panic and worry that they're feeling better. This sounds odd but is quite a common worry. If you've been used to fearing the worst and feeling anxious or low in spirits for a long time, starting to feel consistently better can be scary. I've had clients report back 'I'm feeling much better, touch wood', many a time. I point out that touching wood doesn't affect their continued progress. The only thing that you can rely on to help you continue to improve and maintain a sense of control and rational thinking is yourself. If you stop being mindful of your emotional states and choose to ignore warning signs of slipping back into old ways of thinking, yes, you can start feeling bad again. CBT isn't magic: it's about taking responsibility for your emotional health.

 Think of CBT as involving 'baby steps': taking small steps to improve balance and walking, working hard and consistently to move forward and eventually walking confidently, reaching the places you set your mind to. It involves walking three steps forward and two back as you learn, apply, improve, go back over old ground, reapply and move forward.

> *Take responsibility for your whole life and wellbeing. We make a living by what we get, but we make a life by what we give.*
>
> — Winston Churchill

Only you have the power to take charge of yourself. You may decide for example to equip yourself with a care package for a road trip you are planning, with food, drink, blankets and maps or apps to help guide you. So equipping yourself with your CBT app, ready to face new situations and deal with events, will increase your chances of a successful life journey.

 On a skiing holiday with a group of friends, one day we spent so long in après ski and getting ready to go out for dinner that by the time we went out to find a restaurant, they'd all closed. One person was particularly upset and quite vocal about blaming others in the group for their tardiness. He was making himself quite angry. Without paying too much attention, I threw in my tuppence: 'We aren't responsible for your happiness'. Afterwards, he told me that he was fuming: he found my comment inconsiderate, inflammatory and thought I'd showed little respect for his feelings.

We worked at the same place and over the next few weeks he asked me about CBT and I taught him some of the basics. He related this ski incident to me months later and told me that now he understood why I'd said that. He agreed that no-one else is responsible for his own personal happiness, that he'd changed his views on life and wasn't always looking to others to make him happy.

Other people can add to your happiness; they can often contribute to your sense of wellbeing by their considerate actions and healthy concern for you. But if you demand that others 'make' you happy, you're likely to experience at the very least disappointment, but more often than not, make yourself angry, hurt, depressed and generally feel quite sorry for yourself.

The more you learn about yourself, your personality, your preferred styles of working and what you expect from yourself and others, the more likely you are to make your life rewarding and fulfilling.

Give yourself the best opportunities, be open to experiences and when things get tough, get out your CBT toolkit from Chapter 3 and work on those difficulties.

# Chapter 17

# Adapting to the Inevitable Changes at Work

## In This Chapter

▶ Finding your flexible friend

▶ Coping with work changes

▶ Staying true to yourself

*It is not the strongest of the species that survives, or the most intelligent that survives. It is the most adaptable to change.*

— Charles Darwin

This statement is as true today as when Darwin wrote these words in the 19th century, when he was developing his theories on evolution. Being able to adapt to changing conditions means that you're more likely to cope with life – and be happier and perhaps more successful, too. Although you no longer have to go out hunting for food or live in caves to fulfil your basic needs (unless that particularly floats your boat!), you do have to find food and shelter. You may have swapped the spear for a laptop and your cave for a mortgage or rent, but you still need to find ways to survive – and to prosper happily.

In this chapter, I take a look at the importance of being flexible – don't worry, not in the sense of being bodily bendy! I mean in regards to adapting yourself to the changing situations that life throws at you. I describe how CBT can help you to stay grounded and retain your sense of self even while events around you seem disorienting.

# Accepting the Need to Be Flexible

*Change is inevitable – except from a vending machine.*

— Robert C Gallagher

Humans are born unable to fend for themselves. They're dependent on adults to look after them as babies and children until they're old enough to find a way to support themselves. In most countries, people need to find paid work as they grow up and eventually gain independence from caregivers. All countries have developed at different rates. In transforming from mainly agricultural societies to industrialised and highly technical ones, the types and variety of jobs developed too.

Your chances of earning enough money to support yourself are influenced by your determination, persistence, confidence and, for the focus of this section, your flexibility and adaptability. Generally speaking, if you take the available opportunities to learn new skills, you increase the likelihood of finding work.

You need to be able and willing to adapt and learn new skills when situations are rapidly changing. The days of one job for life and then a sizeable pension, which were prevalent in the 1950s in the UK, for example, have long been replaced by rapid diversification of roles at work, change and uncertainty.

## Diagnosing the problem

You may have an idea of where you prefer your comfort zone to be. Your idea of feeling stable and 'happy in your skin' may be quite different from another person.

Check out Chapter 9 for more on different types of personality and how these affect people's choices of how they live their lives. Some outgoing personalities seek out challenge and change and thrive on variety, unpredictability and excitement. Other more introverted people prefer to work in jobs that require more emphasis on inner reflective and self-contained ways of working. Perhaps you shudder at the thought of working away overseas and changing your projects regularly, whereas your friend relishes the challenge and excitement of moving jobs, countries and homes.

Whichever personality type you feel you're more like, you can find that some jobs you take on don't fit with your preferred way of working. You may conclude that you're 'at fault' somehow and your struggles are caused by yourself.

Not true! CBT can help you work out that the root of your difficulty is the situation, not you as a person. All your working life is going to involve transitions, changes, adaptations and progress. As the Talking Heads' song 'Once in a Lifetime' says, you can arrive at a point in your career that just doesn't seem to be working out:

And you may find yourself in another part of the world
And you may find yourself behind the wheel of a large automobile
And you may find yourself in a beautiful house, with a beautiful wife
And you may ask yourself – Well . . . how did I get here?

## *Treating the symptoms with CBT*

CBT encourages you to take stock of what's happening for you and gives you the tools to be able to investigate rationally the root causes of your thinking – what pressures you're putting on yourself – and to allow you to look at your options.

CBT can help you to see that the situation is what triggers the irrational thinking of 'I must, I have to, I should be able to cope and I'm worthless if I can't'. You can then change your thinking around as follows:

> *I'd prefer to be able to do this job, but at this moment in time it's not the best place for me. I'm disappointed but I'm not a worthless person, I'm just in the wrong place for me. I do have choices; I want to calm down so I can look at what other options exist. It's okay to accept that this job isn't for me. Making myself anxious every day and thinking I don't have any choices isn't helping. They may be tough choices, and I may not have the necessary training and experience to move into a new role yet, but I can start investigating what options I have.*

In my dedication at the back of this book, I include the quote, 'Spirit has no age'.

This came from me questioning myself and having self-doubts about applying to do a writing degree at age 60. I voiced my concerns to my daughter, and she immediately came back with 'Mum, spirit has no age'. I thought this was a great comment; only you can stop yourself from trying new things, and if it doesn't work out, at least you gave yourself your best shot. If you don't have the necessary skills now to make changes, you can start to build up the missing skills you need. It probably won't be an easy option, only you can make it happen.

Even if it goes against your natural preference to work in a safe and secure environment and resist change, you know rationally that flexibility is what you need to move on. The first step in changing is being adaptable enough to allow you to consider other options, so freeing yourself up.

The discomfort you experience in the here and now as you allow yourself to contemplate change is a worthwhile investment in your life and future. Of course, every time you contemplate or actually do something new, you experience some level of discomfort. But feel the pain and do it anyway. Remind yourself why you're doing it.

Use CBT to help you work through the steps of changing your thinking.

People have said to me that they couldn't do some of the things I've done and that they haven't the confidence to travel on their own, change jobs or move on to pastures new. Some even say that they admire some of these things, such as going off to run a ski chalet at age 50! But I explain to them that every time I do something new I feel nervous. It doesn't come easily. I get anxious even filling up a different car with fuel!

What I've learnt, mainly through the CBT training, is to expect discomfort, weigh up the options, push myself through the discomfort zone and make myself take a chance with new ventures. Things don't always turn out how I'd hoped. I make mistakes and unhelpful choices and I get things wrong. But CBT helps me to accept those mistakes, rationalise what went wrong and move on.

## Recognising your preferred environment

Lizzie had always loved working with children and regularly helped out at the chess club in the local area. She enjoyed the challenge of coaching the youngsters in chess and seeing them win competitions. Her own favourite subjects were science, particularly environmental and conservation studies. She graduated in environmental science and trained to be a teacher.

Her first teaching post was in an inner-city secondary school, where her primary responsibility was to teach biology. Lizzie struggled with her job. She found that she didn't enjoy being in charge of large classes. Her confidence reduced as she struggled with maintaining discipline and she became very unhappy. She seemed to be moving further away from her love of environmental science and began to dislike being in the company of the youngsters. Her health suffered and she started to experience panic attacks on the way to work.

Her CBT mentor noticed her distress and arranged a meeting to discuss her situation. Lizzie blamed herself for not being able to do the job and felt like a failure and hopeless. She agonised over the fact that she'd done all the teacher training and felt that she 'had' to do that teaching job. While she felt trapped, her anxiety levels and sense of distress had risen.

Her mentor realised that the root of the distress was that Lizzie wasn't in a role that suited her. Lizzie had many skills, talents and experiences to teach to others, but the large group situation didn't suit her personality. A role outside of the school at the local Environmental Studies Centre as the leader came up and someone suggested that Lizzie try for the job. It would mean smaller groups, subject-specific work in an area she was passionate about and opportunities to develop the educational provision.

This example serves to show that you tend to personalise when jobs get difficult and blame yourself and your perceived shortcomings for anxieties you may experience. This is common, but it's an incorrect interpretation of events. In true CBT terms, as I hope now you are beginning to recognise, it's the situation not you personally that triggers the anxiety provoking thoughts. Lizzie was in a situation that did not suit her; once some thought was given to what exactly was at the root of the anxious feelings, it gave a basis to start to work out what would be preferable for her. She was very successful in her new role and above all, happy and smiling Lizzie again.

Of course, it is not always possible to have a mentor to help you to see what is the root cause of your anxieties, but using CBT you can allow yourself to investigate yourself and consider future possible options.

Here's my adapted version of a well-known mantra, which I say to myself whenever worrying thoughts arise: 'Let CBT help me to accept the things I can't change, not upset myself about the situations and people I can't change, and work hard to sort my negative thinking out and move on'.

# Being Flexible at Work: Transitions, Redundancy and Retirement

Flexibility at work enables you to move on and be prepared to take up new challenges. The reality is that you don't always know what's going to happen next at work. You can feel the impacts of market globalisation and of influences outside your control at any time.

In this section, I lay out some of these potential threats to your equilibrium and how CBT can help you to take them in your stride. You may find instead of making yourself anxious at the thought of changes that may be looming on the horizon, once you get the hang of working things out using your CBT methods you may feel more confident about the future as you feel you have a practical coping strategy to use as needed. Perhaps you could think of CBT as having a satnav in your car . . . when you stray into unknown territory, you have a tool at hand to help guide you through it. Just as your satnav needs to be charged and ready, and have regular updates to check it is current and not gathering dust, so you need to regularly use your CBT if you haven't revised it for a long while.

# Maintaining your skills keeps you confident

Mergers, takeovers, rationalisation, downsizing and closures seem to be frequent words in the world of work these days. The insecurity of the marketplace and the instability resulting from external forces can make for turbulent times. Even retirement doesn't seem to be as simple as previously. New legislation can mean that changes in your retirement expectations, in terms of financial benefits and even the age at which you expected to retire when you started your working life, can be subject to change.

The innovations in technology alone in recent decades indicate how fast work is changing. If you decided in the early 1980s that you were willing to learn how to operate the Sinclair ZX Spectrum computer (remember them?) but refused to 'upskill' your technological skills beyond this, you'd have far less opportunities for work than someone who put in the effort to keep pace with the necessary professional development skills. You can have hopes, expectations and a wish-list of how your working life's going to pan out. You can do your best to work hard, study, invest in training and even restrict your social and family life to give yourself the best chance, only to discover that the opportunities you were after don't materialise or become obsolete.

Equipping yourself to cope with all these work changes is one of the most valuable skills you can arm yourself with. Keeping your skills current and relevant improves your chances of success at work and maintains your confidence too.

# Adjusting to transitions at work with CBT

How you view letdowns and setbacks influences how you react and cope with them.

You may not have much control over the changes at work but you do have the capacity to control how you deal with them. This insight lies at the core of CBT training.

For example, faced with a possible redundancy, you have the freedom to choose how you react to the news:

- ✔ You can jump up and down and rail against the company: You can say how unfair life is – and make yourself thoroughly angry or miserable.

- ✔ You can adopt the philosophical approach of CBT: You can accept that the redundancy is a done deal. You don't like it and you're disappointed and annoyed, but you decide that making yourself angry and feeling hurt doesn't help and in the long run is self-defeating, because you're the one making yourself feel bad.

Taking the latter constructive route allows you to look towards investigating what you can do in your position: trying to find more work.

A potential employer is faced with two candidates of equal standing in terms of qualifications and experience. One candidate is still feeling aggrieved about being made redundant: she feels life is unfair and she has a right to be angry about those circumstances. The other candidate accepted that it was an unfortunate situation, and he'd have preferred the situation to be otherwise, but how would winding himself up help?

Even if the first candidate doesn't verbalise her thoughts about the redundancy, her body language may well convey her distress and count against her at an interview.

# Retaining a Sense of Who You Are

During life's changes and transitions, the external world can influence your life in a major way, perhaps making you feel at the beck and call of your employer's changes. As a result, you can feel that you're losing control over your own life and that these external forces are dominating you. The effect can start the anxious feelings bubbling up. Your self-confidence may start to feel eroded, self-doubts start knocking at your doors of perception. All in all, you can start to feel what I call 'twitchy' about everything. Some people may react by feeling angry a lot of the time, others may feel generally anxious and some may have feelings of helplessness and depression. This incoming tide of changes may feel relentless, but the good news is you can make yourself active in deciding to stem the flow of negative feelings. It won't be easy, just as King Canute found out when he sat there thinking that just wanting the tide to turn would sort out his problems and maintain his regal credibility. You need to be pro-active in taking control, probably just at a time when your energy levels feel pretty low, too.

CBT reminds you that you're the constant in the changing tides of your working life. In a sense, you're your own security.

Whatever the events that occur, no-one can take away your sense of integrity, your moral codes and your standards of working practices. Instead, although you change as you gain in experience, you remain true to yourself. In essence you're the same person – no threats can change that – you're just acquiring different skills, knowledge and wisdom. As a result, your sense of self changes but it doesn't change who you are.

## Keeping perspective through changing times

During tough times at work, CBT is very useful for reminding you of your strengths and core values. It provides a practical coping strategy as follows:

- ✔ During tough times at work, it can help to remind yourself of your beliefs.
- ✔ Strive to keep events in perspective.
- ✔ Take time to look at what's happening to you.
- ✔ Use CBT to rationalise your thinking and restore some balance in your emotional life.

Clients I've worked with actively go back to reading the CBT material and resources I give them to keep reminding themselves of how to get some perspective in their lives. For example, in Chapter 9, I encourage you to examine your personality and, in Chapter 10, I offer suggestions to help you work out your own philosophy and attitudes about work.

If you're responsible for keeping a car running, you probably have to return to the manual occasionally to remind yourself of how to tweak the parts that aren't running efficiently. You need to troubleshoot those problems and apply tried-and-tested methods to restore some balance and harmony. So too with your emotional life: keep a check on it and if you hear some creaks and potential malfunctions, work on them before they let you down.

Give yourself regular emotional MOTs and don't wait until you break down.

### Balancing your roles

You have many parts of yourself to regulate, including many different roles and responsibilities. As a result, you present your 'self' as appropriate to the context. You're still the same person, but your behaviours and interactions change according to the people you're interacting with.

To see what I mean, take a look at the following categories and complete them for your own life. As a bit of fun, I show how a certain famous person may fill in the various points:

- ✔ Yourself: Father Christmas!
- ✔ Roles: Toy factory owner; worker; manager and trainer of enthusiastic but sometimes undisciplined elves; distributor of products on a strict, must-meet deadline.

- Relationships: Married to Mrs Claus; perhaps other relatives such as an uncle, a brother, a cousin, nephew, neighbour; six-foot-tall human called Buddy who thinks he's an elf (a reference to the perfect Christmas movie!).

- Hobbies and clubs: Reindeer Club of the North Pole.

Father Christmas may have realized after doing this exercise and looking at all the roles he fulfils that it is no wonder sometimes he feels pulled in all directions, and not just by the reindeer, and at times feels overloaded with responsibilities and deadlines and experiences fluctuating anxiety levels. Now that Norad has a tracking device to see where he is all over the world on Christmas Eve, there is even more pressure to perform on time (www. noradsanta.org). But he applies his rational-thinking Christmas hat to get his job in perspective. He knows now, using CBT, that it will not help to wind himself up into a state of high anxiety over Christmas that could inhibit his performance of present distribution, but rather he needs to have a healthy concern to do his best but not put unhealthy demanding thinking on himself as that won't help him. Good ole Santa!

### Watching yourself over time

Through the course of your lifetime, your roles and responsibilities change – or more accurately, they accumulate along the way.

### Creating a personal 'timeline'

Map out your life along a line – try and include significant life events along the way, from your early memories to the present day. You may need a long piece of paper for this.

Completing this experiential exercise helps you gain perspective on how your experiences have influenced their present-day self.

Include the following aspects: child, family, school (teenager, friends, college), travel, first job, relationships, hobbies (interests, sports), own family, career, future goals and hopes.

A further extension of this exercise is to look specifically at different areas in your life and expand them. For example, you can map out a family-and-friends cluster group diagram, where you place yourself in the middle and draw stick people to represent significant others in your life. Seeing where you place people, in what proximity to you, can give you an insight into how you see them as situated in your life.

## Staying you through thick and thin

You're the constant during all life's changes: you're essentially the same person, just experiencing many changes.

Use the CBT techniques, such as the ones I describe in Chapters 2 and 3, to help ground yourself. Accept yourself as a valuable human being who's working hard to keep the emotional disruptions to a manageable level. Things may be tough right now, but they won't always be as disruptive.

In the great scheme of things, problems and events that seem huge today will appear less influential in the future. I like Rudyard Kipling's famous poem *If*, which starts with this line:

> *If you can keep your head when all about you are losing theirs and blaming it on you . . .*

It's a long poem full of lots of 'ifs', that is looking at future possible scenarios and encouraging you to have a think about what you can do and what you can't do to keep yourself mentally well balanced when life gets tricky. To read the poem in its entirety, you can look it up online – it's well worth the read!

When you stay as your authentic self and actively deal with difficulties in the best way you can, using CBT to help you to rationalise what's going on, you're being the best you can.

## Affirming your status and sense of worth

During times of change, when you feel more insecure than usual and the creeping self-doubts start to edge their way in, you need to be more aware of what's happening for you.

When the 'wobbles' start to hit, allow yourself to acknowledge that you're feeling unsettled. Use the CBT techniques from Chapters 2 and 3 to identify what exactly you're feeling and work at reducing those negative feelings.

'This too shall pass' is a saying thought to have originated in medieval times. Basically it says that all things are transient; bad and good things don't last forever. Don't think that you can avoid bad things, because that way lies frustration and disappointment. At the time you may feel anxious, scared, distressed or even distraught, but if you can bear in mind that you won't always feel like this, and to hang in there and do everything you can to reduce the overwhelming feelings, you know that you'll eventually feel less disturbed.

You're a worthwhile person. You have value and significance. You will get through the changing times. You may have a rough ride but you'll move on.

# Chapter 18

# Revising and Maximising Your Work Opportunities

*In This Chapter*

▶ Looking at how you handle responsibility

▶ Checking out your options for earning a crust

▶ Considering self-employment

> *In this world nothing can be said to be certain, except death and taxes.*
>
> — Benjamin Franklin

*W*hatever your area of work, you're sure to experience some uncertainties from time to time. The hard truth is that no-one can give any guarantees of stability in work. All you can do is your best to try to achieve balance, continuity and harmony in your work, but you can't demand that life be always fair and reasonable – at least, not without suffering emotional turmoil as a result of holding that belief!

In this chapter, I discuss handling responsibility, considering a change of career direction and musing on whether self-employment is the path for you.

## Assessing Your Thinking about Pressure at Work

Being mindful of why you work in your current job and having some ideas of how you'd like your future to be helps you to make the most of your working life. You're probably living your life at work at a fairly frantic pace, busy reacting to situations that occur and responding accordingly. You're required to fulfil your job description and organise your work in the most efficient way to complete the tasks.

If you hold a managerial role or gain promotion to a more responsible job, the pressure increases even further.

## Experiencing stress and worry at work

Having the responsibility of managing others in a team or department can increase the perceived pressures on you. Managing people isn't easy and often you have no-one to offload your worries onto or run your concerns past. Other people may have expectations of you as well as the demands you put on yourself. In particular, moving from the 'shop floor' by being promoted away from the people you were working with can be a lonely and scary transition.

You're likely to impose a lot of unhelpful 'must, ought and should' thinking demands on yourself. This sort of negative thinking includes the following type of thing:

- ✔ I must be seen to be in control and show people I know what I'm talking about.
- ✔ I should be able to cope with this new job but I'm feeling really anxious.
- ✔ I ought to be able to do this job smoothly and show others I'm worthy of this promotion.
- ✔ I should be confident and assertive.

## Using CBT to handle responsibility

If you've recently been promoted into a more responsible role, or you're the boss of a small, medium or large business, you face the pressure of being responsible for and even keeping employees in work. As a result, you can fall into the sort of negative thinking that I describe in the preceding section.

But your CBT training is invaluable in helping you to identify and deal with such thoughts. Doing so helps you avoid unsettling emotions of anxiety, fear, panic attacks and depressed feelings.

CBT can help you change dogmatic, demanding thinking into a healthier 'preference' way of thinking, which in turn helps to reduce those negative feelings.

No-one is perfect in his job. Accept that sometimes you're going to find your role tough. You're aware that others may resent you, try to be unco-operative and maybe even obstructive. But these people can unsettle you only if you allow their opinions and behaviours to impact on your sense of self.

Accept yourself as a fallible human being who doesn't have all the answers. But you do have the best intentions and will do what's humanly possible to carry out a good job.

# Mapping Your Work Options

*And once the storm is over, you won't remember how you made it through, how you managed to survive. You won't even be sure whether the storm is over. But one thing is certain. When you come out of the storm, you won't be the same person who walked in. That's what the storm's all about.*

— Haruki Marukami

Pinning yourself down to taking a serious look at what you can offer the world of work, in whatever format suits you best, is a helpful exercise. When you write down what you really want to get from work and how your current skills and experiences match up to your goals, you can see more clearly where you want to head.

When writing your own career road map, bear these points in mind:

- ✔ Be bold
- ✔ Be specific
- ✔ Be optimistic

Give yourself some space to consider in depth what options are available for the way you work.

Using CBT techniques outlined in Chapter 2, you are encouraged to look at what options and future constructive behaviour you might consider after you work through an emotional upheaval. This section encourages you to spend some time looking at the possible future choices you might have in order to be pro-active in optimising your future work opportunities. I provide plenty of useful information on assessing your own skills and being realistic.

## Conducting a skills audit on yourself

As the job markets and industries change in fluctuating economic climates, you increase your chances of success when you change your ways of working.

A skills audit involves you sitting down and taking a look at what skills and talents you have. Perhaps you see your skills in terms of what exams you passed and what certificates you acquired.

Creating your own skills audit helps you to stabilise your objective assessment of yourself. Understanding how you can use CBT to stabilise your sense of self as you navigate work and career changes and transitions helps to anchor your emotional states in what can be trying times.

Durham University in the UK has a website where you can check out what a skills audit is and follow the step-by-step suggestions for working out your own. The benefits of doing so are clear. The website quotes the following from a leading IT company boss:

> *Students who invest time and energy in developing their non-academic skills throughout their university life significantly improve their employability upon graduation. They emerge more balanced, self-aware and mature individuals who differentiate themselves in the fiercely competitive graduate recruitment market.*
>
> — James Boddy, IBM

The Durham version helps you assess your skills and it's a useful process, whether you intend to apply to college or university or not. As the website says, the online skills audit encourages you to create your own list of areas for development in the following six core categories:

- ✔ Understanding disciplines
- ✔ Study skills
- ✔ Interpersonal skills
- ✔ Entrepreneurial behaviours
- ✔ Personal effectiveness
- ✔ Understanding the world around you

Check out `https://www.dur.ac.uk/careers/s/employability/skills/audit` for more details.

## *Learning from my experience*

You may think that you don't have many talents and that you'd feel uncomfortable making a list of skills for yourself. But there's no need. To show you what I mean, I provide an example from my own life in this section.

When I returned to the UK after a year working abroad, I felt unsettled. Going back to my old teaching job was difficult and I was interested in learning more about training in stress management. I wrote a list of what I really wanted to do. At the top of the list was: 'Run a stress management consultancy'.

I felt ill-equipped to do so: I had much enthusiasm but no confidence. A colleague suggested I had some careers advice and I went along to a local provider. I opened my session by saying: 'I am just a teacher'.

The careers officer proceeded to show me that I had many skills and talents. I was sceptical and so he demonstrated by giving me a list of what being able to teach classes of youngsters demonstrated in my skills portfolio: it showed the skills of management, organisation, assessment, innovation, record-keeping, flexibility, adaptability, creativity, financial skills and many more.

I was surprised. I hadn't seen myself in that light before. I tended to be proactive, forging ahead and trying new things, some of which were successful, others not. It was always easier to put myself down for the things that didn't work than to take some time to acknowledge achievements. This session gave me the confidence to send my CV to places that employed consultant psychologists, sign up for a course in stress-management training and start to set up my own company. I was given four follow-up business coaching sessions. I saw myself differently afterwards and wrote down my goals, targets and what I needed to do to change my career.

A skills audit – whether via a formal careers adviser or informally by yourself – can help you identify areas for development and opportunities for keeping a rational perspective in the employment arena. In a sense, your CBT toolkit is also a collection of skills, and if you apply it at regular intervals it can help you to stay on track for rational thinking.

Just like physical training or learning any new skills, you need to understand what's involved in learning CBT, practise it, revise it, practise it some more and be mindful of keeping it in your life.

If you don't use it, you lose it.

To stay still is to risk losing the strength you've gained and start sliding back to where you started.

CBT emphasises that change involves a level of discomfort; you need to go through the discomfort zone in order to progress to the next level. You build on each achievement both professionally and personally.

## Focusing on the realistic

When considering the choices you have available for work opportunities, you may want to be mindful that you're looking at options that are realistic for you. If you don't have a basic qualification in maths or faint at the sight of blood, putting brain surgeon as a desired preference may be a bit ambitious (the NHS has enough worries!). That's not to say you should limit your options at this stage, just that you need to keep some perspective of what's realistic for you. You don't have to stay in the job you have, and the chance to investigate a career change is always available (check out the nearby sidebar 'It's never too late' for inspiration).

Doing your skills audit (see the preceding section) helps you to see pragmatically what you may need to add to your skills portfolio if you want to change your job or career. Some changes may be quite basic but others can require a longer-term investment in yourself.

---

### It's never too late

One of my roles as a lecturer was to run the 'Access to Higher Education' training course, which prepares people without traditional qualifications for study at university. No upper age limit or formal entry requirements apply. Most of these students had for some reason not stayed in school to gain their qualifications, but decided later in life that they wanted to learn and study to gain access to higher education. I found that their motivation and commitment levels were high because they were determined to advance their skills and opportunities. The courses are usually offered on a full- or part-time basis, to allow students to continue to work and support themselves and their families and study at the same time. Specific courses are run for access to a variety of degree courses and students went on to study a wide range of subjects such as Business, Law, Health and Social Care, and Education.

The success rate of completing the diplomas was high, showing that it's never too late to further your career. After you decide what you'd like to pursue as a career, you can find that plenty of opportunities open up to you. You may well find that juggling your finances, study, and your domestic and social life is tough, but remember your CBT: in order to progress, you're likely to have to go through some levels of discomfort.

Many colleges and universities run similar schemes: use the Internet to check out the possibilities in your local area.

Use the CBT methods to be honest and plan future goals. You need to research and obtain information about what else is available and then be pro-active in working out what you need to do.

# Striking Out on Your Own: Self-Employment

Traditionally, the majority of people in paid work tend to work for someone else. Youngsters leaving school are less likely to start up their own business, although recent trends in entrepreneurship have seen increasing numbers of youngsters becoming successful business owners. Figures show that more people are setting up their own businesses and becoming self-employed.

An article in a UK national newspaper in 2014 announced: 'Self- employment in UK at highest level since records began'. A report for the Office of National Statistics states that taxi-driving, construction and carpentry are the most common areas for self-employment. With economic instability and the recession, the figures showing that more people are self-employed account for the increase in overall employment numbers. Many people want to have a go at being their own boss. Perhaps with easier access to information and Internet resources available for people to register and set up their own business, they feel more confidence about being their own boss.

On the other hand, I've seen an increase in the numbers of clients from a self-employed background coming along for stress-management therapy. They want to learn some practical coping skills for the anxiety, stress and insecurity that goes with the territory of being totally responsible for making a living on your own. After all, you're responsible for your own finances, production, welfare and livelihood. You can find things tough out there on your own.

More than ever, when you work for yourself the potential for feelings of isolation, anxiety and worry is ever-present.

## Weighing the pros and cons of self-employment

When you're self-employed you're totally responsible for organising your work, from getting your contacts and contracts to organising labour, materials and delivery of the services and goods that your business offers. When you're self-employed, your way of working is more likely to need to be pro-active.

Why would anyone want to take on all that potential insecurity and worry? Here are some of the advantages of being self-employed:

- Being your own boss
- Having control of your working life
- Earning more money, at least potentially
- Setting your own work schedule
- Choosing what work you do
- Enjoying the independence
- Wanting more flexibility

You have to decide whether you have the required talents and personal characteristics to make a go of self-employment. The necessary skills you need to work in this way include the following:

- Ability to put a business plan together
- Creativity
- Determination
- Financial skills
- Initiative
- Knowledge
- Leadership (of yourself!)
- Persistence
- Professional integrity
- Risk-taking skills
- Self-belief
- Social skills to network and sell your business
- Willingness to put in long hours

Disadvantages of being your own boss can include:

- Responsibility: You're on your own with the ultimate responsibility of running the show.
- Finances: Work may become irregular and unpredictable, and you may go for months without being paid.
- Costs: All the running costs – premises, heating, lighting, rent, transport, materials and staff costs – are down to you.

Also, sickness pay doesn't exist when you're self-employed, unless you take out insurance. The worry of getting ill when you rely on yourself can be one of the foremost problems.

This reality is another good reason why taking care of your own mental health as well as your physical health is paramount. If things get tough and you start to rely on unhealthy coping strategies, you just make the situation worse. Stress can have a huge impact on your physical health and so the more you can keep yourself under control and on an even keel emotionally, the better the prospects for you and your business.

In addition, working long hours, not seeing your family or having time to form significant relationships, not taking holidays and feeling isolated can impact negatively on your sense of wellbeing.

Any new project requires intensive work to be successful, but getting into long-term habits of continually working without a break can mean that you lose sight of why you're working in this way.

Feeling that you must keep working, that you should be able to cope and that you mustn't ask for help can trigger anxieties, fears and depression.

Bertrand Russell is quoted as saying: 'One of the symptoms of an approaching nervous breakdown is the belief that one's work is terribly important'.

Of course your work is very important for bringing in the means to allow yourself to live, eat and have shelter, but make sure to keep it in perspective. All sorts of reasons can make you work too hard, beyond wanting to earn a basic living wage. Losing sight of what really matters to you can happen when you get caught up in the process of advancing your business.

## *Letting CBT show you the way*

You may have a great idea for a business and the energy and enthusiasm to want to make it happen, but you always benefit from sitting down and looking at the potential pitfalls as well as the advantages. CBT can be a useful tool to apply to carrying out this cost–benefit analysis.

In Chapter 3, when putting the toolkit into practice, I encourage you to allow yourself to look at the worst possible scenario when working on rationalising your thinking to reduce anxiety and fear. This is a useful exercise to do when considering taking the risk to work for yourself.

Consider the potential worst-case scenarios when you're in the planning stage of setting up your own business and when you're creating your business plan. By facing these fears before they can happen, you help yourself to think clearly and rationally about how realistic your plans are.

You can also apply this CBT method of analysis regularly as your business develops and you grow in confidence – it will help you to take more educated risks about expanding and moving your business forward.

You need to be in a calm frame of mind to manage your business. Sleepless nights worrying about it, working long hours and working in a reactive way send you along the burnout route.

Take some time to reflect on the current situation, acknowledge your worries and insecurities, pinpoint the negative emotions and use some CBT to bring your anxiety levels down.

# Chapter 19

# Exploring Additional Practices for Health and Wellbeing

## In This Chapter

▶ Applying CBT to your whole life

▶ Getting your life into perspective

*T*he main emphasis in this book is on discovering how to apply CBT methods to your work situation. But as I point out in Chapter 16, work is only one aspect of your life. Plus, in the 21st century, the boundaries of your work and personal lives are more blurred than in previous generations, something that partially explains the current rise in popularity of searching for meaning in it all.

The fact is that nothing stands still. You're constantly changing physically and emotionally, and you're repeatedly altering social and personal relationships, making new ones and leaving behind old ones. Plus, your working life status changes as you progress through your life: you can have periods of unemployment, redundancy, redeployment or just get tired or bored of the job you're in or need to find new ways of earning more money.

Whatever your circumstances, change is inevitable. The crucial point is how you deal with the changes, which is greatly influenced by your openness to new experiences and to your attitudes. Every time you experience new situations and come across new people, your senses will be jogged into paying extra attention. You are likely to venture into new territories, and your comfort zone will be challenged. You could lead your life trying to minimise or avoid new situations so that you feel safe and secure. That is fine as long as you don't find that you are losing confidence and missing out on things you would like in your life. If you would like to have a partner to share your personal life and maybe your work life, too, but you never seek to make new acquaintances or accept invitations for social events, you reduce your opportunities for meeting a special friend to be your partner. If you don't apply, or turn down promotion opportunities, you are likely to stay exactly where you are because you were afraid to take a risk. The more opportunities you make to enrich your experiences of life, the more discoveries you will make that enhance your life.

You have your own philosophy of how you want your life to be (refer to Chapter 10), which means that you'll choose resources accordingly that resonate with your way of being. I find that although of course you can apply CBT successfully to all areas of life, I also like to add other personal-development ideas and practices that fit in with my outlook. In this chapter, I give you some ideas for other resources, which you may like to choose in addition to using CBT.

# Gaining a Perspective on Your Whole Being

I have always favoured a 'holistic' approach to life since I have met and worked with some amazing people who practise different types of alternative therapies. As I come from a more scientific background, having studied biology, chemistry and then psychology, I tend not to have come across wider methods of studying the human body and mind. An opportunity to work to help set up an alternative holiday on a Greek island in the 1980s gave me a chance to work alongside other therapists from different backgrounds. I thought at first it was going to be a bit too way out for me and although I like a lot of hippie ideas, but I was wary of mixing them with my professional role as a CBT therapist. I had my outlook broadened as I adopted an open mind and decided to watch, learn and try out as many alternative therapies as I could. 'Don't knock it until you try it' became my motto. I ended up having the great privilege of working alongside some very caring and helpful therapists who shared their knowledge and experience in a professional and empathic way and saw some course participants relax, show improvements in their physical and mental health and go home happier. Even if the effects only lasted that week, and may have been partly due to the wonderful sunny climate, the warm Mediterranean sea and the laughter and camaraderie of the community, the experience seemed to have a lifting effect on many participants.

I decided that, if any treatment was ethical, if it was given by therapists with recognised training, if it didn't encourage dependency and large amounts of money, then whatever helps you to feel better, it is worth considering. These different forms of treatments included:

✔ **Massage:** Using different techniques to massage the body to release tension and to help bring the body back into a state of relaxation. Some of the techniques they used were Swedish massage, Bowen technique, Sports massage, Thai massage and deep tissue massage, Reflexology, Shiatsu Acupuncture Cranial massage.

✔ **Yoga, Tai Chi, Pilates, Qiong:** These practises of movement have their roots in ancient practises which have been used to restore balance in body and mind for centuries. By trying out different classes, you can see if some of them appeal to you. I personally find difficulty in doing yoga because I cannot cross my legs but I loved Tai Chi.

✔ **Meditation:** Described as a form of mental therapy which can be used to treat stress-related conditions or just to be included as a daily practice to maintain a balance of your emotions and to encourage working towards a heightened awareness which can promote clearer perception and a feeling of being open to experience.

Mindfulness has developed into a form of therapy that helps you to move away from your everyday habits. Often you do not realise the emotional and physiological reactions you have during the course of a day and mindfulness encourages you to train yourself to be more aware of what is going on around you and actively manage your mind, which in turn can help calm your body's reactions.

A powerful programme of training which is a combination of CBT and Mindfulness, called Mindfulness-based Cognitive Therapy (MBCT), has been developed by John Williams, John Teasdale and Zindel Segal specifically to help people suffering from depression.

# Understanding that CBT is for Life, Not Just for Crises!

Sorry for that groan-inducing pun, but developing an awareness of your emotional states really is a skill that stays with you for your whole life. It can be a help in times of trouble and when things are hunky-dory. But you do need to keep working at it, in good times as well as bad.

When you know something, you can't unlearn it. When you consciously work to understand and apply the CBT techniques, you integrate them securely into your life. But if you don't refer to the new learning regularly, you can forget certain aspects and you certainly aren't then as mindful of it as you'd like to be.

For example, after you learn to drive a car, your actions became automatic. Instead of constantly checking how to engage a gear, steer and look in your mirrors, with each individual action requiring great concentration, you move on to take control smoothly. Yet an unexpected event brings your attention back to your immediate consciousness. A cat running out in front of the car makes you pay extra attention to the present situation and you adjust your actions accordingly. When dealt with in an efficient manner, you can then return to autopilot mode.

Similarly, when you've learnt the basics of CBT you can draw upon the methods to help you rationalise your thinking when you experience emotional turbulence. Chapter 2 outlines the method in detail and how you can apply it for yourself.

When you feel that you have a grasp on CBT, however, you may want to employ other resources in co-ordination with it. In this section, I describe some of the many different extras that you can add to CBT to enrich and sustain your life. In particular, I focus on a crucial one: paying attention to your social life.

## *Exercising your power to choose additional resources*

Finding which activities help you feel happier is all part of your search for a balanced life. Trying new activities, no matter what your age, gives you more opportunities to discover what 'floats your boat', as well as giving you pleasure.

To help sort the extra activities that you may want to include in your life in addition to CBT, I use the PIES acronym: Physical, Intellectual, Emotional and Social. After all, surely no one with a zest for life can forget PIES!

Joking aside, the activities that I list in this section help you to think about the different aspects of your life that you may choose to attend to. Generally speaking, the more active you are in your life and the more enjoyable activities you take part in, the more balanced and happier you feel. It can be hard when so much of your time is caught up with work, and you come home feeling tired and just really fancy a take away, a glass of your favourite tipple and a slump in a comfy chair. When I lived in California for a year, I joined a leisure club as it was the only facility with a swimming pool for the children to use; I discovered aerobics. I used to do this while the children were joining in their swimming club. I found a form of exercise I really enjoyed doing and felt great afterwards, even though I had done a full day at work starting at 7.30 am. I had had a full medical and fitness check-up as part of the services offered and when they did a recheck six months later, I was amazed at the measurable improvements in my health, wellbeing and fitness. I joined a gym when I got back and made myself go at least three times a week to the aerobic classes. Even though I had to go to later classes, after work and when my husband was home to babysit the children and I might sit in the car parked in the pouring rain, I knew that afterwards I would feel energised and happier and certainly sleep well. Find out what 'floats your boat' and go through the discomfort zones, like in the CBT attitude changing exercises, and you will feel better and happier. I think it is true, 'No gain without pain'. Go for it.

Use your own preferences and current favourite activities to guide your selection from the following activities:

- ✔ Physical: Examples include walking, sports, yoga, Tai Chi, massage, swimming, cycling, dancing, playing music instruments, cooking and gardening.

- ✔ Intellectual: Intellectual pursuits can include reading, listening to music, theatre, concerts, spiritual pursuits, studying, quiz nights, lectures and talks, travel, and challenging computer activities.

- ✔ Emotional: Emotional enrichment is personal to your own tastes and preferences. The study of personality types (refer to Chapter 9), from the angle of how the human brain works, discovered that some people seem to be 'wired' to have stronger connections and emotional responses to different sources.

  Finding which type or pieces of music give you a lift and then listening to them when you're feeling low can actively help you raise your level of happiness. See the nearby sidebar 'When tunes get inside your brain!' for more information.

- ✔ Social: Many work places had social clubs for employees to perhaps form a football team, or plan trips to the theatre, family parties or go to local places on interest or events where you might share a meal or an activity like bowling. These social clubs do not seem quite so many in number now. Interacting with others and making a special effort to go out and mix can have beneficial effects for you. You could join a gym, or running club, or book club, wine tasting, dinner club, rambling, sports team, drama group, dance classes or anything where you get to meet others who may have similar interests. Sharing similar interests and enthusiasms can be uplifting and energising. Social activity is so important that I devote the whole of the next section to it.

## *Becoming more sociable*

Social activities are a natural milieu for you. Humans are essentially social beings who survive more successfully in groups.

## When tunes get inside your brain!

Your reaction to different types of music that you hear elicits varying degrees of emotional responses, as evidenced by the 'strength' of the response in your brain.

Your brain is divided up into different areas responsible for processing sight, hearing, smell, sound, touch and motor co-ordination. Studies show that universal emotions such as happiness, sadness and anger are expressed through music in similar ways across cultures. Just as the development of language follows the same patterns in children all over the world, so responses to music seem to be embedded in people too.

One study by Ferguson and Sheldon in 2013 discovered that people listen to upbeat classical music because they want to feel happier feel their mood lift. For a similar reason, singing in a choir has been resurgent in the UK, with the numbers of people joining popular music choirs for any age rising sharply.

But modern living sees many people becoming isolated in their living situation. The ease of social mobility and opportunities to work away from your origins of birth means that many families are scattered far and wide across the globe. Traditional patterns of extended family support systems have diminished. You may be surrounded by people at work, but the opportunities to form significant relationships through work aren't always that easy.

Your brain is hardwired to form relationships, whether they're with your family, friends and work colleagues, or any special significant intimate relationships you may form.

Psychology professor Arthur Aron, director of the Interpersonal Relationships Laboratory at New York's Stony Brook University, reports that 'Relationships are – not surprisingly – enormously important for health, and there are lots of studies on the biological processes that account for the link between relationships and health'.

The fast pace of work and its demands on your time can mean that you don't have so much time to meet other people to make friends. Yet the rise of Internet dating and social-relationship sites seems to reflect the continuing popularity and need for opportunities to connect with others. Recent figures for just one relationship site show over a billion swipes a day in September 2014.

But making new relationships can be hard. You need to be proactive, plan and make time to succeed. CBT is great for helping you rationalise why you need to plan for goals in your life and take action to pursue them. No magic exists to forming relationships, but you can the social skills you already have to take a few chances, go out there and start talking to people. Push yourself through your discomfort zone; a smile and a readiness to chat is rarely met with a stern and dismissive response.

The more you avoid uncomfortable social situations because of your negative feelings, the more you isolate yourself. But taking educated risks in working towards your goals in life, pushing through the discomfort zones, is more likely to result in a happier you.

You can banish a lack of confidence and low self-esteem with CBT. Check out Chapter 5 for more on the importance of looking after and accepting yourself fully, and how CBT can help you. Use CBT to help you overcome the uncomfortable feelings of anxiety and shyness, as well as a lack of confidence, embarrassment and fear, and take action to increase your chances of happiness.

Here is an example of an exercise that was given to a chap who brought the problem of social anxiety to his therapist. He loved his work, rented a great little apartment, had no money worries but spent night after night sitting in playing computer games and really wanted someone to share his life with outside of work. He didn't necessarily mean for a romantic relationship, but that would have been great too, he said.

His therapist set him this task: this was worked out with the client's agreement. The aim of the exercise was to demonstrate that if he never made a pro-active move to actively seek some company, rationally, he was not likely to achieve that goal. He would be taking a risk and moving out of his comfort zone, but they looked at what was the worst thing that could happen before he did the exercise.

1. Think of three people you like at work and enjoy their company.

2. Ring them or email them to ask if they would like to go to the cinema or some similar activity that the people you ask would enjoy.

The preparation beforehand looked at what the possible outcomes could be.

1. The people declined the invitation in a polite way.

2. The people sounded surprised but thanked the client and said they would think about it and get back to him.

3. The people said 'Yes great, when were you thinking of?'

4. The people screamed and put the phone down.

Each of these possible scenarios was looked at in the safety and relative calm of the consulting room. The client was asked if he felt he could cope with each of the outcomes.

The client responded that, although he wouldn't like some of the options, they weren't life-threatening and although he might feel embarrassed, he would survive. The therapist reminded him how he could use CBT to reduce the embarrassment to disappointment, so that instead of demanding to himself that 'people should be polite and friendly to me and want to go to the cinema', he understood it was not rational to thinking as people can and will say whatever they like. He changed his thinking like that. His rational thinking might go like this: 'I would prefer that people were polite and accept my invitation, but there is no guarantee that they will. I will be disappointed and sad but not wind myself up by feeling embarrassed and that I am a lesser person. If I never make a move to try to increase my chances of mixing socially with others, it is likely that I will stay in the same situation – on my own. Even if some people think I am weird, though, I can stand it'.

It is your fear of how people might react to you that may be holding you back. You may sometimes behave in ways that might seem odd to other people but that does not make you an odd person – only someone who behaves in this way sometimes.

I once decided to give a neighbour's dog some sausages we had as we were going away and the food wouldn't be edible when we got back. The neighbours weren't in when I rang the bell so on impulse, I posted the sausages through the letter box. When we returned a couple of weeks later, we were all in the pub and this mystery of the sausage paper wrapping strewn around our neighbours' house was brought up. It had been a complete mystery to them. Then one of the neighbours looked at me and asked, 'Gill, did you, by any chance, post some sausages through our door?' I confessed I had. It hadn't seemed unusual behaviour at the time. They still stayed friends with me, but just accepted that 'Gill is a friend who sometimes behaves in unusual ways, like posting sausages through a letterbox'.

Take a few risks, push yourself outside your comfort zone sometimes, even if it doesn't exactly work out. You are only human; don't mentally beat yourself up. We all mess up sometimes; it doesn't make you any lesser person. Learn from it and move on.

I have never posted sausages through peoples' letterboxes again – only tins of dog food.

## Checking-in with yourself

Doing a regular health check on yourself (not just your physical health but your mental and emotional health too) keeps you on course for an improved sense of wellbeing. You can use your own time to do this check or arrange a coaching session every few months to reconnect with how things are going for you. For more details, see the nearby sidebar 'Coaching for life events'.

The old proverb says, 'A stitch in time saves nine': in other words, you're better off dealing with problems straightaway. The best approach is to mend problems as soon as you can instead of putting them off until later when things have worsened and need much more repair.

## Coaching for life events

When I worked for the Employees Assistance Programmes (EAP), people had the option to arrange some check-in life-coaching sessions. They didn't have to wait until they had a problem or were in a crisis. They could book a session to use for themselves to just reflect and reassess where they were at in their professional, emotional and social life.

I took a call from an employee who was overwhelmed with work in general and struggling with his home life, trying to give his family enough of his time when he got home as opposed to grabbing a bite to eat and opening his laptop to carry on with work. He had been experiencing headaches, stiff necks and pain in his toe joints; he said he had been feeling that life was hopeless, that he couldn't see any light at the end of the tunnel. In the telephone assessment, some 'risk factor questions' are included to check if the person is in crisis and has had any thoughts of hurting himself or others. He hadn't had any suicidal ideation but was very low. In the six counselling sessions we arranged for him, spending each one-hour session face to face with a counsellor, he had a chance to reflect and assess what was happening in his life. He reported he had found the sessions very helpful to give him a breathing space to let off steam and think about how he could make some changes and manage his time differently. Allowing yourself the 'luxury' of these types of coaching sessions can make a big difference to your emotional wellbeing as life goes hurtling by before you get derailed by illness or full-blown depression.

You can see this logic at work in the way preventative 'medicine' (of whatever sort) helps to identify any looming potential problems, allowing you to alleviate them before they get out of control. For centuries, Eastern medicine and philosophy has looked to enhance everyday health in order to prevent problems, instead of waiting until things go wrong.

## *Rewiring your old brain*

Breaking your old established habits is difficult and you can tend to return to accustomed, but damaging, patterns of behaviour.

In the song 'Old Habits Die Hard', Mick Jagger sings:

But I've never taken your calls
You see, haven't no block on my phone
I act like an addict, I just got to have it
I never can leave it alone

The human brain gets used to repeated patterns of behaviour. You have to work very hard to change your usual ways of reacting and behaving if you want to mitigate any problems you're experiencing. This is where CBT's ABC sequence from Chapter 2 comes in. When you change your thinking, you change your feelings.

Advice to Mick Jagger – you don't have to have it, you can leave it alone, and you just have to work hard with CBT to change your attitude. Going 'cold turkey' to get through the discomfort zones to 'leave it alone' eventually helps you change your habits and break the addiction cycle.

And I can't give you up
Can't leave you alone
And it's so hard, so hard
And it's hard enough to feel the pain

I know, feeling the pain is hard, Mick, but it's necessary!

One definition of enlightened is 'having a rational, modern and informed outlook'. Your informed outlook will come from deciding you want to understand yourself, your joys, your disappointments, your enthusiasms, your struggles, and your wishes for the future. The more likely you are to do something about trying to change the negative things you see in your life, and be pro-active, the more likely you are to achieve more of your wishes and desires.

When the going gets tough, the tough get going.

# Part VI
# The Part of Tens

Enjoy more CBT information at www.dummies.com/extras/cbtatwork.

# In this part . . .

✔ Find ten essential tips for training yourself in CBT.

✔ Learn ten pointers to help you stay motivated and on track so that you give yourself the best chance to achieve a fairly calm and settled emotional outlook about work and at work.

✔ Check out ten tips to keep in mind to help you maintain a healthy perspective on your working life.

✔ Learn about ten different places where you can find more information and resources on CBT.

# Chapter 20

# Ten Top Tips to Train You in CBT

*In This Chapter*
▶ Checking in with the CBT ABCs
▶ Staying mindful of your goals

**Y**ou made a great start to your CBT training for tackling work issues by buying this book. But reading a long book is difficult in one go, and anyway I didn't design it to be read cover to cover in one sitting. Let your concentration levels influence how much you can take in at one time.

I tend to read self-help books with a pencil in my hand, underlining the parts that resonate with me and I find interesting. If I'm serious about trying to take onboard some of the ideas, I then go through the book again and make notes in an exercise book with a biro. Evidence suggests that physically interacting with written material helps the brain to process it and start to leave a memory trace to add to your already huge store of information.

This chapter helps you by outlining ten essential tips for training yourself in CBT.

These tried-and-tested methods are based on feedback from hundreds of clients in the 30 or so years I've worked as a CBT therapist. Read and reread them to squeeze the ideas into your brain!

## Reminding Yourself of the CBT Basics, Again and Again

Chapter 2 of this book introduces the ideas that make up CBT and how it works, which is, essentially, that you feel the way you think.

You'd probably consider yourself pretty heartless and unnatural if you didn't experience some feelings of unhappiness, but how bad you feel and for how long these uncomfortable feelings last depends on how you choose to think about them.

You have responsibility for your own emotions.

Often you can blame other people when bad things happen to you at work and when you're upset. But, logically, they aren't responsible for how you feel – you are! You have responsibility for your own emotions.

Learning any new skill takes time, commitment, practice and determination. As an analogy, consider training for a marathon run – you can't go from sitting around all day unaware of physical exercise to running 26 miles by reading a chapter in a book on running. You're unlikely to last a mile before cramp brings you to the tarmac! You need to work at applying a training regime:

- ✔ Create your best personal training plan, taking into account what you've learnt from others who've trained for the marathon before.
- ✔ Break your plan down into manageable and realistic chunks.
- ✔ Remain mindful of your final goal as you organise your day-by-day targets.
- ✔ Look out for the pitfalls and be prepared for setbacks. Learning any new skill takes time, commitment, practise and determination.

# Revising the ABC Toolkit

The ABC toolkit from Chapter 2 is the key to adjusting your emotional engine. When you experience troubling feelings and difficulties at work, you can get out your toolkit and start to fix the problems. In a nutshell, this toolkit is the sequence for identifying what you're feeling about and at work, and trouble-shooting your emotional disturbances.

You may have difficulty pinpointing the precise emotion, but you need to start by trying. Identify what you are feeling. Here's a menu of just some of the unhappy feelings you may encounter. Recognise any?

- ✔ Anger
- ✔ Anxiety
- ✔ Depression
- ✔ Envy

✔ Guilt

✔ Jealousy

✔ Shame

Although, for example, feeling a lack of self-confidence or self-esteem may seem as though they should be on the list, technically, they aren't emotions. They certainly describe what you're experiencing (and many clients use CBT to help with them), but underlying a lack of confidence and self-esteem issues is the emotion of anxiety. You're anxious or worried about yourself and how you come over to others at work, because you naturally want other people to approve of you, and your anxiety can get in the way.

Turn to Chapter 2 for more on approval issues and the details of the ABC toolkit process.

Connected to this issue are the dangers of 'should, ought and must' thinking, which I discuss in Chapter 5. Just because you believe something should happen or be the way you want it to be, doesn't mean it will be. Here are some examples of this damaging type of thinking at work that you may recognise in yourself:

✔ I shouldn't mess up at work.

✔ I ought to be able to complete all tasks.

✔ I must be perfect.

✔ The firm shouldn't be so unfair in its promotion schemes.

✔ He ought to have more control of the team.

✔ She mustn't give me a bad report.

✔ The company should treat its employees fairly.

✔ This job must be rubbish because it has a high turnover of staff.

Just because you believe something should happen or be the way you want it to be, it does not mean it will be.

When you find yourself thinking along these lines, rationalise those thoughts and change the demanding thinking to preferential thinking. Use words such as 'prefer', 'wish', 'would like' and so on to view your world and the people and events in it.

# Remembering One Example of CBT in Action

When working with clients, I find that remembering one CBT case study helps them to understand the CBT method and apply it for themselves.

Here's an example of how I learnt for myself to remember the ABC sequence of changing irrational, upsetting thinking to rational, less disturbing thinking.

When I was studying to become a CBT therapist, I felt overwhelmed at times with so much information and so many things to remember. The professor was highly organised, gave masses of information at every lecture and regularly set homework on which the students were tested in the next week. He ran the course as he taught CBT to his own clients. It certainly was quite different from other counselling courses I'd been on.

He accepted no excuses, no lateness and set a high workload. The outcome was that having the material drilled into me and having to apply it constantly and being tested on it meant that I got to grips with it. Although I whined at the time (I was holding down a full-time management job and bringing up two children), I was glad that I was held accountable for my own learning. CBT changed my own life as well as the lives of the thousands of clients I've worked with since.

Don't look for a shortcut though, because none exists: only you can work toward understanding the framework and applying it in your own work life.

# Using the ABCs: Considering Your Own Examples

Learning new material is easier when you learn it in the context of something personal to you. You're just more likely to remember personal examples.

Choose an example from your past work that troubled you. Apply the ABC technique from Chapter 2 and identify:

- ✔ C: The emotional Consequence
- ✔ A: The Activating situation or event
- ✔ B: Your Beliefs and thinking about the situation

In fact, I see that's CAB, not ABC. No problem – just remember to call a 'cab' when you need assistance!

I like using CAB because this is the order in which you apply the ABC principles to an emotional disturbance. Write this example out and keep it for future reference. It can act as a reminder of how working on changing your demanding thinking to preferential thinking could've reduced your upset in that instance and so it can in the future as well.

# Reflecting on the Last Week at Work

Taking some time to reflect on what has been happening in your life – say by recording events and thoughts – helps you to keep a perspective on your emotional life. Think of it as like maintaining a garden. You work hard to clear a jungle of weeds and create an ordered and tranquil environment. If subsequently you don't keep a regular check on the frenetic growth of all the plants, your garden soon becomes out of control again. If you feel anxious about the state of your overgrown garden, it can start to be a niggling worry in the background; unless you attend to those anxious thoughts, they escalate.

Make sure that you attend to your emotional garden weekly, checking for negative thinking (work weeds!) and encroaching anxieties (the next two sections describe how). In the long run, you're enhancing your prospects for calm and control.

# Recording Unsettling Work Events

Following on from the preceding section, keeping a diary of your emotional life at work helps you to be mindful of your life. Just ten minutes diary-recording each week is enough to keep track of events and create a record of your activities.

Keeping a check on how often (and when) the negative emotions occur at work helps you to spot any emerging patterns.

Doing so provides you with an invaluable insight into the situations, people and events that impact on you negatively. You may also see a pattern in fluctuations in your physical condition, which may in turn impact on your emotional feelings and behaviours. You may not be aware that impending visits to customers or inspections at work have such a great effect on your levels on anxiety. Planning for extra work on yourself to help keep calm during potentially stressful events gives you a head start on tackling the issue.

# Carrying out Your Own Self-Assessment on the Workweek

The benefits and value of learning to meditate and including meditative practices in your life have been well-known in the East for thousands of years (check out *Meditation For Dummies* by Stephan Bodian [Wiley] and *Mindfulness For Dummies* by Shamash Alidina [Wiley] for more on meditation).

Use yourself as a resource and take time to reflect and use meditation exercises to enhance your sense of wellbeing. Mindful meditation can be a useful addition to your own self-assessment of the workweek (see the two preceding sections).

You can use short mindfulness exercises at work. I had a client who experienced stress-induced asthma who found doing some mindfulness using a download from the Internet and using his headphones at lunchtime very helpful to still his mind and bring down any stress levels which may have been building up. His doctor even commented on how his lung function tests showed improvement after he had been practising this for six weeks.

Some companies requested training sessions from our consultants to provide mindfulness lunchtime sessions for their employees.

# Applying the CBT Toolkit to Each New Event

The more times you decide to apply the CBT toolkit to your unsettling events, the easier and more natural your new way of rational thinking becomes.

Recall when you were learning to ride a bike. You had to concentrate and psyche yourself up to get on that bike and learn all the different aspects of balance, pedalling, steering, speed control and braking (not least getting off the bike without cuts and bruises!). With much effort, your actions became automatic and you were able to relax and look around at the passing scenery.

The same applies to your CBT practice.

Your hard work pays off as you change irrational thinking about work into rational thinking. Your old repeated patterns of self-defeating behaviours occur less and less often as you develop your new perspective on life. Over time you find that the old triggers that used to send you spiralling into negative thinking and feelings no longer elicit that automatic response.

You have less unsettling episodes and more calm and control. Sounds great, doesn't it?

# Working with a CBT Buddy

Sharing your life's ups and downs with another person can be a helpful way of reducing some of the tensions and providing support for each other, especially in the context of work. Research shows that sharing your experiences can be life-affirming and encourage positivity.

One of the first activities on the counselling training courses we used to run was to pair up the new students with a 'buddy'. We always included a structured time slot in each session that allowed for the pairs of buddies to exchange information about how the last week had been for them. The pairings lasted for the duration of the course, from six weeks to a year. Most people found the support they got from their buddy to be a particularly significant aspect of the course. Many firm friendships and professional bonds were created.

In a similar vein, at the start of each course we asked students to write a letter to themselves about their hopes, fears and expectations of the course they were just starting. They placed these letters in envelopes, sealed and self-addressed them. At the end of the course we posted these letters back to each student. The feedback was always positive.

 Consider meeting up with others who have an interest in CBT and mindfulness. Research shows that sharing your experiences with others can be life affirming and encourage positivity. find a CBT buddy at work, perhaps once a month, during your work lunchtime. Continue the process of catching up and debriefing each other in a respectful and confidential environment.

# Creating Your Own Version of the CBT Toolkit

I find that students on courses have many novel and illuminating ideas on how to express CBT ideas and emotional issues, often using pictures and images. In fact, some of the most popular books dealing with emotional topics are in cartoon form or use storyboards; they can offer a very clear way of expressing emotional distress and mental health issues.

An example of illustrating emotional distress such as depression can be seen in the book *I Had a Black Dog,* by Matthew Johnstone. This beautifully illustrated book has become very popular and I often get feedback from clients that they have found it really resonates with them. A fellow student on my writing course was a brilliant cartoonist. I asked her if she could illustrate some of the CBT material in cartoon form with humour as well, and she did a great job. Anxiety is obviously not funny in itself, but sometimes humour can be found in seeing the funny side of how we wind ourselves up with our irrational thinking and engage in some unusual behaviours. Laughing can certainly help release tension and is a social bonding activity.

The more you work on the material to suit your own personality and preferred learning styles, the more personally relevant the ideas are going to be for you.

# Chapter 21

# Ten Pointers to Maintain Your CBT Practice

*In This Chapter*

▶ Monitoring your ups and downs

▶ Recording your emotions

▶ Practising new moves

*I*magine for a moment that the December and New Year holidays are just over: you had a pretty good time and enjoyed loads more food and drink than usual. Hey, why not? You were away from work, relaxing and treating yourself. Now January has started and you've put on a few pounds.

But no worries, because you plan a 'dry January' (go alcohol-free for a month) and you're going to do the 5/2 eating plan to shed that newly acquired weight. You're fired up and enthusiastic: you've read the book and organised your eating plan.

You get back to work and find masses of problems waiting for you. You're racing round trying to sort everything out, but you're fastidious at only eating the packed lunch you made for yourself and you don't have that glass of wine when you get home. So far so good.

But after a few days, you just can't keep the new eating plan up. You hardly have time to go out to buy some sandwiches and crisps from the café, let alone get healthy food, and the thought of that glass of wine is the only thing getting you through the workday.

I expect almost everyone has experienced something similar to this experience, which is why more self-help books are bought in January than any other genre. But try not to let this happen by using CBT: the potential benefits are too large to miss out on! Cash in on your good intentions. Let this book be the one that you persevere with. Plan to get into new and realistic habits. Don't set yourself up to fail.

Here are ten pointers to help you stay motivated and on track. I discuss monitoring your emotions so that you give yourself the best chance to achieve a fairly calm and settled emotional outlook about work and at work.

# Treating Yourself with Patience

You need to plan to be aware of fluctuations in your emotions and use your CBT toolkit to deal with the negative times. When you take baby steps, you increase your skill at dealing with negative emotions. Every time you fall down, simply get back up again (as you did as a baby, strengthening your balancing skills and walking co-ordination as you went). CBT is incremental, three steps forward, two back, and it means that you're on your way – but it takes practice. Another motivator has been found to be if you are working alongside a friend who is also trying to achieve similar goals. The workplace can be used to create a group of like-minded people to support each other and cheer each other on. When I lived in California, the place where I worked organised a 'Club 7' group to help with weight loss. Anyone could join in. You pledged $10 to try to lose seven pounds in six weeks. If you achieved it, you got your $10 back and shared out what was in the pot forfeited by those who didn't achieve their goal. You could have your name up on a graph that monitored the weekly weigh-ins or be anonymous. There was a great spirit of camaraderie and fun. The group helped lift the post-holiday blues that often kick in in January.

 Don't beat yourself up when your best plans get thwarted: you're only human. Use your CBT to accept that today wasn't on target for your plan, but that doesn't mean you're a failure.

Tomorrow's another day. Accept and move on.

# Keeping an Emotions Diary

Drawing up a chart for yourself allows you to watch how events affect your moods and check your ups and downs.

Design a Daily Thoughts and Negative Emotions chart as a way of recording your emotional life and highlighting the unsettling events. Here's an example:

| Day | Emotions | Events | What I Was Thinking |
|---|---|---|---|
| Example | Angry | No milk at work | People should take turns buying milk |
| Monday | | | |
| Tuesday | | | |
| Wednesday | | | |

| *Day* | *Emotions* | *Events* | *What I Was Thinking* |
|---|---|---|---|
| Thursday | | | |
| Friday | | | |
| Saturday | | | |
| Sunday | | | |

You can also keep a small notebook to jot down your feelings about work, or perhaps a sheet that you can collate into a diary. If you prefer a more high-tech approach, check out the next section.

# *Researching and Evaluating CBT Apps*

You can find many resources to help you monitor your emotional life, and handy tips from CBT and general self-help sites.

Being accountable to yourself and engaging in regular recording of your life events encourages you to be mindful of wanting to improve your emotional outlook.

Some great ideas for helping you keep a record of your moods, including 'Mind over Mood. Anxiety and Depression Worksheets', can be found in the book by Dennis Greenberger and Christine A. Padesky; www.mindovermood.com.

Many apps are available for phones and tablets that offer the facility for recording a diary. Here are just two mood trackers and mood diary apps available to help you track your emotional life:

✔ Developer Ronit Hertzfeld describes her app as follows:

'The AWARENESS application is the first tool to use mobile technology to randomly intercept your daily routine, and prompt you to get in touch with what you are feeling; taking you out of your worries and bringing you to the present moment'.

The app encourages and reminds you to record your present feelings. In time, the author maintains that you won't need to use it, because your brain 'rewires' itself to do this as a matter of new habit. You're being encouraged to be in the 'here and now' with your feelings, being mindful of how you're living.

✔ Another app for recording feeling is called the 'ReadyRickshaw' app. The description is advertised as follows:

'Everybody feels, but everybody also forgets. Whether its chronic illness or pain, depression or just normal moods, keeping track of how you feel can give you insight into when and why you feel the way you do. And besides, it feels good to tell someone how you feel, even if that someone is your phone'.

Research into happiness shows that being aware of your feelings and in particular consciously focusing on a positive event and positive feelings before you go to bed at night can help elevate your overall mood.

# Choosing Your Method for Recording Your Emotional Life

You can find so many different suggestions for ways of recording the events, activities and emotions in your life that you need to choose a method that fits with you. Clients always amaze me at the novel and interesting ways they find to help them stay on track with their plans to incorporate CBT into their everyday lives. CBT encourages personal responsibility; it's the essence of the therapy. People are encouraged to do their homework, which they have agreed to in advance, and report back the next week. If a few weeks go by without the clients completing the tasks, my job is to point out that I wouldn't be doing my job if I allowed them to continue having sessions.

Some companies I work for, who provide a counselling service, state that if a client is a 'DNA' ('did not attend') no further session can be arranged without further communication from the company. If you're a self-funding client, you're wasting your money if you don't commit to your agreed CBT plan.

Considering that the aim of CBT is for clients to become their own therapist and have the skills and tools to help themselves to create and maintain an emotional equilibrium; CBT therapists are doing themselves out of a job if they do a good job!

# Analysing Your Emotional Data

Take a look at your attitudes, expectations and beliefs about how you think life at work should be for you. If you encounter difficulties and problems that you upset yourself about, applying some CBT can help you to break the negative cycle.

For example, perhaps you find that your job goes well at first and then you seem to have major conflicts with work colleagues and your bosses. If so, analysing your emotional data may reveal that you're repeating patterns of behaviour that contribute to these situations.

Look at the charts or the screen shots of the recordings of your emotional diary (see the preceding three sections): you'll probably surprise yourself when you see patterns emerging. The more insight you have into yourself, the better you can plan your life to maximise your happiness. (The same applies to the timeline that I suggest you create in Chapter 17.) The choices you've made at various points in your life are influenced by your personality, your experiences and the events that take place. The one constant throughout this timeline is you.

Here's a mantra I repeat throughout this book because it's so important: if you always do what you always did, you always get what you always got. If you keep choosing similar jobs and behaving in repeated ways, you'll have similar experiences.

# Assessing Your Work Performance

Some of you may have a regular appraisal at work, with specific targets, goals and feedback at regular intervals. Even if this task is scheduled in for you, making your own appraisal at regular intervals is still worthwhile. Keeping in touch with your job aims and achievements means that you don't 'stagnate'. Often the job you find yourself doing may be quite different from the one you applied for as you may be required to take on new responsibilities and roles as the years go by. You do need to be flexible these days and often a contract will include this requirement in the job description. You may discover that the extra roles and responsibilities that evolve with your job result in a situation that you are less comfortable with. One of my jobs in a college changed from psychology lecturer, to be required to include head of counselling training, faculty manager for human and physical resources and ultimately I was asked to take over manager of sports and leisure as well. The last request to take on that responsibility was my tipping point. After a few sleepless nights and raised anxiety levels, meetings and protestations that I had neither skills, qualifications nor interest in being in charge of sports and leisure, I started looking for another job.

# Identifying Areas You Want to Improve

Check out if you're getting bored or underwhelmed by your job. Bear in mind a plan to move forward in the future. You can plan short- and long-term goals. You may need to factor in some extra training to enhance your transferable skills and give you more options for the future.

In the previous example, I spent some time looking at what sort of work I would prefer to do. I actually booked a session with a careers advisor, which was available locally. I was 44 years old then and felt a bit embarrassed at first as I assumed careers advice was for youngsters at school. The advisor was most encouraging and helped me make a skills audit list, and guide me to look at the type of work I would prefer to do. I decided to find out about some training in stress management; I did a course in how to run your own business and went on to set up a stress management consultancy.

# Creating a Plan of Action

Draw up a chart or use an app to create your plan of action. You can devise a forward-thinking timeline and set your goals in a timeframe.

Using the example above, the careers advisor conducted the first session by structuring it in this way:

- ✔ Reviewing past jobs
- ✔ Identifying the positive aspects of each job and then the negative
- ✔ Looking at each of the positive aspects and discussing why it was enjoyable
- ✔ Putting together what would be 'the dream job'
- ✔ Identifying what skills would be needed to do the 'dream job'
- ✔ Comparing the list of skills I already had and identifying what other skills would be needed

Homework:

1. To research for jobs that might meet some of my preferences
2. Identify what might be required to expand on my skills and experience to work towards a new job/career
3. To draw up an action plan (see Chapter 12)

# Implementing and Recording Your Goals

Make the goals in your action plan realistic and achievable. Also, make yourself accountable to visiting your plan regularly and checking out your own progress. Being mindful of a game plan for work keeps you fresh and interested.

Where I mention discussing the 'dream job' earlier in this chapter, this is really to help you free yourself of constraints and allow your imagination to wander. Obviously, just wanting a dream job and actually achieving that goal are miles apart. Wanting to be a world-class tennis player and never having had tennis lessons or being physically inactive for 20 years does indicate that that goal is unrealistic. However, identifying that you would like to work in a sports environment could be a start. There are many training courses for the leisure and tourism industry that might make an inroad for you. You could sign up for part-time evening courses and continue in your current job (you will need to pay the bills!) while you build up your portfolio of new skills.

Re-training and expanding your experiences is hard work at any age. CBT echoes this sentiment. You might forego short-term pleasure like your evening sitting at home after work, or social activities with your friends in order to maximise your chances of achieving your new long-term goals.

The road to achievement necessitates hard work and at times, sacrifices of the things you might prefer to be doing.

You may find reading some biographies of high achievers interesting. Many of them have been through tough times and triumphed over adversity. I like the memoir of Michael J Fox, *Lucky Man*; there is a man who has fought many battles and describes his highs and lows and how he coped with them.

# Making Sure that You Practise, Practise, Practise

No shortcut exists to understanding and applying CBT practices to yourself in the workplace. As with physical training, no-one else can do the training for you. You can throw vast amounts of money at your emotional struggles but ultimately your own commitment to learning CBT and applying the methods when the going gets tough is what sees you leading a happier, more emotionally settled life at work.

# Chapter 22

# Ten Tips for Maximising Success in the Workplace

*In This Chapter*
▶ Being enlightened and happy
▶ Laughing at your silly behaviour
▶ Living your life in the here and now

*H*ere I describe ten tips for you to bear in mind to help you to keep perspective on your working life.

Abraham Maslow, a psychologist who pioneered humanistic psychology in the early part of the 20th century, said:

> *The most beautiful fate, the most wonderful good fortune that can happen to a human being, is to be paid for doing that which he passionately loves to do.*

You may not reach this state of nirvana in all your jobs, but you can do your level best to make the most of your time while doing them. To help, bear in mind the points in the following table. It contains ten conclusions that I've reached from working in dozens of jobs in 40 years of working life (so far!):

| *My Personal Experiences* | *CBT Interpretations* |
| --- | --- |
| People are just weird sometimes | People can behave in unpredictable ways |
| People can be mean | Not all people behave in a generous and considerate manner |
| People can get jealous of you | Not everyone cheers for you when you do well |
| People are competitive | Others can behave in ways that protect their self-interests |
| Life isn't fair | Where is it written that life would be fair? |

| My Personal Experiences | CBT Interpretations |
|---|---|
| Any job is work experience | You're a constant factor in all your employment roles |
| It's not your parents' fault if you mess up | You're responsible for your own actions<br>No point whining about stuff<br>Accept tough times and move on |
| Being snippy with people can come back to bite you<br>If you decide to do something you don't like, do it with good grace | Low frustration tolerance in relationships isn't helpful<br>Use CBT to move to a state of acceptance |

# Developing Enlightened Self-Interest

Look after yourself first, before you can function at your best. This doesn't mean acting in negative selfish ways, but that you keep in mind the needs of others too.

Mutual co-operation at work enhances the chances of success for everyone. You have a vested interest in ensuring that the workplace functions well for your own wellbeing. Your ability to act in this way is influenced by your own confidence and self-acceptance. CBT training helps you to look out for yourself in a healthy context, not acting in self-defeating ways by letting others trample over you or forging ahead with no regard for others or the good of the whole organisation.

# Creating a Philosophy for Work

Developing your own philosophy for work, so that you can keep your life in perspective and achieve a good balance of work and personal life, is an important skill that you can work on. Chapter 10 shows ways of helping you to work out what your own philosophy is and how you may want it to be in the future. Allow yourself to have regular checking-in moments and updates to see how your work life is progressing. No-one can take away from you your own code of behaving and standard of ethics. You may find times when you seem to be surrounded by others who're operating different standards of behaviours and codes of ethics, which is at the very least disappointing and a challenge to work with. But you can use your CBT to keep yourself calm.

You can't change other people's behaviour, but you can change the way you view others to avoid winding yourself up into a state of anxiety, anger or even depression.

# Being a Fallible Human Being

No matter how hard you try to be perfect or do the best you can, at times you're going to make mistakes, mess up or just not cut it. You can then choose whether you mentally beat yourself up for your incompetence, ineptitude or just lack of experience, or you use your CBT skills to accept that sometimes things just don't work out as you hope or like them to.

Accept yourself as a fallible human being, like everyone else, and move on. Learn from your mistakes and work on finding out what you can do in the future to minimise the chances of repeating mistakes.

To err is human, to accept is healthy!

# Keeping a Healthy Perspective

Being conscientious at work, responsible and reliable are great assets, but taking yourself too seriously all the time can work against you. Work can get very demanding and the pressures of meeting targets, completing projects, arranging meetings and travelling can put you in potentially scary situations. But taking some time out to step back for a breather is very beneficial for you.

Regular and scheduled breaks for refreshments and meals are far less common in the workplace these days. You may find that you're constantly racing around, eating food at your desk, grabbing a drink on the go, missing meals or eating unhealthily because you can only access convenience foods.

Try to step back sometimes and plan for a break. Just ten minutes downtime, perhaps shared on a break with a friend, where you can catch up and maybe even have a laugh, is a great investment for the rest of the day.

# Laughing at Yourself

*I do take my work seriously and the way to do that is not to take yourself too seriously.*

— Alan Rickman

Laughter is a great tension breaker. The purpose of laughter has been greatly debated, but certainly it brings many positive physiological and social benefits:

- Increases blood flow to the heart, which can help prevent heart attacks
- Raises immunoglobulin levels in the blood, which helps fight infections
- Acts as a great stress-buster, relaxer and conflict-defuser
- Releases endorphins into the body, the feel-good hormones
- Promotes group bonding
- Increases your attractiveness to others

Laughter can help you see situations from a different perspective, such as helping to reduce the perception of threats around you.

So be good to yourself, plan for fun and for tension-breaking activities. Also, laugh at your irrational thinking. When you laugh at yourself, you're really laughing at your own behaviour or actions produced as a result of your thinking.

I found CBT particularly helpful in clarifying what laughing at yourself really means. If you find you want to defend yourself and hang on to your own viewpoint and attitude, even when all the evidence around you seems to indicate that your plan of action may not be the most helpful, taking some time out to re-evaluate your actions can help you to rationalise your thinking.

Hanging on doggedly to your viewpoint without any willingness to consider options is just being stubborn. When you allow yourself to look at options, you may well see the humour in your previous behaviour.

## Exercising Your Mind and Body

Getting a balance of intellectual and physical activities is a great investment for you. If your job involves mostly sitting at a desk in front of a computer, you don't have many opportunities for exercising your body.

But you can make a conscious decision to use the stairs instead of lifts and go out for 30 minutes at lunchtime to walk briskly around the block. Perhaps walk a couple of bus stops or park farther away or even cycle in for a few miles from where you park. Walking helps you process information and get a different perspective from the heads-down-at-desks view. Only you can make this happen. Not many managers or bosses actually suggest you take more breaks!

Including outside work activities, perhaps in a social group situation, can help you achieve a healthy balance of work and play. Even though you may be very tied up with work, family life and struggling just to keep going sometimes, building in a regular break for yourself to pursue some activity you find enjoyable, stimulating and relaxing is vital for your overall wellbeing.

Put yourself first and arrange time to share with a significant other in your life – or it's unlikely to happen.

# Accepting Yourself

Accepting yourself is absolutely key in the CBT programme of training. In Chapter 5, I discuss the idea of working towards accepting yourself, warts and all, instead of changing your view of yourself every time you get negative feedback. Low self-esteem doesn't exist for you if you can fully accept yourself as basically a good, well-intentioned human being who sometimes makes mistakes.

Unconditional self-acceptance means saying goodbye to ever getting down on yourself. These phrases are just no longer in your vocabulary:

| | |
|---|---|
| I'm a failure | I'm rubbish |
| I'm useless | I'm a bit of a loser |
| I'm unlovable | I'm not good enough |
| I'm incompetent | I'm a fool |
| I'm stupid | I'm inferior |

You're made up of loads of different aspects, talents, skills, attributes and quirky behaviours. If you mess up sometime and get things wrong, it doesn't mean that you've lost all your other skills and positive attributes. It just means that in that particular instance, things didn't go so well for you and you didn't behave in your best interests. In such cases:

✔ Accept, move on and learn from what happened.

✔ Don't spend the rest of your life mentally beating yourself up about it.

✔ Wear the virtual badge: 'your approval isn't necessary'.

✔ Take responsibility for your behaviours and actions, but don't be too hard on yourself.

Perhaps many other people are ready to be hard on you and try to give you a hard time. If so:

✔ Nod and smile.

✔ Accept and agree that at times you don't behave perfectly.

✔ Decide to learn from the experience and move forward.

You aren't giving in and giving up: you're working with CBT to maximise your chances of a calmer life by rationalising out the less favourable incidents in your life.

# Empathising with Other People

While you're working on not judging yourself too harshly, also have a think about how you judge others. Sometimes you can find that you wind yourself up into a state of anger about the behaviours of other people. But they too are imperfect human beings who, at times, behave in ways that are self-limiting and potentially harmful towards others. You can choose whether to judge them negatively and focus on their negative behaviours or not. You can use CBT to rationalise that though you don't like how they're behaving towards you and others, you can accept their foibles. After all, how is getting angry or anxious about them helping you?

In the past, I read a book called *Happiness is the Best Revenge* by Chuck Spezzano (Hodder & Stoughton). I don't advocate revenge as such, but looking after your own happiness is a healthy way of being. So see those irritating people for what they are, fallible human beings acting in negative ways.

# Remembering that Life Isn't a Rehearsal

As Guy Lombardo says in the lyrics of a song:

Enjoy yourself, it's later than you think
Enjoy yourself, while you're still in the pink
The years go by, as quickly as a wink
Enjoy yourself, enjoy yourself, it's later than you think

To get the most out of your life, you'd like to experience the least stress, anxiety and depression. CBT shows that you do have choices over how you view life and ultimately how you feel about events, people and the world in general.

Sometimes all your choices and options may be pretty tough, but you can allow yourself to look at them. This can be liberating and not as scary as you might imagine. If you allow yourself to consider what choices you actually have, you can start to find a way to deal with them, use the CBT to move you to making a choice, accepting it and thus move on to effectively manage and live your life.

Use the CBT method to rationalise your thinking and change unhealthy negative emotions into healthy positive emotions. If you love your job, get along well with your colleagues and earn as much as you need to fulfil your basic needs with enough for other activities, you appear to have your life in balance. The more you can understand about yourself and the more hard work you put into developing your thinking and actions, the more you get out of life.

Paul Tsongas is credited with saying: 'No-one on his deathbed ever said, I wish I'd spent more time on my business' (though some people may have loved their job so much that they'd have wanted to spend more time there, or may have liked to leave more provision for their family). A palliative care nurse, Bronnie Ware, listened to many people in the last 12 weeks of their lives and recorded the top five regrets they shared with her:

- ✔ I wish I'd had the courage to live a life true to myself, not the life others expected of me.
- ✔ I wish I hadn't worked so hard.
- ✔ I wish I'd had the courage to express my feelings.
- ✔ I wish I'd stayed in touch with my friends.
- ✔ I wish I'd let myself be happier.

The emotional content of the regrets was quite revealing. Incorporating the use of CBT techniques can help you with the last item in the list. Allow yourself to be happier by making conscious choices not to think in negative ways that reduce your happiness.

# Prioritising Your Life

*A 'no' uttered from the deepest conviction is better than a 'yes' merely uttered to please, or worse, to avoid trouble.*

— Mahatma Gandhi

If you don't prioritise your life and make some conscious decisions, you can bet your bottom dollar that others will do so for you. Always wanting to please others and putting their needs, wants and demands before your own ensures that you lead a life chosen for you.

If putting yourself first isn't in your nature, and you need some serious retraining of your automatic habits of responding in the same obliging ways, keep referring back to the CBT methods and examples in this book to help you keep on track. Expect to go through uncomfortable transition phases as you forge out your calmer, more self-enlightened life.

You have nothing to lose but your old unhelpful ways of thinking. Build the career and life you want, push through the tough bits and improve your self-calming skills by being prepared to examine your thoughts and concerns.

As William Shakespeare wrote, 'There's nothing good or bad, but thinking makes it so'. Think yourself happy; you can do it!

# Chapter 23

# Ten Invaluable Ideas for CBT Resources

*In This Chapter*

▶ Gathering helpful information

▶ Finding resources that work for you

*O*bviously this book is the best one available on CBT at work anywhere in the world, indeed the cosmos, and will never be surpassed. (You wouldn't expect me to say anything else, would you?) But you can find plenty of other information sources about CBT, whether in book form or to download as an app, which may also be helpful to your self-understanding and CBT practice.

## Reading Yourself toward Feeling Better

My old professor used to refer to books that help in learning about therapy as *bibliotherapy*. But as regards digesting information, different formats appeal to different people at different times. For example, when life gets tough, you may not fancy a detailed analysis of therapy and so one of the great cartoon therapy books may be more appropriate.

Check out the library or look online for books that appeal to you.

## Getting Techy Help

Checking out how you're getting along with CBT and recording your progress can be aided by downloading an app or two – if you like this format.

Many, many apps are available to help with depression, anxiety, stress reduction, sleep diaries, relaxation, health and diet, and general topics around psychology and therapy. Only you can decide which ones are helpful and which appeal to you.

You may want to check out the online programme 'Beating the Blues' in the UK, which has been designed and developed by the National Health Service and is intended for use by patients who've been given access to the programme by their doctor. Check out `http://www.nhs.uk/Conditions/online-mental-health-services/Pages/beating-the-blues.aspx`.

Working in conjunction with a health professional helps you take a comprehensive approach to monitoring your physical and emotional health.

# Surfing for CBT Websites

All sorts of websites offer resources for using CBT. When I did a search for 'CBT websites', I got over a million results! So you need to be discerning about which resources you use.

The qualifications and training required to be an accredited CBT therapist vary hugely in different countries. CBT is still a relatively new therapy and its popularity has rocketed in the last 30 years or so. This fact is reflected in the large increase in available resources and therapists advertising their services.

Nationally recognised training schemes and strict accreditation criteria exist in different countries. Generally speaking, a four-year training course with over 250 hours of hands-on, supervised therapy practice provides a benchmark for becoming a therapist.

Before you make a commitment, check out a person's training and qualifications when you're looking for a therapist or online therapy.

# Hearing All about CBT

Audio resources offer a great user-friendly way to discover more about CBT and participate in exercises.

Obviously, don't take part in relaxation exercises while you're driving. Instead, find a quiet space to be mindful where you won't crash into a lamp post!

I've worked with clients who download a suitable relaxation resource and even sit at their desk at lunchtime and take 10 or 15 minutes of 'time out' to relax. The more times you can go over the principles of CBT and discover more about it from different resources, the more likely you are to get to grips with it and make progress towards a calmer frame of mind and happiness.

# Sitting Down with a CBT Movie

I like to watch videos and films of CBT in action. Some great resources are available on popular video sites. Plus you can buy professionally produced films of CBT sessions conducted by experienced therapists on recognised training courses and institutions.

Of course, not all resources are going to be relevant to you. Unless you're thinking of training to be a CBT therapist, the level and detail of the information may not be as useful to you as other resources.

The most important resource is yourself. You're the one who has to implement what you have learnt, and there ain't no way around that!

# Thinking about Training Courses

You may decide that you want to do some training in CBT. If so, many courses are available worldwide that offer training at different levels.

Consider taking an introductory course in basic counselling skills to find out whether you'd like to study further. Counselling skills training can be useful for customer-interface work, because the skills are useful in many situations. You can search for counselling and specifically CBT training courses in your area via the Internet and find out what's required at entry level.

As this book describes, CBT is useful for managing people and dealing with a variety of situations at work. In fact, it has the advantage of not only helping others in the workplace but also yourself. Therefore, taking part in training can be a worthwhile investment for all concerned.

# Considering Talking to Friends and Family

Your family and friends can often be a great source of support and encouragement when times are tough at work: you're likely to be met with sympathy and a friendly welcome.

But they can help you only so much. Because they're closely involved with you, they may want to protect you or give you their opinion of what you should be doing to help yourself, which although well-intentioned, may not be what you need to hear at the time. You can also hold back on what's really happening because you don't want to worry them.

As a result, your best resources are independent people, preferably professionals who are trained to look out for warning signs of emotional ill health and are trained to help you.

# Accessing National Directories

Concern for a nation's emotional health is often seen as a major worry in the 21st century. Many charitable organisations as well as national social healthcare programmes appreciate the value of education for mental health as a major factor in preventative care.

You can find the national directories of counselling organisations, as well as countries' help lines, on the Internet. These sites can be a great source of information and some operate 24-hour help lines to assist people in distress. The confidential help lines are often freely available. Plus, Employee Assistance Programmes can be accessed if your company has an arrangement with them.

# Staying Local

Your local provision of help (free voluntary organisations and privately funded resources) can include healthcare providers that you access to through your doctor or other health schemes. You can also find independent, private services by searching on the Internet.

Provision of emotional support can vary enormously depending on where you live (whether rural or urban), how much your employer has put in place for employees, and your own financial situation if you access care through an insurance scheme.

Your first point of call when you find yourself struggling is your GP.

# Employing Mind and Body Resources

Looking after your whole self, body and mind, in a holistic integrated way, is important. The two aspects are so inextricably connected that you can't afford to ignore one or the other. You can access many mind–body resources that help balance your mental activities with physical activities: exercise, yoga, meditation, Tai Chi, massage, dance, music and many more.

A point to keep in mind could be:

> *To keep the body in good health is a duty ... otherwise we shall not be able to keep our mind strong and clear.*

Take good care of yourself and others in your life and work. Use everything at your disposal to learn from and incorporate your new-found knowledge in your activities, and move forward in the best way you can.

# Index

## • A •

ABC framework (or model)
  in action, 25
  applying
    at work, 188–190
    to your problem, 112
  CBT toolkit, 40, 42, 44
  in CBT workshops, 239, 240
  considering your own examples, 306–307
  outline of, 25
  revising, 304–305
absenteeism, 53
accepting (acceptance)
  by agreeing to differ and not
    losing face, 157
  colleagues, 164
  difficult emotions, 107–108
  flexibility, 272–275
  friends at work, 174
  mistakes, 129, 321
  people you work with, 154
  that you are struggling, 22
  yourself, 323–324
    as a fallible human being, 321
accountability, 16
action(s)
  becoming conscious of your, 179–180
  conflict between beliefs and, 14–15
  dissonances between your
    beliefs and, 152
  practising before, 180
  realising that the time has come
    for, 182–183
  speaking louder than words with, 183–186
activating event, in ABC model, 25
active learner, deciding to be an, 196
active listening, 248–249
addiction to work, 89
additional resources, 294–295

admitting
  that something is wrong, as essential
    first step, 108
  unhelpful characteristics, 138
  your mistakes, 217–218
  your struggles, 15
adrenalin, 27, 76, 106, 157, 185,
  186, 188, 264
advocate, moving from sceptic to, 203
advocating the use of CBT at work, 218–223
affirming your status and sense of
  worth, 280
aggression, dealing with, 95
alert button, activating the, 40–41
alerting strategies, CBT toolkit and, 43–44
ambassador for acceptable behaviour,
  acting as an, 214–215
American Psychological Association, 84
analysing your emotional data, 314–315
anger
  "glad" game and, 120
  at work, 98
anxiety
  discovering what pushes your buttons, 31
  generalised, spiralling negative thoughts
    and, 186–187
  social, 228
  about work, 100
  working out the thinking and beliefs that
    give rise to, 189
appearance, 167
applying for jobs, 81, 83
appraising
  colleagues, 163–164
  what you want from work, 149
  work culture, 206–207
  your job, 93–94
apps, CBT, 313–314, 327–328
Aron, Arthur, 296
assertiveness, 89

assessing your work performance, 315
atmosphere at work, uncomfortable, 156
attitudes
  toward work, 147–151, 153–154
  in workplace, 55–59
    comfortable conditions, 57–58
    exploring new attitudes, 58–59
    overview, 55–56
    recognising the importance of
      attitudes, 56–57
audacity, 89
audio resources, 328–329
auditioning for the part of your job, 143–144
autopilot, 75, 267, 294
availability of resources, conflict at
  work and, 55
AWARENESS application, 313
awareness of your overall emotional
  situation, maintaining, 267–270

• *B* •

balance
  of intellectual and physical
    activities, 322–323
  work-life
    boundaries of your job and, 87, 89
    by dividing your time, 123
    in general, 18, 70, 214, 262
    in 1960s and 1970s, 262
    as potential source of difficulty, 23
    through exercise, 266
    working to live or living to work, 262
balancing your roles, 278–279
Beck, Aaron, 24
behaviourist psychology, 238
beliefs
  in ABC model, 25
  conflict between actions and, 14–15
  deciding if they need changing, 39
  dissonances between your
    actions and, 152
  unhelpful
    halting, 188
    identifying and disputing, 35, 189–190
    overview, 33

pinpointing, with CBT, 155–157
possible origins of, 34
tweaking with CBT, 139
viewing others in terms of your, 35
benefits of cognitive behavioural
  therapy (CBT)
communicating to other people, 213–230
  acting as ambassador for acceptable
    behaviour, 214–215
  advocating the use of CBT at
    work, 218–223
  demonstrating rational
    thinking, 215–216
  offering to present your CBT
    understanding to a group, 220
  overview, 213–214
  reaping what you sow, 217
  recognising the different levels and
    depths of CBT, 222–223
  testifying to CBT by your example, 214
overview, 16–18
best friend, being your own, 71
bibliotherapy, 219, 327
bio dots, 44
blessings, counting your, 121–122
Boddy, James, 284
body
  chemical changes in, 185
  reactions to perceived threats, 184–185
body language, positive, 119–120
boldness, 89
bonding, in friendships, 172
books, self-help and therapy, 219, 303, 327
boss, managing your, 94
boundaries
  with friends at work, 174
  of your job, going beyond, 87–89
brain muscles, exercising your, 43
breaks, taking
  to gain a little peace, 45
  in general, 321
British Psychological Society, 126
buddy, CBT, 309
bullying
  definition of, 102
  at work, 102

## • C •

Carnegie, Dale, 122, 129
catastrophising thinking, 38, 41, 43,
    148–149, 186
CBT. *See* cognitive behavioural therapy
CBT apps, 313–314
CBT buddy, working with a, 309
CBT toolkit
    adjusting workplace emotions with, 59–60
    alerting strategies and, 43–44
    applying to each new event, 308–309
    building yourself a, 39–41
    choosing to use your, 42–45
    components of, 39
    creating a, 32
    creating your own version of, 309–310
    deciding when to implement your, 44
    deploying, 193–195
    exercising your brain muscles and, 43
    gaining a little peace with, 45
    in general, 32
    keeping your toolkit prepared, 41
    needing to earn a living and, 69
    practising the routines, 44–45
Centre for Economic Performance's Mental
    Health Policy group, 233
change. *See also* transition management
    communication during, 245–246
    normal reactions to, 242
change management, CBT-based, 202
changes
    keeping perspective through changing
        times, 278–279
    management of, 198
    retaining a sense of who you are, 277
character types, 164–165
checking-in with yourself, 298–299
chemical changes
    depression and, 133
    inside your body, 185
chemical composition of tears, 107
children
    as natural philosophers, 125
    roles of, 171

Churchill, Winston, 269
Clance, Pauline, 101
closed questions, 253
coaching
    executive, 204
    facilitative environment for, 247
    for life events, 299
    during transition, 242
cognitive behavioural therapy (CBT)
    applying the technique to your
        problem, 112–113
    basics of, 11–13
    being an ambassador for CBT, 17
    benefits of, 16–18. *See also* benefits of
        CBT, communicating to other people
    brief history of, 24
    as brief therapy, 20
    brightening your work future with, 130
    components of, 20–21
    counselling compared to, 196
    deciding whether you want to use,
        21–22
    Epictetus and, 151
    as evidence-based theory, 16
    finding an example where CBT could've
        helped, 112
    implementing, at work
        applying the ABC model, 188–190
        becoming conscious of your
            actions, 179–180
        body's reaction to perceived
            threats, 184–185
        deciding when to implement CBT
            toolkit, 44–45
        deploying your CBT toolkit, 193–195
        doing your homework, 178
        drawing up a plan of action, 195–196
        gaining insight into yourself, 177–180
        halting unhelpful thoughts, 188
        handling problem situations, 191–195
        observing the thinking-feeling link in
            operation, 184
        overview, 110–111
        realising that the time has come for
            action, 182–183

cognitive behavioural therapy *(continued)*
  reflecting on and tackling your tricky
    areas, 190–191
  seeing CBT methods in action, 180
  speaking louder than words with
    actions, 183–186
  spiralling negative thoughts out of
    control, 186–188
  understanding your motivation, 178–179
  overview, 1, 9, 60
  as positive force in the
    workplace, 197–198
  appraising the work culture, 206–207
  communicating a consistent
    message, 204–205
  engaging employees, 199–200
  including HR in feedback and evaluation
    of CBT courses, 203–204
  maintaining trust in relationships, 210
  "manager's special," 200–201
  reacting to broken trust, 211–212
  relationship issues at work, 209–210
  senior staff members' reluctance or
    opposition, 201–203
  standardising your company's
    strategic aims, 206
  sustaining human resources, 208–209
  transition management, 198
  winning customer respect, 210
  simplifying methods of, 24–25
  Stoicism and, 158
  tackling tough times with, 13–14
  ten essential tips for training yourself
    applying the CBT toolkit to each new
      event, 308–309
    creating your own version of the CBT
      toolkit, 309–310
    recording unsettling work events, 307
    reflecting on the last week at work, 307
    remembering one example of CBT in
      action, 306
    self-assessment on the work week, 308
    using the ABCs, 306–307
    working with a CBT buddy, 309
  ten essential tips for training yourself in
    overview, 303–304
    revising the ABC toolkit, 304–305

  toolkit. *See* CBT toolkit
  transferring CBT skills to new situations
    believing in using your skills and
      experience, 260
    combining emotional and physical
      health, 263–265
    contextual clues for CBT use,
      258–259
    flexibility of CBT approach, 258
    holistic approach, 265
    identifying your own working
      pattern, 261
    outside of work, 260–266
    overview, 257
    personal life, 263
    stability and consistency across entire
      life, 267–270
    taking confidence into new
      environments, 259
    widening the application of CBT
      skills, 258–260
  transition management and, 198
  understanding, 19–23
  for work-related problems, 110–112
  workshops
    3-hour interactive, 241–243
    5-hour manager-training, 243–246
    engaging employees, 199–200
    general session objectives, 241
    including HR in feedback and evaluation
      of CBT courses, 203–204
    leading, 235–243
    managing directors (MDs) and, 204
    moving from sceptic to advocate, 203
    outline of topics, 236–241
    parts of, 242
    senior staff members' reluctance or
      opposition, 201–202
    transition management, 80, 198
cognitive dissonance, 56, 152
colleagues (co-workers; employees)
  accepting, 154
  categorising your, 162–163
  dealing with people you can't
    stand, 166–167
  engaging, 199–200
  sharing CBT with interested, 219

spotting specific emotional problems in, 227–230
taking a hard look at your, 162–167
college, 179
comfortable conditions, challenging your expectations of, 57–58
communication
  during change, 245–246
  consistent, throughout company, 204–209
  guidelines for effective, 245–246
  lack of clear, 55
  looking at basic skills, 246–247
  mass communication to groups, 247
  reflecting for better, 249–251
community, helping, to cope with change, 205
company, introducing CBT methods to your, 231
  balancing the costs and benefits, 234–235
  economic benefits, 232
  evidence for CBT's benefits, 233
  overview, 231
  potential benefits, 232
concentrating on what you're thinking, 30
confidential helpline, 110
confidentiality, 243, 253
conflict, meaning of, 53
conflicting influences about work, 53–55
conflicts
  handling, 94
  in professional and personal views, 154–155
  unresolved, 53
conflicts of interest, 54
Confucius, 33, 67, 154
conscience, what you want from your job and, 150
consciousness, of your actions, 179–180
constructive feedback, converting criticism to, 221
context, placing yourself in, 73–74
contextual clues for CBT use, 258–259
control, locus of
  finding your, 90
  increasing, 59
  overview, 54

counselling
  active listening technique, 248–249
  CBT compared to, 196
  creating a trusting environment, 247
  by probing with questions, 251–254
  reflective skills in, 249–251
  talking in a respectful and professional manner, 248
counselling skills, 209–210
counting your blessings, 121–122
courses
  objectives of, overview, 244
  transition management, 200–201
    including HR in feedback and evaluation of, 203–204
    objectives of, 244
co-workers (colleagues), as not always caring, 72
creative industries, 48
creative types, depression and, 141
criticism
  being prepared for, 221
  converting to constructive feedback, 221
crying at work, 107
culture, influencing the work culture, 93–95
customers, respect of, 210
cycle of loss, 203, 242

damaging beliefs (unhelpful beliefs)
  halting, 188
  identifying and disputing, 35, 189–190
  overview, 33
  pinpointing, with CBT, 155–157
  possible origins of, 34
  tweaking with CBT, 139
Darwin, Charles, 271
de Botton, Alain, 149
decisions, making tough, 159–160
demands
  stress and, 86
  of yourself in a helpful way, 45
depression
  causes of, 133
  creative types and, 141

depression *(continued)*
  endogenous, 133
  exogenous, 133
  Mindfulness-based Cognitive Therapy
    (MBCT), 293
  professions tied to, 142
  about work, 100
detective of your emotions,
    becoming a, 26–27
diagnosing the problem, 272–273
differences, in attitudes toward work, 153
directories, national, 330
discomfort. *See also* distress
  addressing, one step at a time, 111–112
disputes, handling, 94
disputing unhelpful beliefs, 189
dissonances between your beliefs and your
    actions, identifying, 152
distress
  signs of, 109–110
  talking freely about your, 110
dividing your time, work-life
    balance by, 123
doctor, visiting a, 109–110
dress
  for business, 74
  for success and to impress, 168
Durham University, 284
dynamic employee, taking responsibility
    for yourself as a, 85

• *E* •

EAPs (Employee Assistance
    Programmes), 234–235
Einstein, Albert, 101
Ellis, Albert, 24
embarrassment at work, 105–106
emotional consequence, in ABC model,
    25, 26, 40
emotional enrichment, 295
emotional flash points, holding bay
    for, 156–157
emotions (feelings)
emotions diary, 312–313

empathy
  importance of, 324
  trusting environment and, 247
Employee Assistance Programmes
    (EAPs), 234–235
employees (colleagues)
  accepting, 154
  categorising your, 162–163
  dealing with people you can't stand, 166–167
  engaging, 199–200
  sharing CBT with interested, 219
  spotting specific emotional problems
    in, 227–230
  taking a hard look at your, 162–167
end of the day, reflecting at the, 121
endogenous depression, 133
engaging employees, 199–200
engaging with other people, 122
enlightened self-interest, 63, 64, 320
environment
  psychological, 50 *See also* working
    conditions (work environment)
  recognising your preferred, 274–275
  trusting, 247–248
Epictetus, 151
errors (mistakes)
  accepting, 129
  being the first to admit your, 217–218
  in general, 321
  at work, 106
European Research Council, 265
Evans, Jules, 158
executive CBT coaching, 204
exercising
  seeking balance through, 266
  your mind and body, 322–323
exogenous depression, 133
expectations
  of best outcome, 118
  exceeding your own, 91
  of friends, 154
  going beyond what's required, 90
  meeting, 86–87
  of work, 155
  of work/employer, 155

experience, being open to, 126
expressions, 167
external locus of control, 90
extroverted people, 57, 89, 131–133, 141
extroverts, choosing jobs, 141
eye contact, 168

## • F •

facial expressions, 167
fallible human being, being a, 321
family, talking to, 330
fear(s)
  of being unworthy, 83–84
  conquering, 182–183
feedback
  constructive, converting criticism to, 221
  from employees who participated in
    workshops, 242
  reacting to, 137
feelings (emotions). *See also*
    *specific feelings*
  accepting difficult, 107–108
  analysing your emotional data, 314–315
  becoming a detective of your, 26–27
  chemical changes in your body, 185
  connecting thinking and, 29–30
  identifying the event that triggered, 189
  keeping a diary of, 312–313
  maintaining an awareness of your overall
    emotional situation, 267–270
  negative (unhealthy), 20–21
    assessing your, 139
    example of, 239
    maintaining vigilance for, 113
    spiralling, 186, 187, 191, 309
    trigger for, 28
    warning signs of, 39–40
    at work, 37
  positive. *See also* optimism
    expecting the best outcome, 118
    "glad" game and, 120
    optimising chances of a positive work
      climate, 128–130
    as optimistic thinking, 117–121
    overview, 117

positive body language and, 119–120
    reflecting at the end of the day, 121
  recognising your, 27
  tackling unsettling, 29
  taking charge of your, 10–11
  thinking rationally to troubleshoot
    your, 11–14
  unsettling, 107–108
  wobbly
    CBT toolkit and, 40, 43–44
    maintaining vigilance for, 113
    overview, 26
  about work, 51
fight or flight reaction, 27, 44, 95, 106
five-hour day course, 243–246
flash points, holding bay for, 156–157
flexibility
  accepting the need for, 272–275
  of CBT approach, 258
  overview, 271
  at work, 275–277
Ford, Henry, 268
fortune (luck)
  expecting, 127
  increasing your, 126–127
  turning bad luck into good, 127
Franklin, Benjamin, 281
Freud, Sigmund, 238
friends (friendships)
  best, 71
  bringing to psychotherapy sessions, 225
  expectations of, 154
  making, at work, 172–174
  as sources of anxiety and distress, 173
  talking to, 330
frustration at work, 106–107
furniture, 49

## • G •

Gallagher, Robert C, 272
Gandhi, Mahatma, 325
"glad" game, playing the, 120–121
goals
  conflicts of interest among, 54
  implementing and recording your, 316–317

Goffman, Erving, 73
Greeks, Ancient, theory of personality, 132
Greene, Robert, 162
grimacing, smiling and, 169
guilty feelings, 104
gut feelings, 126

### • H •

habits. *See also* work habits and routines
  breaking your old, 299
  maintaining vigilance for, 114
handbooks, for CBT courses, 204
happiness
  adopting role of a happy worker, 143
  definition of, 262
  "glad" game and, 121
  responsibility for your own, 70–71
  three aspects of (Seligman), 160
Harwig, Kathryn, 128
head movements, 168
health (healthfulness)
  checking-in with yourself, 298–299
  combining emotional and
      physical, 263–265
  defined, 73
  going to work ill, 104–105
  investing in your overall, 73
  making efforts to assist your, 75–77
  of work habits, 71–72
healthy perspective, keeping a, 321
healthy preference thinking, 241
healthy work routines, implementing, 60
hedging your bets at work, 129
help
  asking for, 22
    at work, 227
  professional, recommending that people
      seek, 224–227
helpful beliefs
  identifying, 35
  viewing yourself in terms of your, 34–35
helplessness, feelings of, 59, 90, 277
helpline, confidential, 110
Hertzfeld, Ronit, 313

hierarchy, valuing, your place at
    work, 92–93
holding bay, for emotional flash
    points, 156–157
holding pattern strategy, 40–42, 44, 60, 98,
    99, 122–123, 156, 157, 184, 196
holistic approach, 265, 292–293
homeostasis, 179
homework, doing your, 178
honestly, viewing yourself, 64–65
HR, including in feedback and evaluation
    of CBT courses, 203–204
human resources, sustaining your
    firm's, 208–209
humanistic psychology, 238
hunches, 126, 191
hypothetical questions, 252–253

### • I •

icons used in this book, 5
"if I knew then what I know now"
    exercise, 190
illness, 53
Imes, Suzanne, 101
importance of self, rationalising, 68–69
imposter syndrome, 101
impression, dressing to make an, 168
impression management, 65–66, 73
improvement, identifying areas
    for, 315–316
Improving Access to Psychological
    Therapies (IAPT), 233
Ingham, Harrington, 87
initiative, taking the, 89–90
"inner child," 125
insight into yourself
  gaining, with CBT, 177–180
  identifying problem areas, 97–107
  reacting to personality feedback, 137
  remembering how you were before
      work, 170–171
intellectual activities, 295
intellectual attributes, positive, 138
internal locus of control, 90

interviews, job, 84, 190–191
intrinsic motivation, 178–179
introverted people, 57, 132, 133, 141, 272
intuition, 126–128

## • *J* •

James, PD, 127
job description, 54
job descriptions, analysing, 81–82
job interviews, 84, 190–191
job-hunting
    analysing a job descriptions and, 81–82
    fear of being unworthy, 83–84
    job interviews, 84, 190–191
    negotiating your pay, 84
    preparing for, 81
    using CBT while, 79, 80
jobs. *See also* workplace
    changing reality of, 159
    choosing a job you can enjoy, 140–141
    getting what you want from your, 150
    staying put or leaving your, 157–158
Johari window, 87–88
judging others at work, 174
Jung, Carl, 132–133

## • *K* •

Kelly, Gary, 172
Kubler-Ross, Elizabeth, 242

## • *L* •

laughing at yourself, 321–322
laughter, as stress releasing, 125
Layard, Richard, 233
leading questions, 254
listening
    active, 248–249
    framework for, 248–249
    to silences, 249
locus of control
    finding your, 90

increasing, 59
    overview, 54
losing face, agreeing to differ and not, 157
luck (fortune)
    expecting, 127
    increasing your, 126–127
    turning bad luck into good, 127
Luft, Joseph, 87

## • *M* •

management, transition, 198
managers, basic communication
        skills, 246–247
"manager's special," 200–201
Manager's Transition Management
        Programme, 201
manager-training day, 5-hour, 243
managing directors (MDs), offering to
        enlighten, 204
*Managing OCD with CBT For Dummies,* 75–76
Marcus Aurelius, 178
Marukami, Haruki, 283
Maslow, Abraham, 57, 319
massage, 293
MBCT (Mindfulness-based Cognitive
        Therapy), 293
meditation, 293
memories, as internal thinking triggers, 28
mental health
    economic cost to countries of mental
        ill-health, 238
    professions tied to, 142
mental health problems, spotting when
        colleagues have, 227–230
mindfulness, overview, 124, 127
Mindfulness-based Cognitive Therapy
        (MBCT), 293
"misery loves company," 119, 165
Mission Statements, 206–207
mistakes (errors)
    accepting, 129
    being the first to admit your, 217–218
    in general, 321
    at work, 106

monitoring
  actions, 97
  emotional states, 267
  feelings, 27, 97, 180
  in general, 16
  self-esteem, 103
mood rings, 44
motivation
  intrinsic, 178–179
  understanding your, 178–179
movies, CBT, 329
music, 36, 124, 295, 296

• **N** •

National Institute for Health and Clinical
    Guidance (NICE), 233
NATs (negative automatic
    thoughts), 118, 148
negative automatic thoughts
    (NATs), 118, 148
negative emotions
  in CBT workshops, 239
  changing unhealthy, to healthy negative
    emotions, 240
negative feedback, 221
negative feelings
  examples of, 29
  about work, 51–52
negative stress, 31
negative thinking
  assessing your, 139
  example of, 239
  maintaining vigilance for, 113
  spiralling, 186, 187, 191, 309
  trigger for, 28
  warning signs of, 39–40
  at work, 37
neglected at work, feeling, 101–102
negotiating your pay, 84
Nettle, Daniel, 141
new activities, 294–295
NICE (National Institute for Health and
    Clinical Guidance), 233
nodding and smiling, 122–123
non-judgmental interactions, trusting
    environment and, 247

non-verbal characteristics, of
    colleagues, 164
number one, allowing yourself to be, 63

• **O** •

obsessive compulsive disorder (OCD),
    75–76, 228–229
obstacles, dealing with, 60
OCD (obsessive compulsive disorder),
    75–76, 228–229
open questions, 252
opportunities
  catching important
    opportunities, 125–127
  lucky people and, 126
opportunities at work, revising and
    maximising your
  assessing your thinking about pressure at
    work, 281–283
  focusing on the realistic, 286–287
  mapping your work options, 283–287
  overview, 281
  self-employment work, 287–290
optimism, studying, 129
optimistic thinking, 117–121
optimists, choosing jobs, 141
organisation, benefitting the, 91–95

• **P** •

pace, 168
palm reading, 128
panic attacks, 109, 185, 186, 188, 274, 282
paraphrasing, 250–251
past problems, looking at, 190
patience, treating yourself with, 312
patterns in behaviour, identifying, 191–192
pay, negotiating your, 84
Persaud, Raj, 140, 141
persistence, 158
personal life, using CBT in, 263
personal space, 49
personality (personality types)
  choice of jobs and, 142
  choosing jobs, 141
  of colleagues, 163–165

comfort zones and, 57
imagining the worst at work, 142
Jung's theories of, 132–133
linking to different jobs, 139–142
origins of, 133–134
overview, 131–132
psychometric tests, 134
taking a look at your, 136–139
testing for, 134–135
working environments and, 49
perspective
    keeping, through changing times, 278–279
    putting your job into, 123–125
    on your whole being, 292–293
pessimists, choosing jobs, 141
philosophy
    creating a philosophy for work, 320
    definition of, 147
    discerning your values about
        work, 150–151
    gaining a new perspective on, 160
    learning from people who went
        before, 151
    of life, 148
    Stoicism, 158
    survival, 149
    what you want from your job, 150
physical activities, 295
    balance of intellectual activities
        and, 322–323
physical health
    combining emotional health and, 263–265
    going to work ill, 104–105
physical surroundings, looking at
    your, 48–50
physician, visiting a, 109–110
PIES (Physical, Intellectual, Emotional and
    Social) activities, 294–295
Pilates, 293
plan of action, creating a, 316
positive attributes, identifying your, 138
positive body language, 119–120
positive feelings
    examples of, 29
    about work, 51
positive thinking. *See also* optimism

expecting the best outcome, 118
"glad" game and, 120
optimising chances of a positive work
    climate, 128–130
as optimistic thinking, 117–121
overview, 117
positive body language and, 119–120
reflecting at the end of the day, 121
positivity, increasing a company's, 16–17
post traumatic stress disorder
    (PTSD), 229–230
posture, 168
practising, before acting, 180–181
"prefer" thinking, changing "should"
    thinking to, 139, 178
presentation
    on CBT, 220
    of self, 167–169
presenteeism, 70, 105
presenting yourself to your current or
    potential employer, 143
pressure at work, assessing your thinking
    about, 281–283
prioritising
    the work, 86
    your life, 325–326
    your working day, 123–124
probing skills, 251–254
problem situations (tricky situations)
    handling, 191–195
    reflecting on and tackling, 190–191
procrastination, 13, 76, 112
productivity, increasing a
    company's, 16–17
professional help, recommending that
    people seek, 224–227
professional manner, talking in a
    respectful and, 248
professional views, conflicts in personal
    views and, 154–155
proximity, 168
psychoanalytic psychology and
    therapy, 238
psychological environment, 50–53
psychology, in CBT workshops, 237
*Psychology For Dummies,* 237

psychometric tests, 134
*Psychometric Tests For Dummies,* 134
PTSD (post traumatic stress disorder), 229–230
public, dreading facing the, 135

## • Q •

Qiong, 293
questions
  asking effectively, 252
  closed, 253
  hypothetical, 252–253
  leading, 254
  open, 252
  probing with, 251–254
  unhelpful, 253–254
  why, 253

## • R •

rational thinking, demonstrating, 215–216
ReadyRickshaw app, 313
realistic options, focusing on, 286
reality check, 188
reaping what you sow, 217
recording
  an emotions diary, 312–313
  CBT apps, 313–314
  choosing your method for recording your emotional life, 314
  unsettling work events, 307
  your goals, 316–317
redundancy, adjusting to transitions and, 276–277
reflecting
  for better communication, 249–251
  at the end of the day, 121
  on last week at work, 307
  and tackling your tricky areas, 190–191
  on your behaviours, 65–66
reflective skills, 249–251
rehearsal, life isn't a, 324–325
relationships (at work). *See also* colleagues; friends
  appraising colleagues, 163–164

categorising your workmates, 162–163
character types, 164–165
dealing with people you can't stand, 166–167
facing up to relationship issues, 209–210
impression you give, 167–172
maintaining trust in, 210
making new, 296–298
overview, 161
taking a hard look at your colleagues, 162–163
repeated patterns in behaviour
  changing, 192–193
  identifying, 191–192
repetitive thoughts, 104
reputation, company's, 207–208
resilience, 158–160
  knowing yourself builds, 159
Resilience Training programmes, 160
resources, CBT, 327–331
respect
  of customers, 210
  talking in a respectful and professional manner, 248
  treating yourself with, 67
  trusting environment and, 247
respectful, of friends at work, 174
responsibility
  taking responsibility for yourself, 67–68
  as a dynamic employee, 85
  using CBT to handle, 282–283
  for your own happiness, 70–71
  for your own wellbeing, as central premise of CBT, 63
restating, 250
retirement, 276
rewiring your old brain, 299–300
Rickman, Alan, 321
roles
  acting in your own best interests, 144
  balancing your, 278–279
  coping with changing, 10
  getting into character, 145
  seeing yourself in different, 171–172
  of successful, happy worker, 143
Roosevelt, Franklin, 149
Russell, Bertrand, 289

# • S •

scared feelings at work, 104
scientific methods, 16, 24, 126
searching for work (job-hunting)
  analysing job descriptions and, 81–82
  fear of being unworthy, 83–84
  job interviews, 84, 190–191
  negotiating your pay, 84
  preparing for, 81
  using CBT while, 79, 80
Seasonal Affective Disorder (SAD), 133
secondary emotional disturbance, 157
Segal, Zindel, 293
self-acceptance
  in general, 84
  replacing low self-worth with, 103
self-actualisation, 57
self-assessment, on the work week, 308
self-confidence
  in general, 84
  lacking, at work, 100–101
  retaining a sense of who you are, 277
self-defeating thoughts and behaviours,
    138, 139, 182, 308, 320
  tweaking with CBT, 138
self-employment, 287–290
self-fulfilling prophecy, 91
self-help and therapy books, 219, 303, 327
self-interest
  acting in your own, 144
  enlightened, 63, 64, 320
selfishness, replacing with enlightened
    self-interest, 64
self-medication, noticing damaging levels
    of, 226–227
self-presentation, 167–169
self-responsibility, 68
self-worth, low, replacing with self-
    acceptance, 103
Seligman, Martin, 160
senior staff, reluctance or opposition
    of, 201–203
Seuss, Dr., 268
Shakespeare, William, 326
shame at work, 105–106

"should, ought and must" thinking
  changing, 241
  changing to "prefer" thinking, 139, 178
  examples of, 305
  in general, 240
  secondary emotional disturbance as, 157
silences, listening to, 249
simplifying CBT, 24–25
sinking pit feelings, 53
skills
  maintaining your, to keep you
      confident, 276
  recognising your, 82–83
  self-employment, 288
  skills audit on yourself, 284, 285
  transferring CBT skills to new situations
    believing in using your skills and
        experience, 260
    combining emotional and physical
        health, 263–265
    contextual clues for CBT use, 258–259
    flexibility of CBT approach, 258
    holistic approach, 265
    identifying your own working
        pattern, 261
    outside of work, 260–266
    overview, 257
    personal life, 263
    stability and consistency across entire
        life, 267–270
    taking confidence into new
        environments, 259
    widening the application of CBT
        skills, 258–260
smiling
  emotional contagion and, 169–170
  nodding and, 122
sociability, 295–298
social activities, 295–298
social anxiety, 228
social attributes, positive, 138
"sorry," not always the right word, 218
space, personal, 49
spiralling negative thoughts, 186,
    187, 191, 309
status, affirming your sense of worth and, 280

Stibich, Mark, 169
stigmas, facing, 22
stoical attitude, adopting a, 222
Stoicism, 158
strategic aims, standardising, 206
strategic objectives, 206
stress
  definition of, 86
  distress and, 31–32
  negative, 31
  prioritising the work, 86
  resilience and, 160
  spotting symptoms of, 264–265
  stressing out at work, 10
  at work, 282
struggles
  admitting your, 15
  telling another person of your, 108–110
  using your CBT experience to help in, 223
success, dressing for, 168
suicidal thinking, 230
summarising, 251
'Sunday-evening school-night' feeling, 50
surroundings, physical, 48–50
survival philosophy, 149

• T •

Tai Chi, 293
taking care of yourself
  recognising the need for, 68
  responsibility for, 15–16
taking responsibility for yourself, 67–68
  as a dynamic employee, 85
talk therapy, 102
team power, 171
tears, chemical composition of, 107
Teasdale, John, 293
tensions, picking up on, 156
tests, psychometric, 134
The National Institute of Economic
  Review, 234
therapy. *See also* cognitive
  behavioural therapy
  bringing friends to, 225
  recommending that people go to, 224–225
  saying yes to, 22

Thich Nhat Hanh, 170
thinking
  catastrophising, 38, 41, 43, 148–149, 186
  concentrating on what you're, 30
  connecting feelings and, 29–30
  negative
    assessing your, 139
    example of, 239
    maintaining vigilance for, 113
    spiralling, 186, 187, 191, 309
    trigger for, 28
    warning signs of, 39–40
    at work, 37
  philosophically, 124–125
  positive. *See also* optimism
    expecting the best outcome, 118
    "glad" game and, 120
    optimising chances of a positive work
      climate, 128–130
    as optimistic thinking, 117–121
    overview, 117
    positive body language and, 119–120
    reflecting at the end of the day, 121
  practising a new way of, 180
  scientifically, 24
  suicidal, 230
thinking psychology (cognitive
  psychology), 238
thinking-feeling link, 184
threats
  identifying, 27
  reactions to, 27
three-hour interactive workshop, 241–243
time, dividing your, 123
time frame exercise, 124
timeline, creating a personal, 279
tone, 168
toolkit, CBT
  adjusting workplace emotions with, 59–60
  alerting strategies and, 43–44
  applying to each new event, 308–309
  building yourself a, 39–41
  choosing to use your, 42–45
  components of, 39
  creating a, 32
  creating your own version of, 309–310
  deciding when to implement your, 44

deploying, 193–195
exercising your brain muscles and, 43
gaining a little peace with, 45
in general, 32
keeping your toolkit prepared, 41
needing to earn a living and, 69
practising the routines, 44–45
Top 100 small businesses, 207–208
training
    in counselling skills, 209–210
    courses, communicating a consistent
        message in, 204–209
    experienced facilitator needed for, 223
    transition management courses, 200–203
training courses, 329
transition courses, CBT-based, 200–201
transition management
    5-hour manager-training day, 243–246
    using CBT in, 198, 200
    workshops, 80, 198
transitions
    adjusting to, 276–277
    negative water cooler and, 119
treating yourself
    with respect, 67
    valuing yourself, 66–67
    as your own best friend, 71
tricky situations (problem situations)
trust
    reacting to broken, 211–212
    in relationships, maintaining, 210
trusting environment, creating a, 247–248
Tsongas, Paul, 325
typecasting people, avoiding, 136

**• U •**

unhelpful characteristics,
    admitting your, 138
unhelpful questions, 253–254
unhelpful thoughts and beliefs
    halting, 188
    identifying and disputing, 35, 189–190
    overview, 33
    pinpointing, with CBT, 155–157

possible origins of, 34
tweaking with CBT, 139
unsettling emotions, 107–108
unsettling work events, recording, 307

**• V •**

values
    cognitive dissonance and, 152
    about work, discerning, 150–151
valuing
    your place at work, 92–93
    yourself, 66–67
vigilance for your emotional outlook,
    maintaining, 113–114
vigilante group of one, 114
voice, 168

**• W •**

warning signs
    of negative thinking, 39–40
    that using CBT toolkit would be
        helpful, 32
    watching for, 225–226
watching yourself over time, 279
water cooler, negative, 119
weaknesses, becoming aware of your, 87
websites, CBT, 328
wellbeing. *See also* health
    psychological environment and
        sense of, 50
whole being, gaining a perspective on
    your, 292–293
why questions, 253
Williams, John, 293
Wiseman, Richard, 118, 121, 126
wobbly feelings
    CBT toolkit and, 40, 43–44
    maintaining vigilance for, 113
    overview, 26
work. *See also* jobs
    adapting to changes at
        accepting the need to be
            flexible, 272–275

work. *(continued)*
   affirming your status and sense of worth, 280
   diagnosing the problem, 272–273
   flexibility, 275–277
   keeping perspective, 278–279
   maintaining your skills to keep you confident, 276
   overview, 271
   recognising your preferred environment, 274–275
   retaining a sense of who you are, 277
   staying you through thick and thin, 280
   treating the symptoms with CBT, 273–275
  anxiety about, 100
  appraising what you want from, 149
  asking for help at, 227
  assessing your feelings about, 51
  assessing your work performance, 315
  attitudes toward, 147–151
  attitudes towards, 153–154
  being neglected at, 101–102
  bullying at, 102
  character types at, 164–165
  conflicting influences of, 53–55
  crying at, 107
  digging deeper into your experience of, 52–53
  discerning your values about, 150
  embarrassment and shame at, 105–106
  engaging with other people at, 122
  feeling depressed about, 100
  finding out how you prefer to, 137
  frustration at, 106–107
  identifying how you view, 148–149
  identifying problem areas at, 97–98
  imagining the worst at, 142
  implementing CBT at work
   applying the ABC model, 188–190
   becoming conscious of your actions, 179–180
   body's reaction to perceived threats, 184–185
   deciding when to implement CBT toolkit, 44–45

   deploying your CBT toolkit, 193–195
   doing your homework, 178
   drawing up a plan of action, 195–196
   gaining insight into yourself, 177–180
   halting unhelpful thoughts, 188
   handling problem situations, 191–195
   observing the thinking-feeling link in operation, 184
   overview, 110–111
   realising that the time has come for action, 182–183
   reflecting on and tackling your tricky areas, 190–191
   seeing CBT methods in action, 180
   speaking louder than words with actions, 183–186
   spiralling negative thoughts out of control, 186–188
   understanding your motivation, 178–179
  increasing favourable interactions at, 121–123
  lacking self-confidence at, 100–101
  making friends at, 172
  making mistakes at, 106
  observing your behaviour at, 34–39
  philosophy of life and, 148–149
  physical surroundings at, 48–50
  picturing yourself at, 168–170
  positive feelings of, 51
  recording unsettling work events, 307
  reflecting on last week at, 307
  relationships at. *See also* colleagues; friends
   appraising colleagues, 163–164
   categorising your workmates, 162–163
   character types, 164–165
   dealing with people you can't stand, 166–167
   facing up to relationship issues, 209–210
   impression you give, 167–172
   maintaining trust in, 210
   making new, 296–298
   overview, 161
   taking a hard look at your colleagues, 162–163

remembering how you were before, 170–171
scared feelings at, 104
selecting the work life you want, 17
valuing your place at, 92–93
work colleagues
accepting, 154
categorising your, 162–163
dealing with people you can't stand, 166–167
engaging, 199–200
sharing CBT with interested, 219
spotting specific emotional problems in, 227–230
taking a hard look at your, 162–167
work culture
appraising, 206–207
influencing the, 93–95
work habits and routines
assessing healthfulness of, 71–72
obsessive compulsive disorder (OCD), 75–76
replacing, 74–75
work opportunities, revising and maximising your
assessing your thinking about pressure at work, 281–283
focusing on the realistic, 286–287
mapping your work options, 283–287
overview, 281
self-employment work, 287–290
working conditions (work environment)
assessing, 48
comfortable, challenging your expectations of, 57–58
dealing with obstacles, 60
gaining a little peace with CBT toolkit, 45
healthy work routines, 60
overview, 47
physical surroundings, 48–50
working day, prioritising, 123–124
working pattern, identifying your own, 261
working styles, identifying your preferred, 58
work-life balance
boundaries of your job and, 87, 89

by dividing your time, 123
in general, 18, 70, 214, 262
in 1960s and 1970s, 262
as potential source of difficulty, 23
through exercise, 266
working to live or living to work, 262
workmates (colleagues)
accepting, 154
categorising your, 162–163
dealing with people you can't stand, 166–167
engaging, 199–200
sharing CBT with interested, 219
spotting specific emotional problems in, 227–230
taking a hard look at your, 162–167
workplace
assessing the situation, 85–86
benefitting the organisation, 91–95
conditions
assessing, 48
comfortable, challenging your expectations of, 57–58
dealing with obstacles, 60
gaining a little peace with CBT toolkit, 45
healthy work routines, 60
overview, 47
physical surroundings, 48–50
coping with changing roles in, 10–11
damaging beliefs at, 36–37
looking after yourself in, 15–16
placing yourself in context, 73–74
recognising problems in, 14–16
stressing out in, 10
tips for maximising success in, overview, 319–321
working out where you stand, 92
workshops, CBT
3-hour interactive, 241–243
5-hour manager-training, 243–246
engaging employees, 199–200
general session objectives, 241
including HR in feedback and evaluation of CBT courses, 203–204
leading, 235–243

workshops, CBT *(continued)*
managing directors (MDs) and, 204
moving from sceptic to advocate, 203
outline of topics, 236–241
parts of, 242
senior staff members' reluctance or
opposition, 201–202
transition management, 80, 198

World Health Organization (WHO), 73
worry at work, 282
worth, sense of, affirming your
status and, 280

"yes," saying, to therapy, 22

# About the Author

**Gill Garratt, M.A. Psychol. M.A. Prof. Writing, B.Ed. Hons, Senior Accred. REBT Therapist,** is an accredited psychotherapist in the U.K. who specialises in using Cognitive Behavioural Therapy in the workplace. She has 30 years experience in the public and private sectors both in the U.K. and internationally. Gill has incorporated CBT into individual and group training in a wide variety of workplace settings. These include global financial organisations, the education sector, pharmaceutical industries, Central U.K. Government departments, including H.M. Treasury, prisons and even cruise ship guest lecturing. She wrote a CBT-based Transition Management programme which was piloted and rolled out nationwide within a major financial organisation and continues to write customised courses for Change Management. Gill has worked for an International Employee Assistance Programme, Lifeworks, as a Consultant for 15 years, as well as having a practice in Falmouth, Cornwall, U.K.

Her first book was *An Introduction to CBT for Work* (Icon, 2012) and her second book is *Your Dog and You. Understanding the Canine Psyche* (Veloce, 2015).

# Dedication

To anyone who has found work tough going.

# Author's Acknowledgments

Thanks to all the great teachers I have learned from – the academics, researchers, writers, philosophers, educationalists, health care professionals, artists and wise friends. Thanks to Iona Everson, Andy Finch and Kerry Laundon at Wiley for their guidance and encouragement and giving me this opportunity to share my knowledge and experience on work and life. I have felt very encouraged and supported from start to finish by the Wiley team throughout. I am impressed with their organisation and their empathy toward me as a writer, who sometimes struggles with self doubt and anxiety like any other person.

Thanks to Donald Robertson, a fellow CBT therapist, author and keen technical editor for this book.

To the hundreds of individuals I have had the privilege of working with and sharing their concerns and struggles – I have been alongside as you worked hard to learn about CBT and apply it to yourselves and bring some rational thinking back into your lives.

This book is a testimony to your determination and authenticity.

I would like to thank the team at Falmouth University Professional Writing Masters Course, who took me on as the oldest student and gave me an opportunity to learn to articulate my thoughts and beliefs and to express them in the written form.

Thanks to BJ for your patience and IT support during the long winter months of writing. Finally I'd like to thank Charlotte and Johnny for your encouragement of your Mum, and reminding me that you are never too old to try new things and that 'Spirit has no age'.

## Publisher's Acknowledgments

**Acquisitions Editor:** Ben Kemble

**Project Editor:** Iona Everson

**Development Editor:** Andy Finch

**Copy Editor:** Kerry Laundon

**Technical Editor:** Donald Robertson

**Production Editor:** Siddique Shaik

**Art Coordinator:** Alicia B. South

**Cover Image:** KieferPix/Shutterstock